THE A-TO-Z BOOK OF
MANAGING
PEOPLE

THE A-TO-Z BOOK OF
MANAGING
PEOPLE

VICTORIA KAPLAN
AND ROBERT KUNREUTHER

BERKLEY BOOKS, NEW YORK

THE A-TO-Z BOOK OF MANAGING PEOPLE

A Berkley Book / published by arrangement with
the authors

PRINTING HISTORY
Berkley trade paperback edition / December 1996

The Putnam Berkley World Wide Web site address is
http://www.berkley.com/berkley

ISBN: 0-425-15459-9

BERKLEY®
Berkley Books are published by The Berkley Publishing Group,
200 Madison Avenue, New York, New York 10016.
BERKLEY and the "B" design
are trademarks belonging to Berkley Publishing Corporation.

PRINTED IN THE UNITED STATES OF AMERICA

10 9 8 7 6 5 4 3 2

CONTENTS

AIDS • Alcohol • Alternative Work Schedule •
Answering Phones • Appraisals and Reviews • Awards
and Bonuses • Blood Donations • Bullies • Calling In,
Unscheduled Absences • Car Pool, Need to Develop •
Car Pool, Problem With • Cleanliness, Work Space •
Cliques • Coffee Breaks • Company Time • Competition
Among Employees • Computer Games • Computers,
Personal Use • Cooking • Counseling • Day Care, Elder/
Child • Death in the Family • Decor • Desk Audits •
Disabilities • Discrimination Complaints •
Documentation • Dress Codes • Embezzlement/Theft •
Emergency Preparedness • Emotional Problems •
Employee Assistance Programs • Employment at Will •
Equipment for Personal Use • Express Mail,

Unnecessary • Falsification of Documents • Family
Medical Leave Act (FMLA) • Feuds • Fighting (Physical
Contact) • Flirtations • Food • Gambling • Gays and
Lesbians • Gifts • Glass Ceiling • Gossip • Holidays •
Illness, Extended • Injury Compensation • Job
Descriptions • Job Sharing • Jury Duty • Keys to the
Office • Know-It-Alls • Late Completion of Work •
Layoffs • Leave Abuse, Vacation and Personal Days •
Lunch Breaks • Lying • Maternity • Negative Attitude •
Nepotism • Organization Charts • Overqualified
Employees • Overtime, Fair Labor Standards Act •
Parking • Parties • Perfectionists • Performance
Evaluation • Personality Clashes • Personnel Files •
Personnel Policies • Phone Calls, Personal • Physical
Fitness • Political Campaigning • Privacy • Probationary
Period • Procrastinators • Promotions • Quality
Improvement Teams • Questionnaires and Surveys •
Radios/Music • Raises, Annual • Reimbursements •
Resignations • Romance • Rumors • Second Job •
Security • Severance Pay • Sexual Harassment • Shift
Work • Short-Timers • Sick Days • Sleeping on the Job •
Smoking • Suggestions • Tardiness • Temper Tantrums •
Temporary Employees • Testing, Lie Detector and
Honesty • Testing, Alcohol and Drug • Tests, Aptitude •
Theft • Threats • Time Clocks • Trade Secrets • Training,
Requests for Tuition Reimbursement • Travel Expenses
• Turnover • Unemployment Compensation • Union
Organizing • Vacation and Personal Days • Vehicles,
Company • Whiners • Working Late and Weekends •
Zeros

FOREWORD

How did you get here? How can this book help you?

We know too many people who have quit a job because of a boss, a supervisor, or a manager. Often it had nothing to do with work assignments, lack of ambition, or coworkers. Some of those people were despairing. Some were completely fed up. But all knew they couldn't put up with the boss anymore. More than one have had to seek employee assistance or outside therapy to deal with the emotional stress of working for a bad boss.

We've known equally depressed and frustrated managers. In some cases, they're trying to deal with people whose behavior is so anti-social or counter-productive as to make them seem like caricatures of bad employees. Despite our admonitions to the contrary, these managers carried their workplace frustrations home with them. Some even dreamt about office problems—leaving them exhausted before the work day even began.

Then there's the largest group: coworkers. When a manager and employee start to weigh on one another, all but the most obtuse coworkers recognize and are affected by the situation. Likewise, when an employee is getting away with something because the manager is unwilling or unable to act, resentment builds within the workforce. Eventually, should problems with a bad boss or undisciplined coworker persist, the best of the workforce may leave.

A manager—or supervisor, or boss—is a person who controls the work life of others. She is responsible for the health, well-being, and productivity of her employees. In our experience, most people take on the job of managing people in one of two circumstances. The first is that of the entrepreneur who realizes the business has grown and requires more bodies to accomplish the task at hand. The second is that of an employee who's selected because of technical competence—he knows how to do the "stuff" of the business, whether it's building a truck or selling lipstick.

Only a few managers and supervisors entered the workforce with ambitions of leading other people. People become managers not because they want the increased stress, have all the answers, or want more responsibility. Most do it for the money. In large and medium-sized organizations, one must eventually accept a management job if she is to continue advancing. Most entrepreneurs become managers for the same reason. Without employees, they simply can't grow the business.

The role of the manager is much more complicated than it first appears. As with teachers and parents, success is predicated on the attentive care and feeding of "subordinates." The notion that managers are superior in the feeding chain makes it hard for them to see themselves as serving the employees. Much as a teacher has to maintain control *and* meet the needs of the student, the manager has to keep everything together *and* meet the needs of the employee.

This book is aimed at those needs that most managers are least equipped to handle and those concerns that occupy much, if not most, of their time—namely people. This book is a browser's guide. We've attempted to list workplace issues that can slow organizations down or disrupt relationships. We've tried to add ideas that would make the work lives of manager and employees a bit easier and more cooperative.

It's often been said that ten percent of the workforce occupies ninety percent of management's time. Allowing for the exaggeration, the sentiment is true. Most management philosophers choose to ignore the anti-social, immature, and incompetent employees, believing their behavior will change as managers do. Become more assertive, and they'll fall into line. Become more caring and benevolent, and they'll show their appreciation. Become a coach, and their performance will improve. Our response is "Sometimes yes, sometimes no . . . and what happens if the outcome is negative?"

In some aspects we're very traditional. For instance, we believe there are many circumstances when employees can and should be fired. In other areas we're more progressive, believing that not only should employees help managers make workplace decisions—their opinions should be actively solicited. Overall we believe that a positive, concerned employer can solve many of the problems listed in this book . . . before they even occur. We do not, however, see attitude and skills as the cure for all problems.

If employees are going to leave your employ, let it be for a better job, a different geographical area, or a career change, but not because you're a jerk, you didn't hear what they were saying, or you didn't act when action was required. We hope this book will provide you with the tools to create a workplace that's not only more productive, but also more enjoyable—for you and your employees.

As much as possible, we've tried to use male and female pronouns equally. We believe "he" and "she" make for better sentence construction, and also make for better workplaces.

CHAPTER 1

LARGE VS. SMALL ORGANIZATIONS

THE DIFFERENCE BETWEEN managing employees in a large bureaucracy and in a small business is enormous. While the problems facing supervisors are generally the same, the way problems manifest themselves and the latitude supervisors have to deal with them will vary significantly.

In a small organization, you have much more flexibility to respond to employee problems (and to problem employees). This is the good news. It's great because you're not bound by volumes of personnel rules and regulations. The "corporate culture" is yours to design. If you want to develop a workplace where open communication and decisive action are encouraged, you can. If you have a crisis that requires immediate attention, you don't have to wade through layers of management to get a response—you can just handle it.

The bad news is that there are no rules and regulations to follow—save federal, state, and local laws governing things like minimum wage, workers' compensation insurance, unemployment insurance, and the like. You really are left to make it up as you go.

When you're successful at creating an open, friendly workplace full of satisfied, productive employees, it can be very exhilarating. When you run into problems, or have a screaming employee who's making you crazy, it can be very frustrating to be on your own.

If you're managing employees in a small organization, you may want to consider options for developing colleagues. (This is also a good strategy to improve your financial management skills too.) Find out if your industry has an association—and if the association has a local chapter. Check out your local Chamber of Commerce. Often neighborhood Chambers have business roundtables. They're very useful for creating a forum to air problems and share solutions.

Those of you in large organizations have a separate set of issues. It's likely you'll have a human resources department (what we used to call "personnel"), complete with a policies-and-procedures manual. Managers in this environment must focus more on conformity than they would if the organization were theirs to manage.

If you work in an enlightened organization, you may have wide latitude for dealing with employee problems. There will likely be clearly defined procedures for dealing with some issues—discrimination, harassment, and holidays, for example—while others may be left to your discretion. Knowing the difference is one of the most important things a supervisor must learn in a large organization.

If the place where you work doesn't offer an orientation for new supervisors, try to get them to create one. Although it will still require trial and error to learn the rules and to figure out this business of supervision, you'll do a better job if you're informed in advance about how far your authority goes.

(**NOTE** to small-business owners: When it comes time to hire someone else to supervise your employees, remember this. If you tell her what you expect, she'll be able to give it to you more easily than if she has to guess.)

Regardless of where you work, we believe managers should be empowered to make their own decisions. As you will see throughout this book, we are assuming the reader has some latitude to make decisions and to act.

It's always important to consider the organizational culture of your workplace. However, we believe the more authority supervisors have to manage employees as they see fit, and the more open supervisors are to input from employees, the more likely you are to have a productive workforce.

CHAPTER 2

MAXIMIZE YOUR ASSET UTILIZATION, OR: WHATEVER HAPPENED TO PEOPLE?

AFTER LULLING EVERYONE into a semi-conscious state at the retirement party, the senior manager uttered the predictable cliché: "Our people are our most valuable resource." Before he could join the group for food and drink, the press of "business" overtook him and it was off to another meeting. The scenario is not unusual.

When unskilled and semi-skilled labor was all the employer needed, employees seemed expendable. Fire this one and hand a shovel to the next one in line. In most organizations today, things are different. You depend on customer satisfaction, and your customers depend on the people who work for you. From the receptionist and clerks who answer phones to mechanics who service cars to engineers who design systems, individual employees determine organizational success.

In most organizations, the numbers drive the manager, while the manager, in turn, drives the workers. After all, the numbers are indicators of success. Where they're lacking, attention is required. But why not stop and consider reversing that philosophy? Have the employees drive the numbers . . . with you providing knowledge, support, concern, and attention that keep them motivated. Let them see the numbers, let them drive themselves and each other, and let yourself clear the way.

The most typical employee complaints are that they're not heard, understood, respected, and so forth. With each complaint discussed over lunch comes less interest or commitment upon returning to work. That's normal and human, but you should realize that employee attitude directly impacts customers, quality, and "the numbers."

While discontent is growing at one level of the organization chart, supervisors and managers are lamenting their own endless problems. Many involve people—sometimes the same ones over and over again. More and more managers miss using their technical skills that were so valued in the past. They feel at sea with personnel issues, which require the experience of a psychologist more than those of a computer programmer, machinist, or sales rep who was promoted along the way.

So managers withdraw even farther into their "work." It's easier, more interesting and certainly less frustrating than dealing with the personnel issues. Employees sense management is becoming even more remote and begin "acting out" at the lack of attention and interaction. Eventually, the grapevine starts up with . . . STOP THE MUSIC!

This is management, sir and madam! Your people *really* are your most valuable resource. They really do *require* "care and feeding." They are both your subordinates and your customers. You are both their master and servant.

Employees are a real priority—like the meeting you have to attend tomorrow morning, the report you must complete by week's end, and the dental appointment next week. Where are they on your calendar? What's your commitment to attend to them?

Your old job is gone. You may be a "working manager" and still have one foot in the technical stuff. But if the other is planted in meetings and administrative matters, your most valuable resource may be losing its value.

Take a look at where the money (in your budget) goes. How

much is devoted to people—salaries, benefits, training, etc.? Now look at your calendar and see how you're managing your resources. Perhaps it's time to maximize your organization's biggest investment. We hope the pages that follow will help.

CHAPTER 3

DISCIPLINE FOR GROWN-UPS

MANY OF THE entries in this book concern employee misconduct. Some of the recommendations suggest taking disciplinary action against the employee. The difficulty is that everyone has a different idea as to what discipline means. Our best definition is this: Discipline is action taken by management in response to an employee violating rules, policies, procedures, laws, or commonly accepted behavior.

Most texts advise managers that disciplinary action is intended to correct problems, not punish people. While this is sound advice, it's often difficult to follow. People who violate policies and rules often try our patience. Some managers correctly feel as if they're being tested and must respond decisively. As one person appears to have created the problem, so it is that person at whom the discipline is directed.

While disciplining the individual is altogether appropriate, managers often lose sight of the problem. The power to take such action, up to and including firing, rests with management. When such power is exercised vindictively, or in an attempt to get back at someone, the problem often escalates rather than subsiding. In labor-relations circles, discipline taken more as punishment than corrective action is genteelly referred to as a "urination competition." The problem is not solved, and the employee, manager, and coworkers are adversely affected over a period of weeks or longer.

Disciplinary matters differ from job-performance issues. Performance problems relate to knowledge, skill, ability, and work habits. As stated above, disciplinary matters focus on rules, policies, laws, etc. In essence, performance evaluations and actions concern achievement over time. Discipline focuses on rules and rule-breakers.

It's a lot like being back in school, where performance problems were reflected in report cards, and discipline was meted out in the principal's office. Fail to do your homework or study for a test, and over time your grades would suffer. Shoot spitballs in class or talk back to a teacher, and you were sent down the hall, often to collect a note to carry home to your parents.

If we only focus on the negative side of employees for a moment, where a person *can't* perform the work assigned to her, the issue is more in the realm of performance and should be handled through performance evaluations. Where an employee *won't* perform as required by the rules, disciplinary action should result.

Some examples are in order. An employee who becomes angry and resentful when coworkers point out his mistakes represents a performance problem. While job knowledge and skills are not an issue, his ability to work with others and accept their criticism certainly is. There's no specific incident where organizational rules or policies have been violated. Rather, the individual needs to work on and improve his work habits and overall job performance.

Now, assume the same person left checks out on his desk upon leaving work yesterday. If check-handling procedures have been made clear (either verbally or in writing) and it's just as clear he's violated those procedures, discipline is the appropriate response. In some organizations, he would receive a reminder or even a chewing out. In others, he might be fired. Whatever the case, management's response is immediate and focused on a single incident rather than a practice, habit, or recurring deficiency.

The line between performance deficiencies and disciplinary infractions is often less than apparent. A secretary who's been advised to proofread correspondence before mailing, but fails to do so, has violated a procedure, while also showing a deficiency in work habits. In such cases, it's your call.

In many cases, however, the line is clear. Discipline is for people who come to work late, overstay their lunch break, steal, come to work intoxicated, are insubordinate, falsify information, etc. These are matters of right and wrong. They're matters where the phrases "He should've known better," "She was told not to," or "Our policy is clear" come into play. In other words, disciplinary action is taken against those who are *irresponsible*, not those who are *incompetent*. The former require a stern hand, while the latter require assistance and training.

As discipline is predicated on specific incidents of misconduct, management's response is most effective when taken quickly. Those requiring discipline are often behaving as children, so it's easiest to think of effective discipline in the same terms. When a child runs into the street without looking for traffic, discipline should follow immediately. So it is with an employee who calls his supervisor an "incompetent moron." The more timely the response, the more effective the action.

Disciplinary action usually involves some type of sanction or action intended to change employee behavior. These could include reminding the person of the rules, writing a letter to go in the employee's personnel file, or taking removal action. The remedy or sanction in your case depends largely on your organization's past practices and your management style.

Perhaps the most sensible way to decide on an appropriate remedy or action is to consider the following factors. Some may weigh in the employee's favor, and others against her. Try to be as objective as possible.

1. What's the nature and seriousness of the employee's offense? (Did he arrive late at work or punch a coworker in the stomach?)
2. Does the employee have a past record of disciplinary infractions?
3. Is this a senior or high-performing individual?
4. If similar problems have occurred in the past, what was the organization's response?
5. Has the employee's behavior affected your organization's public image?

6. Was the employee warned or advised of the policy or rules?
7. How has your confidence in this individual been affected?
8. What's the employee's side of the story? Were there mitigating circumstances?

Perhaps it's best to begin at the end of the list—with the employee's side of the story. It's better to hear her reasons, her version of events, an apology, denial, or explanation before deciding what to do. Such a discussion should be open-ended, allowing the employee to do the talking and to tell her story—"Tell me what happened yesterday as you were leaving work." Ask for clarification where you're unsure what he said or what he meant—"You said you waited a while. How long do you mean?" Take notes.

During such discussions, managers often become upset if employees appear to be fabricating their version of events. The natural response is to want to attack apparent lies and the liar along with them. This may not, however, be the most intelligent response. Don't cross-examine or try to trap the employee in his own web of deceit. Just allow him to create his version and document it. You will review your notes and impressions to determine whether discipline is appropriate and what penalty will correct the problem. Those who seem to be lying will usually suffer greater penalties.

Many employers rely on the concept of progressive discipline—beginning with the least severe action and progressing with a heavier hand until the problem is corrected or the employee is fired. Such models usually follow what's known as the "hot stove" approach—when one touches a stove and gets burned, touching it again without checking is less likely.

As the heat is turned up, employers move from letters to unpaid suspensions to demotion or termination. Rather than disadvantage themselves as well as the employee by sending her home from work, employers are avoiding suspensions and disciplining in terms of paper only. You may, for example, offer the employee a suspension from work or a letter in lieu of suspension. If he chooses the latter, the letter will reflect his decision. In some cases, the employee is asked to forfeit grievance or legal appeal rights in making such a choice.

Progressive discipline, regardless of how you define the penalties, only works where minor infractions are involved. In some cases, removal is warranted for the first offense. Examples include theft, falsification, violence, sexual harassment, etc. In cases involving probationary employees, termination during the probationary period may prove much more expeditious than progressive discipline.

For most managers, the hardest aspect of this process is confrontation. Most of us can think of bosses who let problems go on far too long before squaring off with the employee. Some never did. Some of us left before finding out. Because the lack of discipline frustrates the more mature and productive employees, we recommend you get on with it.

CHAPTER 4

GETTING PERSPECTIVE

MOST MANAGERS WORK too hard. There are administrative details to tend to, endless meetings, and a myriad of reports and personnel matters requiring time and thought. Over time, the wear and tear begins to show. The time spent focused on work narrows the vision of many managers.

This section is a plea for sanity. We want you to consider the possibility you're cutting yourself off from energizing, thought-provoking activities. Employees are adversely affected by your myopia—your family probably suffers—but mostly we're concerned about how you're treating yourself.

If you really want to be an effective manager, you need to get out of the office. We believe if you spend several hours a month away from your normal routine, it will pay off in increased energy, creativity, and enhanced relationships with your employees. Here are some suggestions for ways to give your brain time to imagine new approaches to old subjects.

Watch Television on Company Time!

Go to the public library and rent videos on management. There's a wide range of topics and presenters available. Personnel management techniques, Total Quality Management, marketing campaign development—you name it, it's out on video. Get someone else's opinion on how things can be done. Bad videos may prove more effective than good ones. Think about where and why they missed the mark and where others would agree. Then see if they do.

Go on a Field Trip

Visit other organizations with similar numbers of employees, markets, or organizational structure (but not competitors!) and talk to them about how they do things. How do they maintain discipline and motivate employees? How does information flow through their organization? From filing systems to birthday parties to payroll disbursement, their way may help you see yours more clearly. Come to think of it, your employees may benefit from a few field trips as well.

Create a Nest

Make your office comfortable and welcoming. Within reason, let your office reflect your personality rather than just the organization. Unless you're a total slob, what's comfortable for you will likely be comfortable for your employees. Bring one of your bowling trophies in, your favorite photograph, set up a comic/cartoon bulletin board, etc.

Meet Your Employees

Get out there and talk to your employees about something besides work. Get a clue about who they are. Find out what they do evenings and weekends. If they have kids, what are their kids up to? We don't mean pry into their personal lives . . . we mean, let employees see that you view them as people, not just workers.

Free Lunch

Even though people will try to tell you there's no such thing, take your employees out to lunch once in a while. Go someplace besides the same old dive down the street. If there are too many employees to take at one time, take them in groups of three or four. Make it clear you're trying to get a new perspective.

One Picture Is Worth . . .

Next time you have a problem to solve, draw a picture of the problem. It doesn't matter whether or not you know how to draw, the exercise will force you to think about the problem differently.

The idea here is not to tell you what to do, but just to provide you with some examples of productive ways to alter your routine. These breaks will offer you time for new ideas and perspectives you don't otherwise get when you're running in the same rut forty, fifty, or more hours each week. We believe managing employees can be rewarding and exhilarating, as well as frustrating and overwhelming. Changing routines from time to time will give you a new way of knowing the same old situation, which may help in creating new circumstances.

TOOLS OF THE TRADE

There are ten useful tools that will be used repeatedly throughout the book. To avoid repetition, in each entry the tools will be referred to by name in italics.

1. *Be consistent*

Employees count on you to be fair. When you make rules, they expect you to apply them consistently. If you treat different people differently or stray from established rules/procedures, you should have a good reason and be ready, willing, and able to articulate it. *continued* . . .

2. Conduct regular staff meetings

Staff meetings are an excellent vehicle for exchanging information, getting to know one another, and reinforcing teamwork. They provide a forum for employees to share ideas. Staff meetings that are regularly scheduled and have agendas can be a major asset to managers who are focused on improving communication and teamwork. Special attention should be given to schedules, time limits for talking, and opportunities to raise new issues.

3. Follow the Golden Rule

Before making decisions that affect your employees, consider how you would want to be treated in a similar situation. Don't jump to conclusions. Ask for their side of the story . . . and really listen to it. Judge them with the same regard you would expect from your own best boss.

4. Think it over

Give yourself a chance to respond to emotions, without losing your cool. Sometimes it is smarter to adjourn, or take a break, than maintain a calm, businesslike appearance (when you are neither calm nor businesslike). Count to ten, walk around the block, or sleep on it—but don't respond too quickly. Except in extreme emergencies, it is always appropriate to say, "I'll get back to you." Give the employee a reasonable time frame for your response, and then follow through on it.

5. Let the employees solve the problem

The best managers are often catalysts for decisions, not arbiters. Ask employees how they would solve the problem. Define the parameters, provide them with ideas, but encourage them to decide. You will develop a more responsible, involved workforce if you let employees have a hand in solving their own problems.

One thing to remember—an employee's response will seldom match your own. However, it may prove more valuable just by being his.

6. *Say it again*

Don't assume the employee understands what you have said. Either ask her to summarize your words, or do so yourself. Her frame of reference may be completely different than yours. By asking her to restate what you've said, you can help minimize confusion.

7. *Define the problem*

Begin by defining the problem at hand—in writing. Determine what parts of the problem are attributable to the person's competence or behavior and which result from miscommunication and/or office working conditions.

Only address an individual on matters that are within his control. Competence and behavior are within the employee's ability to change. Miscommunication, equipment problems, or other physical office screw-ups are generally management problems.

8. *Say what you mean*

This may be the most important tool available to a manager. Employees need to know your mind, just as you need to know what really pleases and displeases your own boss or customer. You may think you have told an employee what you wanted, but chances are you have not been definite.

Be very specific in dealing with a problem. If you narrow it down to the specific problem, you are more likely to change the behavior than if you attack it globally. "You always...," "She never...," and "Whenever he..." are more reflections of your frustrations than they are statements of the problem, and are likely to invite a defensive response. *continued ...*

9. *Consider the costs vs. the benefits*

Every manager faces budget constraints. Decisions concerning human resources (salaries, firing, snack facilities, etc.) should be weighed in the same manner as decisions regarding supplies and equipment. Many personnel decisions involve costs in terms of hours lost, lower morale, diminished confidence in management, etc. Benefits may include increased loyalty, improved communication, enhanced credibility, etc.

Because such factors are not easily translated to dollars and cents, managers may shy away from doing a cost/benefit analysis on human resource decisions. This omission can cost both time and money.

10. *Get another opinion*

As a general rule, those involved in a problem are less than objective when it comes to solving it. If you can define the problem, (see Tool 7) present it to a spouse, a friend, or another manager. Keep in mind that how you ask the question might determine the answer.

If you try this, make a special effort not to evaluate or reject the suggestions you receive. Merely thank the other person (after all, they did what you asked), and then consider the differences between their perspective and your own.

THE A-TO-Z GUIDE TO MANAGING PEOPLE

AIDS (ACQUIRED IMMUNE DEFICIENCY SYNDROME)

"One of my employees let me know his sister has AIDS, and he will be wanting some time off to help take care of her. I don't know whether I have to give him time off with pay."

AIDS in the workplace has become a serious problem for more and more managers. Whether it is accommodating employees who are suffering from the disease, dealing with employees who have ill family members or friends, or addressing the fears of fellow employees, AIDS has become a visible workplace issue.

Under the Americans with Disabilities Act of 1990 (ADA), AIDS is considered a disability, and must be dealt with accordingly. (It should be noted that the ADA only applies to organizations with fifteen or more employees. Although we believe it's good business to develop and maintain a diverse workforce, in small organizations hiring the disabled is not legally required.)

The key to understanding an employer's obligation to AIDS-infected workers lies in the legal term "reasonable accommodation." The law requires employers to accommodate disabled workers in any number of ways, as long as they're not cost-prohibitive. While the line between reasonable and unreasonable accommodation is a matter of judicial case law, it's management's obligation to determine what physical or policy changes would be required to allow an impaired individual to work productively.

Things such as flexible work schedules, a change in furniture or equipment, or the possibility of telecommuting are ways employers can enable employees with AIDS to continue working productively. If such accommodation(s) causes an organization "undue hardship," then a decision not to hire or to terminate employment is not considered illegal.

In any case, the employer's obligation is not to make assumptions. Employees or applicants should be advised of the job requirements and asked in what way, if any, they are prevented from or limited in performing such job duties. Particularly in the absence of a policy, managers will have to be prepared to be flexible in dealing with employees who have AIDS.

The same applies to employees who have family members with AIDS. The Family and Medical Leave Act (FMLA) requires employers (with fifty or more employees) to give up to twelve weeks of unpaid, job-protected leave during a twelve-month period for birth or adoption of a child, care of a spouse, child, or parent with a serious health condition, or the serious health condition of an employee. Again, for organizations with fewer than fifty employees, we believe it's just good business to be flexible in working with employees who have friends or family with AIDS.

The issues of how and when to integrate ADA and FMLA, both of which can be relevant to questions around AIDS, are complicated. If you have specific questions regarding AIDS in the workplace, check with the EEOC, and talk with an attorney who is versed in employment and discrimination law. Keep in mind, this is a rough guide to AIDS in the workplace and not the final word on the subject.

Approach to Take:

There are really three separate problems for consideration in dealing with AIDS: one is the employee who is ill; one is the employee who has a family member who is ill; and the third is providing training to combat fear and increase understanding on the part of other employees.

A. We'll begin with the AIDS-infected employee.

1. If you manage in an organization with more than fifteen employees, you are bound by the ADA to try to accommodate the employee to be able to continue working. We believe, regardless of the size of your business, you should start the process by *following the Golden Rule.* Consider what you would want your employer to do for you if circumstances were reversed.

   This does not mean you sacrifice your business for the good of one sick employee. It does mean that you make every effort to accommodate that employee and, above all, that you don't discriminate against her on the basis of her illness.

2. As long as the employee is able to complete his job tasks, and there is no legitimate, non-discriminatory reason for termination, start to work together to evaluate what might be needed to be able to continue the employment relationship. *Let the employee solve the problem.* Ask him what accommodations would enable him to continue being a productive employee.

3. As mentioned above, consult an attorney regarding your obligations under FMLA. If you're in a company that's covered by the Act, you may be required to provide up to twelve weeks unpaid leave for the employee.

4. If the employee is no longer able to work productively, you must have a clearly defined business reason for termination. We suggest you evaluate your choices re-

garding termination to see what, if any, options you can afford the employee in the way of insurance benefits, etc. Keep in mind the morale of the rest of your workforce, as well as your legal obligations to the employee in question.

B. In the case of the employee who has a family member who has AIDS and who requires care, you are again in the position of balancing your legal obligations, your moral obligations, and economic reality.

1. As noted above, depending on the size of your organization, the FMLA may require you to provide up to twelve weeks leave (per twelve-month period) for the employee to take off to take care of an AIDS patient.

2. In the case of an organization that's *not* covered by the FMLA, we urge you to *consider the costs vs. the benefits*. It may be possible to strike a compromise with the employee. If you allow a twelve-week leave (without pay, but with job protection), maybe the employee helps you find a temporary replacement. Or maybe you allow a six-week leave, with an additional six weeks of part-time employment.

3. Another option is to *let the employee solve the problem*. Try to work this out together. In the case where your organization is not large enough to be covered under FMLA, explain to the employee the problems her absence creates for you, and try to negotiate a plan together. In the long run, morale and productivity are enhanced by accommodating employee needs at a time like this.

4. *Follow the Golden Rule.* Think how you would feel if a loved one were afflicted with a terminal illness, and you had to choose between spending precious time with that person or keeping your job. Although no one expects you to put your business seriously at risk for the emotional well-being of one employee, consider

whether there are ways to accommodate this need and still maintain your economic health.

C. The third issue to consider is providing training to combat fear and increase understanding on the part of other employees.

1. If you have an employee assistance program (EAP), this is a time to use it. *Get another opinion.* Talk to a counselor who's well-versed in AIDS training issues, and follow the recommendations.
2. Call a local hospital or public health clinic and tell them you're seeking training for your employees about AIDS. Make it clear to employees that you consider this an important issue, and make the training mandatory for everyone.
3. If you are working in an area where no training resources are available, call your state public health department and have them send you information. This is definitely our last choice, but the point is to get clear, straightforward information about the disease.

   As always, if you have specific questions about how to treat an employee, check with an employment attorney. Don't make termination decisions without expert advice.

Preventive Measures:

Factual training about AIDS, diversity, and other emotional issues can go a long way to defusing problems in the workplace. Although it's not always easy to justify the time away from work, we believe this kind of training is important for everyone. Obviously, it's much easier to impart objective information about AIDS before it's an issue in your organization. *Consider the costs vs. the benefits* of doing ongoing training (at least for supervisors) on these issues.

For more information on employee education see *HR Mag-*

azine, May 1995, "Employee Education Programs Replace Fears About AIDS with Facts," p. 99.

ALCOHOL

"One of my employees appears to be drinking too much. Not only is she having problems getting to work and getting started, but I suspect she may be drinking during the lunch hour."

Alcohol is far and away the most abused intoxicant in the Western world. Oddly enough, moderate consumption of alcohol can maintain or enhance the job performance of someone who is dependent on the drug. Other forms of drinking can prove more destructive to the employment relationship—including binges, excessive drinking in social situations, and "latter stage" alcoholism.

If you as a manager are willing to accept the opinion of the AMA and the Congress, then alcohol dependence should be viewed principally as a personal problem. Until and unless the individual seeks treatment (detoxification, active Alcoholics Anonymous participation, admission to a treatment facility, etc.), there is little a manager can do to solve the underlying problem.

Alcohol dependence has often been described as "the disease of denial." Indeed, the AMA and the ADA define alcoholism as an illness and, in some instances, a handicap. Unlike most other medical conditions, individuals who suffer from alcohol dependence will, as a rule, do whatever it takes to mask their symptoms and avoid diagnosis.

Many employers have in-house or access to contracted employee assistance programs (EAP). Such programs provide intake and referral counseling services regarding personal problems that may be affecting job performance or conduct. If an EAP is available to you, make contact with a counselor and ask how he recommends you proceed.

One of the most difficult problems in confronting a suspected problem drinker is the likelihood that he will almost invariably steer the conversation away from the subject of alcohol.

Approach to Take:

1. *Define the problem.* Write down the specific performance-related issues. You will want to confront the employee concerning the on-the-job symptoms you are experiencing, such as absenteeism (especially on Monday or Friday) or moodiness.
2. *Say what you mean.* Be very specific. Have your facts in front of you at the time you meet with the employee. Such things as attendance records, notes from past meetings or incidents, complaints from other employees, other departments, or customers, or a list of deadlines missed will help you focus on the problem rather than on the employee.
3. Be firm. Threaten performance-based demotion or removal if job-related problems continue. "If you don't get help and follow the advice of a health professional, I may have to fire you." Make it clear there's help available. Be in touch with some counseling services—call the United Way, Alcoholics Anonymous (AA), or the county mental health department. Have names and numbers available for the employee. Remember it is the employee's responsibility to make the call—it is your responsibility to be supportive and/or to follow through on your threatened action.
4. Establish a timetable for review.

   Alcoholism is now considered to be a handicap under the ADA, so the EEOC requires managers to offer employees a "firm choice" between a prescribed choice of treatment and loss of job.

Preventive Measures:

Consider providing employees with the benefit of an EAP. Many health maintenance organizations, hospitals, and other public and private health organizations provide them on a contract basis. They are usually priced on a per capita basis.

If you suspect someone has a drinking problem, you're usually right. Most people don't err on the side of indictment. Confidentiality is important. Remember, there is a social stigma associated with alcohol dependence. People charged with driving while intoxicated (DWIs), who drink at lunch, or who come to work under the influence probably have a problem.

Have a rule about alcohol in the workplace, and consumption of alcohol before work and during the lunch hour. Definitely develop a rule regarding operation of company vehicles/equipment.

ALTERNATIVE WORK SCHEDULE

"A few of my employees have approached me concerning more flexible work hours. Right now all employees must arrive before 8:30 and stay until at least 5:00."

The opportunity to use alternative work schedules only presents itself in those organizations where fixed hours aren't absolutely necessary in order to serve customers. For instance, security patrols may not be adaptable to flexible schedules, but interior designers may. Most managers implement alternative work schedules only at the insistence of employees or unions—believing that fixed schedules are necessary to ensure all employees are supervised and productive. However, many employees prove more productive when left to schedule their own hours.

Alternative work schedules may refer to "flex time" in which start and quitting times are at the employees' discretion. In some flex-time environments, "core work hours" require the presence of every employee at work during certain times of the day. Many organizations have also moved to "compressed work weeks." Employees are allowed to work ten-hour days in exchange for four-day work weeks, or nine-hour days in exchange for an extra day off every other week.

Deciding on alternative work schedules is seldom easy for managers. We suggest balancing the needs of the employees (child and elder care, personal business, special transportation issues, etc.) against needs for regularity, customer service, and oversight. Many employers have experienced increased morale after implementing alternative work schedules. Others report abuses of the privilege and an eventual change in thinking in which a benefit is perceived as an entitlement. In those cases, morale and productivity benefits may start to be lost.

We believe that wherever possible managers should at least experiment with alternative work schedules. We think it helps create a climate of trust. Only individuals who betray that trust should be required to "clock" in and out. Problems to look out for include: a workforce where some of the employees could work flexible hours, while others are needed 9:00 to 5:00; a situation where customer service could be seriously impaired if scheduling problems arose; and employees who are already behaving irresponsibly and don't need any excuses for worse behavior.

Approach to Take:

1. Alternative work schedules should not be introduced as an all-or-nothing proposition. We suggest *letting the employees solve the problem*. A committee of volunteers should be allowed to propose a system. Once reviewed and modified, it should be implemented for a trial period, after which *everyone* is given a chance to evaluate successes and failures. From this gradual approach, a manager can adopt either a permanent plan or run a second trial with modifications.

2. It must be acknowledged that in many organizations cer-tain jobs will adapt easily to flex time and compressed work weeks while others will not. *Say what you mean.* Make it clear to management and employees alike that adoption of alternative work schedules must maintain or improve *overall* morale and productivity, not just in one segment of the organization.

3. As far as concerns over customers go, *follow the Golden Rule.* Many times we forget that our customers are part of our management team. Do a survey of your customers and ask them how they would feel if you were only open four days a week. Another option is to explain that you're going to do a six-month trial and it's important to you to get feedback from them. Your goal should be providing flawless service the four days a week you are open.

4. Management should be open to employee ideas and sug-gestions for making alternative work schedules effective. Few of us enjoy working for bosses who are rigid in their assumptions and uninterested in seeing the world of work from an employee perspective.

5. For suggestions and examples of what's been tried other places, call the U.S. Department of Labor, Wage and Hour Division, for literature regarding alternative work schedules.

ANSWERING PHONES

"I can't seem to get my employees to understand that we need to answer the phone in our office—and answer it quickly."

The telephone is your lifeline to customers and suppliers. In many cases, it is the first contact these people will have with your company or department. You know from your own ex-perience there's nothing quite as annoying as an unanswered business phone. It leaves a bad impression about the compe-tence of the company.

Unfortunately, like you, employees are often too busy or unavailable at the very time their hand should be reaching for the receiver. Interrupting concentration or putting a caller on hold while another call is answered is never a simple chore.

Approach to Take:

1. This goes to the top of the agenda for the next *staff meeting*. Make sure everyone involved is present. Your first question should be, "Who covers phones during the meeting?" You can voice your frustration with the situation, but it is important to let employees assist in figuring out a solution. They are most likely to be responsible for implementation.
2. *Say what you mean.* Explain to the employees why it is important the phone gets answered in a timely fashion. Make it clear who is responsible for answering phones, and establish a system for phone backup. It's okay for employees to go to the bathroom, but someone has to cover the phones. See also the section on JOB DESCRIPTIONS.
3. Take a turn answering the phone yourself. It will help you understand the employees, allow you to get to know customers and suppliers better, and give you a clearer understanding of what people want when they call your office.

Preventive Measures:

Call your local phone company or a telephone consultant and figure out better options than just letting the phone ring endlessly. Such services as call waiting, two-tone ringing, and voice mail could alleviate some of your problems.

Without notifying employees, monitor incoming calls for brief periods of time. Determine the number of calls per hour, average rings per call, percentage answered by different individuals, etc. You may wish to use this information in formulating a solution.

APPRAISALS AND REVIEWS

"Our policies and procedures require an annual written performance evaluation at the end of the fiscal year. The fiscal year ended two weeks ago, and I don't know what to do or say."

For many managers, periodic, formal evaluations of employee job performance are their most dreaded task. As with report cards for students, adults in the workplace demand and require feedback concerning their overall performance. Almost every organization of ten employees or more has a structured system for conducting performance appraisals. Some use checklists, while others rely on work plans, goals, and objectives or defined performance standards.

The problems for the manager is that no one wants to receive bad news, evaluations are often tied to salary determinations, and documentation on performance and productivity is often unavailable, incomplete, or unreliable.

Everyone does performance appraisal differently. The only thing that's consistent is that none of the methods is adequate or appreciated. Almost all of them create a certain level of tension between employee and supervisor. We'll briefly present one straightforward method we find works pretty well.

Approach to Take:

1. *Think it over.* Document what you want to say. Refer back to your evaluation form and/or any written performance standards or objectives. Get your notes together. Go back in your own calendar. Remind yourself where you were at the beginning of the rating period. Make an outline or a set of notes you can refer to during the meeting.
2. *Define the problem.* Decide on an objective for the meeting. Do you want to rate or grade the employee's work during the past year or six months? Consider whether you will be making salary adjustments and termination or pro-

motion decisions based on this evaluation. Acknowledge your own biases concerning the employee. These may include such things as attendance at the same church, whether he is the only other man in the office, whether you have developed a personal relationship, etc.

3. Schedule a meeting in a place where neither you nor the employee will be interrupted.
4. Explain what work you have done in compiling information: reviewing documentation, consulting customers and other employees, etc.
5. *Say what you mean.* Deliver the news. Most authorities advise that you lead with the employee's strongest suits. Point out deficiencies later in the conversation, and then go back and re-emphasize the positive.
6. Ask for the employee's response, comments, and additional pertinent information. If and/or when they speak, listen carefully and *take notes.* Do not argue, debate, or contradict.
7. At the end of the discussion, summarize your assessment, as well as the employee's. Advise her as to how and when the appraisal will be finalized, and its subsequent use (bonuses, retention standing, raises).
8. When performance evaluations are final (some are narrative, others numeric, some merely indicate "acceptable/ unacceptable"), consider discussing changes and improvements desired during the coming evaluation period. We believe appraisals can be an effective tool for performance management in addition to being used for performance review.

Preventive Measures:

1. Develop an ongoing file to keep information about each employee's performance on an *ongoing* basis. This eliminates a lot of panic and confusion over what you're going to say at the end of the rating period.
2. Conduct quarterly, bimonthly, or monthly informal discussions. You'll both have a better idea where the em-

ployee stands, and you'll develop a greater sense of comfort with each other.

3. Work together with employees to develop and define the evaluation criteria that will be used to assess job performance.

   In large organizations, check with your human resource department to get performance appraisal forms and procedures. As mentioned above, consider the possibility of meeting more often than required.

AWARDS AND BONUSES

"At the end of last year I gave each employee $30 times the number of years they'd worked here. This year was not as good for us financially, yet the employees are expecting the same if not more."

More than one employee, when asking about award or bonus money, has been told, "Your bonus is that you get paid every two weeks." Hardly a morale booster! Many employers currently find that salary alone is an insufficient incentive or motivation. In order to maintain the energy and performance of workers, many organizations offer awards or bonuses, thus encouraging employees toward extra effort.

People generally consider the term "bonus" as a scheduled increase in pay or an annual payout in cash. Employees may ask one another, "How much was your bonus this year?" Awards, on the other hand, are generally considered as less predictable events. These are often tied to special projects, unusual events, or mere whim. Where an organization uses awards, an employee might ask, "Did you hear that Sally got Friday off for handling a difficult customer the other day?"

There are different techniques for rewarding employees. Some employers prefer a year-end payout or gift-giving event. Others like to reward individual employees after reviewing their annual performance criteria. Some bonuses come in the form of salary increases, others as separate checks, and still others as gifts ranging from turkeys to certificates for nights out. The one thing most bonuses have in common is an element of uniformity or predictability.

The importance of a bonus to the management of an organization is that it positively impacts employee performance. Whatever form it takes, the bonus serves as an incentive motivating the receiving employees toward greater loyalty, customer service, or productivity. Therefore, it may be as important to consider the means of presentation of a bonus as its form or amount.

Awards, for purposes of this book and in many organizations, have a certain air of unpredictability. In fact, the greater the spontaneity, the more positive the impact in many cases. The intent is more to excite and enthuse than to assess the value or status of an individual. What's more, awards can become a very creative business.

Organizations have come up with award ideas that were unthinkable ten years ago. Some reward people for ideas that never made it off the ground—an incentive for continued suggestions and improvements. Others reward employees who took risks—regardless of whether they succeeded or failed. A more common award is the preferred parking space for an "employee of the month." Less visible to outsiders would be a "helping hand" award, where nominations come only from coworkers.

The impact or success of an award is tied to three components: the form (check, gift certificate, or personalized jacket); the focus (five years of service, a particular project or event, or a complimentary remark); and the presentation (private, organizational meeting, or special ceremony).

The greatest difficulty surrounding the issue of bonuses and awards is the potential for hard or hurt feelings. Where some employees receive recognition and others don't, resentments are likely. Likewise, when last year's bonus was greater than or equal to this year's, employee expectations may not be met.

One thing is certain. When rewards become expectations, they lose their impact.

Approach to Take:

1. *Consider the costs vs. the benefits.* More and more studies indicate that the monetary value of a bonus or award may have less motivational impact than its presentation and relevance to the employee. Therefore we suggest the following:

    Consider budgeting for bonuses and awards as you do other expenses for the coming year.

    Create a system for reminding yourself to review the award situation at various points throughout the year.

    Make the form and/or amount of an award known to others. Trying to make awards and bonuses confidential may backfire, especially where employees are close to one another and communicate freely.

    Avoid a scheduled cycle for awards. As employees begin to anticipate both the timing and amount, the potential for disappointment increases. This can result in the irony of giving to the employee a reward that actually demoralizes him.

    Always consider how your decision will positively impact future performance. Although a bonus usually focuses on past deeds, it must be designed to maintain or improve that employee down the road.

2. As outlined above, we urge you to consider awards and bonuses separately. We recommend judicious use of bonus money in an effort to retain the services and productivity of most valued employees. They should be especially aimed at people who are less likely to be promoted and, therefore, may begin to feel their skills and experience are under-recognized.

    In this context, bonuses should be considered as a close adjunct to salary expenses. Whether you use them as a means of increasing an employee's pay or as an annual cash dividend, the idea is to boost their earnings and maintain their loyalty. This will inevitably lead to disparities among employees. We know of no way to acknowledge individual differences without running this risk. Consider which is worse: a mediocre employee who becomes disaffected or an exceptional worker who finds a better offer.

3. In the area of awards, you need not be extravagant nor must you exclude anyone. We recommend you use awards to get people excited. Employees who never know what good things may happen when they come to work often want to come to work . . . if only to find out. Consider a cold-cut tray from the local supermarket at lunchtime, the appearance of a magician on a Tuesday morning, or a raffle for airline tickets next month. While work is not a carnival, it can be made more enjoyable through the strategic use of awards.

   Unlike bonuses, awards also lend themselves well to employee input. *Let the employees suggest* the form or category of a new award. Let them nominate or vote for coworkers. You may even want them to have certain awards for managers as well. A combination of upward, downward, and peer recognition can prove quite motivating.

4. Look for awards that cost little if anything. Certificates can be formatted on a word processor, and blanks bought for pennies apiece. Etched plaques cost little, as do frames and photographs. Some managers have become experts in novelty gifts, using them to poke fun at themselves, other management officials, and, eventually, employees, once people are sufficiently relaxed. For example, go back and look up the names of the Seven Dwarfs in Disney's *Snow White*. Now consider seven different awards in seven categories relating to each of these—even Grumpy and Dopey. It could actually be fun—especially if the employees become involved.

   The key is to begin where you are. If employees are not used to having fun at work, start slowly. Never risk embarrassing someone until you're confident he can take it in the right spirit. Also ensure your choice of awards

does not offend people's sensibilities. A gorilla-suited bal-
loon bearer may be far wiser than a birthday stripper.

5. Lastly, remember different people are motivated differently. For some, nothing is more important than a check.
Others desperately need to feel appreciated or noticed.
It's your job to know who's who and what makes them
go. In many ways, this is the essence of management.

6. Many employers choose to share profits or savings with
the employees who produced them. We recommend this,
especially where profitability and/or cost savings can be
attributed to employee effort. Payouts are usually computed as a percentage and may be distributed in equal
shares or calculated in ways that acknowledge base pay
and/or seniority. One thing to keep in mind is to *be consistent.*

   Such bonus systems have the positive effect of unifying
a workforce toward common purposes. When one shares,
all share, and if one is left out, so will the others be. Its
disadvantage is that it lacks the personal touch that individual or small group bonuses and awards foster. Perhaps
a combination of the two is the best solution. In most
cases we find the time and attention devoted to bonuses—their calculation, cost, and presentation—are outweighed by the motivational benefits they offer.

Preventive Measures:

Try to avoid creating specific expectations that may now or in
the future not be met. When confronted by an employee who
feels under-acknowledged, tell the truth. Own up to any mistakes on your part in that regard.

As with so many other topics in this book, we believe honesty
is the best policy. If you're having a bad year, and aren't in a
position to distribute sizable bonuses, let your employees know.
As we said above, in the absence of monetary rewards, you can
still plan events to let them know you appreciate their efforts.

BLOOD DONATIONS

"I recently hired an employee who, in the past, had been allowed off work (with pay) every two months to donate blood."

For years, the American Red Cross has encouraged employers to establish a cooperative blood donation program. The civic benefits associated with employers who facilitate blood donation are presumed to outweigh the expense—which usually comes in the form of time and limited use of facilities (i.e., the Bloodmobile taking up space in the parking lot).

In large organizations, you may have the luxury of having the Red Cross come to you. This makes decisions about work-release time considerably easier, because the time involved is minimal compared to having to leave work to donate blood. In small organizations, the burden of allowing employees time to donate blood is disproportionately larger. You may be looking at one additional paid day off—or one day off without pay, and this leaves you without the services of one employee.

Approach to Take:

1. Allowing time off for blood donation is a civic-minded gesture. The needs of the community should be balanced against your organization's need for the employee's services. In no case should the employee's desire for time away from work, or even ongoing community blood supplies, dictate your decision. Many employers allow employees to leave work at midday to donate blood, and allow the remainder of the workday as recovery time— assuming the employee has donated a pint of blood.

2. Where an employee appears to have abused the privilege of blood donation time, talk to the employee. *Say what you mean.* Normally a first instance will be chalked up to

"misunderstanding," while any subsequent problems would be considered disciplinary infractions.

Preventive Measures:

Contact your local office of the American Red Cross. Ask if they have guidelines for setting up an employee program.

Develop a written plan or policy concerning blood donations. Be sure that each donation is considered separately and that your approval is required in advance.

Also, provide guidance for those who are not allowed to donate for reasons of health or time constraints. If they can't donate, they must come back to work.

BULLIES

"One of my employees has been with us for years. We just hired someone to work with him, as he had complained there was too much work for one person. Since the new hire arrived, he has been pushed around, harangued, and generally had his life made miserable by the longtime employee. I fear that one or the other will leave, whether or not I intervene."

There are times when it seems as if students of abnormal psychology should be required to observe people at work. Bullies represent only one behavior problem among many, such as paranoia, passive aggressiveness, etc. Bullies warrant particular attention because their particular behavior is so apparent and disruptive.

Often known as pushy, demeaning, and abrasive, bullies take a serious toll on their coworkers. Whether they occupy similar, greater, or lesser status in the organization may or may not affect the bullies' behavior. For instance, a receptionist can bully and control higher-level employees just as one of them could make a receptionist's life miserable. One thing's for certain. If bullying becomes a feature of someone's behavior, it's difficult to change the situation.

People are bullies for reasons that are no longer apparent or traceable by the time they enter the workforce. Their audacity and insensitivity will not be remedied by management counseling, or other forms of persuasion. Making matters even more difficult is the likelihood that you as a manager are intimidated from confronting them as openly and honestly as you would a more reasonable person.

Approach to Take:

1. Bullies operate by leveraging their power. When confronting such people, you must do the same. While you can use techniques such as *letting the employees solve the problem, considering the costs vs. the benefits,* etc., if you're unable or unwilling to bully the bully, your chances for success are less likely.

   Think it over. Put in writing what you want to say before you meet with the employee. Be prepared to tell him what you expect in the way of changes, over what time period. Make it clear that these changes are not negotiable. Remember that you're the boss—you must retain the power in this situation. Trying to reason with a person who behaves this way is probably counter-productive. Don't argue, don't debate, and don't spend too much time explaining.

2. Where a bully has you concerned regarding issues of violence or of coworkers resigning, intervention should be swift and decisive. We suggest you consult an attorney as to whether you may preemptively remove or demote the offending employee rather than anticipating the consequences of inaction.

Preventive Measures:

Aggressive employees are usually tolerated by managers long after the problems they present have become apparent. The best technique for preventing bullies from disrupting the work-place is to act early and assertively. Many managers lack the personal characteristics required in such situations. If this is the case, we suggest skill-building in the areas of confrontation, negotiation, and assertiveness.

CALLING IN, UNSCHEDULED ABSENCES

"Yesterday was Monday, so I could've predicted our com-puter operator might be sick or have some kind of emer-gency. I was right, but what made me angriest was waiting until 9:30 in the morning for a call."

Absences due to illness or injury can never be anticipated. Managers are left holding the bag—figuring out how to adjust assignments and hours to insure work gets done and customers are not adversely impacted. Personal emergencies follow a sim-ilar pattern. The only difference is a presumption that employ-ees may have a bit more control over events in their personal lives than over their health.

In either case, the unscheduled absence demands early no-tice. The workplace is not like school or summer camp and bosses shouldn't be burdened with a morning head count. Nor should a coworker have to approach management to ask if Sheila or Wally has called in as no one has seen him.

Approach to Take:

1. Unscheduled absences create two distinct problems. The first concerns the truth of the matter. Is the employee really sick? Is the car really broken? If you're asking such questions, there is probably a fundamental breakdown in trust based on the employee's pattern of behavior to date.
2. Where the principal problem centers on the notice given management and coworkers, it would be wise to create and enforce a clear policy. For instance, you may require

employees to call and report any unscheduled absence between 8:00 and 9:00 A.M.

Your policy may also discourage calls from family members where the need to communicate with employees directly is important. Some policies also require callers to ask for a management official—not merely report an absence to a coworker with an understanding the message will be passed "upstairs."

Again, we urge you to distinguish between issues of pragmatism and trust. Rather than become angry or concerned regarding the status of an employee, why not pick up the phone and call her? *Say what you mean.* Developing an honest relationship with employees is a two-way street. If you're disappointed, or feeling betrayed, say that.

3. Where employees fail to adhere to the organization's call-in policy, progressive discipline is probably your best response. Clear confrontation and counseling, followed (if needed) by letters to the individual with copies filed in the personnel folder, is a logical series of steps. Any employee requiring such corrective measures is probably suffering a personal problem or has lost commitment to his work.

4. Where individual employees have frequent unscheduled absences and/or problems calling in on time, consider your employee assistance program or other counseling services. The problem could be violence in the home, substance abuse, depression, or just about anything. What should be clear to you is that the employee's behavior is abnormal and probably requires greater attention than you're trained or capable of giving. See EMPLOYEE ASSISTANCE PROGRAMS (EAPs).

Preventive Measures:

Where employees care about their work, their coworkers, and those who supervise them, their tendency is to give the earliest and clearest notice possible regarding an absence. This has probably been the case for you as well. If untimely calls or evasive measures are not unusual, consider why workers are willing to treat each other and you with such disregard.

CAR POOL, NEED TO DEVELOP

"My employees and I aren't sure whether or how incentives to carpool will work."

The cost of single-occupant-vehicle commuting is not only high in environmental terms, but in business costs as well. The annual cost to provide an employee parking space in downtown Seattle can run as high as $150 per month. Additional costs related to single-occupant commuting are: unreliability (due to traffic); public relations perceptions of a lack of community commitment; and employee morale.

Employer facilitation of car-pool planning is required in certain state and municipalities. In addition, in almost any geographic setting, it will be seen as a positive gesture.

Approach to Take:

1. *Get another opinion.* Call your local or state department of transportation. They can give you information on providing employee incentives, and also give you particulars on scheduling, van pools, and savings estimates.
2. *Let the employees solve the problem.* Have a *staff meeting* to discuss the subject. Ask for volunteers to put together a proposal for review of the group. Be sure to establish a timetable for receiving information.
3. Build in incentives so employees will be encouraged to participate. Consider giving away a Friday afternoon a month to the car pool that has the highest ridership. Remember to make arrangements for car-pool members to park when they are required to drive alone. (Don't punish employees by taking away their parking space and then

not making provisions for emergencies.)

Keep in mind that car pools are great, but they won't necessarily work for everyone in your organization. Try to strike a balance between building enthusiasm for the idea and creating a stigma for those unable to participate. Be sure to include the needs of handicapped employees in your planning.

4. *Consider costs vs. benefits.* You may find the economics of establishing a car-pool system allow you to give more bonuses, or you may see that the time spent on administering the system is not worth the effort. You won't know until you've looked at the details.

CAR POOL, PROBLEM WITH

"Since we instituted carpooling arrangements, the program has proven somewhat beneficial but has also created several problems."

In addition to certain economic advantages, car pools can instill certain aspects of teamwork and cooperation. Unfortunately, when members of the team have to arrive early, stay late, attend to personal business, etc., the arrangement can prove burdensome.

Approach to Take:

1. *Define the problem.* Is the problem one of scheduling, or morale, or is it really economic? Before you can make a decision about the solution, you need to get clear about the problem. If scheduling is the problem, maybe everyone needs to strive to meet deadlines more effectively. If productivity really is suffering, it may be more than just arrival and departure times causing the problem.
2. *Do a cost/benefit analysis.* As much as possible, quantify the costs of retaining the car-pool option. In your analysis,

include the costs of: providing public transportation, retaining parking spaces that are only used occasionally, and
having a person assigned to do scheduling. On the benefit
side, consider the public relations benefit in supporting
carpooling. Also consider the advantage of added reliability involved in carpooling. Also be mindful of any local
regulations regarding car pools.

3. *Let the employees solve the problem.* Send a memo to
your staff explaining the problems. Ask them for suggestions about solving them, and then have a *staff meeting*
to review them. It's a good opportunity to get their input
and, if you are open to the information, to get them invested in finding a solution.

CLEANLINESS, WORK SPACE

"This morning I asked an employee for a file, having told
the customer I'd review it and get back to her immediately.
It took him two hours of digging through all the junk in his
office before he could locate it and get it to me. His apology
hardly seemed to matter."

If we were more ethical as authors, we would have someone
else compose this section. On the other hand, our experience
as slobs affords us an insight the more meticulous lack. To gain
perspective on issues relating to cleanliness, consider an old
and a new maxim: "Cleanliness is next to godliness" and "A
clean desk is a sign of a sick mind."

A clean workplace carries two implications—one relating to
health and sanitation and the other to organization and appearance. Where the former are issues, action on the part of
management is always appropriate. The health and safety of
employees, as well as customers, should never be compromised. Where hazardous materials are improperly stored, food
items left out in the open, or inventory unsafely stored, action
must be taken.

Where appearance is the issue, management judgment is required. Stacks of unread items, unanswered mail, folders with action pending, reference items that haven't been reshelved, tools that have been used but not replaced, all may or may not require action. In many cases, such a mess has no particular impact on productivity or customers. In others, however, serious problems may be right around the corner.

Approach to Take:

1. As you probably know by now, a manager's job involves working with (and sometimes around) a multitude of personalities. It also demands you adjust your own personal and cultural styles to suit a diverse workforce. In the case of cleanliness, *consider the costs vs. the benefits* of imposing standards and holding people accountable. Obviously, if you run a restaurant or fitness center, this is an issue of paramount importance. If you are a telemarketer or a consulting engineer, it may not be such a big deal to have a spotless work space.

2. In all cases where sloppy work habits or appearances have a negative impact on safety or efficiency, take action. *Define the problem.* Managerial action in the form of progressive discipline, is usually required in the following cases:

   a. in matters that might affect employee or customer safety;

   b. in matters where public or personal health could be adversely affected;

   c. when customers are likely to draw a negative impression of the entire organization;

   d. where productivity and efficiency are impaired due to an inability to locate necessary work items.

   If an offending employee fails to maintain her work area, common areas, or areas frequented by customers as you have instructed, take disciplinary action in a progressive manner.

3. In other cases, we assume that personal taste regarding appearance and/or hygiene is the central issue. The manager should attempt to balance the employee's need to do things his own way against the "norm" that management or coworkers would prefer imposing. *Say what you mean.* Say how you and/or other people feel, and see what kind of response you get from the employee.

Preventive Measures:

Health and safety issues should be defined in policies rather than individually. Employees should be reminded of these periodically. If problems are not occurring, we suggest annual updates.

CLIQUES

"A small group of professional employees in our office eat lunch together every day and socialize after hours. Over time, they've begun to see themselves as elite or special, and treat coworkers as outsiders. Most of the office is fed up with their clique."

Any manager who hasn't heard or read about the value of teamwork is following in the footsteps of Rip Van Winkle. But cliques and teams are quite different. The latter is intended to be *inclusive* while the former is *exclusive*. Cliques can actually destroy workplace cooperation and team spirit, because part of the workforce sees themselves as outsiders while those in the clique enjoy insider status—regarding gossip, opinion, and even necessary information.

It's not up to you as a manager to decide who among your employees will be friends. It is, however, your responsibility to foster a peaceful workplace where morale and productivity can develop and increase. A clique can quicken the deterioration of a bad situation, and undermine a good one.

One of the biggest issues with cliques is that, like so many issues addressed in this book, the manager is often the last to know. Try to spend enough time getting to know your workforce that you're not caught off guard by this kind of problem.

Approach to Take:

1. *Be consistent.* To the best of your ability, all behaviors that affect productivity and morale should be dealt with quickly and honestly—whether the problem is with clerks, foremen, or senior staff.

   Direct management counseling and appropriate use of performance evaluations may solve the problem. For example, if you have a private group who uses the conference room for their own exclusive lunch period, they should be advised that others resent their exclusivity as well as the limited access to a common area.

   If you have some clerical staff who get together regularly after work, but who have excluded a minority of the group, they should be advised that a single unified work group or team is the objective. Anything less is detrimental to efficiency and morale.

   A foreman who reserves the premium work assignments for her old buddies should be reminded that "playing favorites" can have consequences such as grievances and discrimination complaints.

2. *Say what you mean.* In all of these cases, those participating in cliques need to know that their performance ratings may suffer if their behavior doesn't change. Each can be told specifically what different behaviors are preferred (office-wide potluck lunches, a system for assisting every clerical worker during heavy workloads, or logging amounts of time spent with every subordinate).

   As you discuss these matters, employees are likely to find fault with or blame those excluded from the clique. While these accusations may be valid, they cannot serve to justify a clique.

3. *Consider the costs vs. the benefits.* Where personality problems seem irreconcilable, hiring a professional me-

diator/conciliator may prove more cost-effective than on-going civil war. Reassignment is usually only an effective way to avoid dealing with the problem.

Preventive Measures:

You and other managers must set the tone to develop a productive workplace. Managing by example, you must make it clear that teamwork is a valued trait in your organization.

Diversity problems may be the basis for cliques developing in your office. Consider investing in long-term diversity training. In addition, there are several good reference books on both teamwork and diversity.

COFFEE BREAKS

"I want to give my employees the benefit of a short break in the morning and afternoon. My problem is I can't afford to lose any more productivity."

The old adage "Eight hours work for eight hours pay" may seem violated by the notion of paid coffee breaks. The loss of twenty, thirty, and in some instances up to sixty minutes per workday appears, at first blush, to be a handicap. Breaks can easily exceed one hundred work hours per year—a serious commitment to employee convenience and mental health.

The fact is that coffee breaks hold many positive benefits for employers. They often include necessary trips to the restroom, and refresh employee concentration. Managers who are committed to maximizing quality and customer satisfaction often suggest paid breaks as a means of ensuring clear focus.

Coffee-break abuse (the stretching of ten minutes to twenty or twenty-five) can prove both annoying and counterproductive. An employee who has coffee, a snack, a conversation, a personal call or two, and a trip to the restroom may stretch an intended break in concentration into much more than originally intended.

Approach to Take:

1. When an individual's coffee-break habits appear excessive, meet individually and privately to discuss the matter. *Say what you mean.* Don't hint around about the problem. Be clear and honest with the employee. When the employee responds, be sure to listen. Don't interrupt. With the exception of a medical problem (which should be documented), there is no good reason for consistent break abuse.

2. Employees should be reminded periodically regarding the policy. The smartest way to remember is to put semi-annual reminders in your calendar for staff meetings.

3. If you're having problems with several employees, *let the employees solve the problem.* When bringing up the subject of breaks in a *staff meeting,* ask employees whether they serve their intended purpose (a break in concentration), whether the privilege is being abused by coworkers, and for any suggestions or recommendations for improvement.

   Allow for anonymous, written responses—especially as concerns coworker abuse.

   Consider extending work hours or shortening lunch hours to accommodate both the employees' desires and the needs of the business.

Preventive Measures:

Before breaks become a problem, decide what your policy is. Do you want one break in the morning and another in the afternoon? Approximately how long should they be? At any time will you monitor them?

COMPANY TIME

"An employee left this morning to pick up a prescription and come right back to work. He was gone for forty-five minutes. I don't know whether to write this time off or ask him to make it up."

Fewer and fewer organizations rely on time cards to log people in and out of work, paying only for those hours actually spent productively engaged. As workdays are more frequently considered to be eight-to-ten hour blocks of time, accounting for time away from work becomes more and more difficult.

Many employees are already working more than forty hours a week. In these cases, time off to take care of matters unrelated to work may not be an issue. Others may be giving the organization fewer than the forty hours for which they're being paid each week, leaving the manager less likely to allow time away from work for extraneous matters. The difficulty arises when both types of employees are present in the same setting and consistency or policy becomes the issue.

Generally speaking, most organizations prefer supporting salaried (or "exempt") employees by allowing company time to be used when warranted. Where hourly employees are involved, company time is less likely to be granted. Where these practices exist, resentment between lower- and higher-level employees may become a morale issue.

Many employers are adopting alternative work schedules—allowing employees to account for their own time. In these cases, company time may not be as much an issue since starting and quitting times are adjustable based upon the number of hours the employee has actually worked. (See ALTERNATIVE WORK SCHEDULE.)

In some cases it may be in the organization's interest to grant paid time away from work. Where being at work might raise issues of health or safety, when adverse weather circumstances dictate that an employee arrive late or leave early, etc., many employers prefer carrying the employee on company time rather than docking pay or making them use vacation time.

Approach to Take:

1. While a written policy concerning when and under what circumstances company time will be granted seems appropriate, in reality it's very difficult to write. The variations among the reasons for needing time off and the employees who take it are too many to distill into a coherent policy. Unfortunately, this leaves you with two basic options: prohibit any use of company time at all, or allow it on a case-by-case basis.

   Banning company time altogether can seem somewhat heartless or extreme in certain circumstances. Clearly if employees can leave their duties to go to the bathroom, have a cigarette, or purchase a snack, why not allow time for more pressing circumstances. *Consider the costs vs. the benefits.* Often granting company time can be a greater morale booster, and a better investment of company resources, than not allowing any time off for personal errands.

   We suggest you overlook absences of up to ten or fifteen minutes, yet account for longer ones. This would involve allowing employees to request small increments of vacation time, or to add short absences together until they equal a full day. While some employers would prefer docking pay for each hour absent, we believe the use of vacation time is a more agreeable option. *Be consistent.* If you establish a policy, enforce it.

2. If you choose to grant company time on a case-by-case basis, we strongly urge you to keep a list or record of these cases. At a minimum, note the date, amount of time, employee, and the reason(s). As a history develops, check for patterns, disparities, and/or potential abuse that may require corrective action.

   A manager who grants company time on such a basis, without any records, allows herself little chance of correcting disparities and is more vulnerable to accusations of partiality.

COMPETITION AMONG EMPLOYEES

"Due to a scheduled retirement, a key position will be opening up in a month or two. Three employees are beginning to vie for the job by outdoing one another. Each is trying to work longer hours, be more visible, and generally show himself to be more worthy. I worry that two of them will resent whoever gets this job."

With the advent of Total Quality Management (TQM) concepts through the 1980s, management philosophers have urged greater and greater emphasis on teamwork and cooperation in the workplace. While individual achievement is to be admired, collective or organizational advancement should come first.

In previous eras, competition among workers was believed to improve and increase productivity. It also was considered effective in promoting a form of social Darwinism in which those who came out on top were felt to deserve their status.

The truth lies somewhere in the middle. Organizations are seldom egalitarian, which leads individuals to seek personal rewards and gratification, sometimes at the expense of others. By the same token, any organization that allows the devious, the egomaniacal, or the aggressive to achieve superior status may jeopardize its long-term health.

In designing certain organizational features, such as promotion, bonuses, performance evaluations, etc., management can encourage or temper internal competition. Striking a balance requires continual attention and a willingness to make adjustments whenever initiative suffers or cooperation is devalued.

Approach to Take:

1. In a work environment that offers many incentives for competition, competitive people will thrive. Likewise, where such incentives are lacking, the potential for mediocrity is increased. The key is to provide incentives to reward both individual and collective achievements.

   Despite much rhetoric and genuine efforts to promote internal cooperation and support, specific features (bonuses, salaries, promotions, perks, training opportunities, etc.) must be designed to minimize competition—without diminishing each employee's willingness to achieve.

2. Bonuses or awards should be allocated to both teams and individuals. Among factors for promotion, the ability to work with others should be made an important criteria.

   Where it seems to be part of an individual's character to vie with coworkers for recognition, even when they are not participants in the contest, a solution may not be found. Such employees are often more likely to poison the atmosphere in an otherwise healthy workplace than change their ways. As a manager, you risk both demoralizing and losing loyal and better-adjusted employees if competitive personalities cannot be reined in. Often the only solution is to get them out of the organization.

Preventive Measures:

The best preventive measure is to recognize competitive employees and let them know their chances for advancement are limited by their inability to gain the support and cooperation of coworkers.

COMPUTER GAMES

"Brad really knows how to nail it when it comes to computer Solitaire. It's hard to tell how many minutes or hours a day he spends playing video card games when he should be working."

Video games have become a standard feature of most personal computers. What's more, they have a certain addictive attraction, as do slot machines and more common arcade attractions.

As with sleeping on the job, personal phone calls, and E-mail abuse, playing computer games is offensive primarily because it violates the tenet "Eight hours work for eight hours pay." Some employees may argue if their work is caught up with, why not relax over a few hands of Solitaire. No problem—unless a few hands of Solitaire represents hours each week that could have been devoted to work.

Generally speaking, if employees have to sneak or disguise an activity like computer games, it's likely the endeavor is not in the organization's best interest.

Approach to Take:

1. In this area, a manager wanting to make a unilateral decision has three basic options:
   a. establish a policy prohibiting computer game-playing throughout the organization;
   b. create a policy that allows the practice under defined circumstances; or
   c. let it go altogether and trust employees to know when it's time to work and when it's time to play.

   In most subject areas, we would recommend the last option, believing that trust between management and employees is a fundamental key to quality and productivity. However, computer games, like gambling, possess a certain addictive quality that must be acknowledged. Having scored seven hundred points, many people feel obligated to play just one more round in hopes of topping their previous effort. In some organizations, it might be cheaper to provide a video or computer gaming station than to trust employees to know when to stop.

Recently the federal government ordered all of its agencies to remove games from their computer hard drives. While some may find this absurd, others reading this book may want to follow suit.

2. Another alternative a manager faces is to *let the employees solve the problem.* At one of your *regular staff meetings,* put computer games on the agenda. Listen to what the employees are saying. Give them a chance to provide input at the meeting, or form a committee with a specified date for getting back to you with recommendations. It's a good way to involve the employees in the decision, continue to build trust, and get the problem solved.

Preventive Measures:

As mentioned above, one possibility is to attempt to remove all games from all computers. This doesn't seem to us to be particularly effective, since it's so easy to replace them via floppy disk. The best preventive measure is just to be honest with the employees, and create an atmosphere where they believe productivity is in their best interests.

COMPUTERS, PERSONAL USE

"While an employee was on vacation last week we needed to access a file on his computer. I was shocked to find a file containing hundreds of documents relating to the Little League he helps organize."

During the past twenty years, personal computers have become ubiquitous at the workplace. While many blue-collar employees remain unfamiliar with the operations of personal computers, most white- and pink-collar employees are.

It's impossible to know how much computer time is spent on the organization's work and how much may be devoted to personal use. Common personal items include correspondence, volunteer activities, games (see COMPUTER GAMES), personal financial records, and documents relating to outside employment.

As with personal phone calls, computer games, and other entries in this book, a manager's primary concern may be the use of organizational time for personal reasons. The adage "Time is money" is certainly applicable in such cases.

Many employees take personal time on a computer only during non-work hours. Therefore, a secondary concern is the use of computer storage for files and documents unrelated to work. Finally, there's an ethical concern related to converting equipment to personal use without permission. (See the section on EQUIPMENT FOR PERSONAL USE.)

Approach to Take:

1. *Say what you mean.* Where an employee has been found abusing your organization's data-processing equipment, she should be confronted. Rather than obliterate the files or software discovered, ask her to purchase diskettes and remove the personal items on her own time.

2. Where policies are already in place and employees have disregarded them, enforcement or reassessing the policies are your only viable options. *Be consistent.* Administrative disciplinary action taken against violators serves not only to correct their behavior, but also to put others on notice. As in many other cases, the simple act of discovering computer abuse and confronting the employee may be the only deterrent needed. In the end, whatever sanction you choose is dependent on the individual circumstances and your own management style.

3. Our experience in this area is that coworkers often know of the source and extent of misuse long before management ever discovers it. Coworkers are usually reluctant to

blow the whistle on one another. While some may disdain the abusive behaviors, others may imitate them. You should be mindful of this when dealing with cases of computer misuse and consider termination in cases of repeat offenders.

Preventive Measures:

Make sure your policies concerning the use of office computers and peripherals are clear, understood, and reiterated periodically. Also be sure that your policies can be easily accepted by both you and the employees you manage—year in and year out.

You may wish to have a flexible policy that allows for limited use of the organization's equipment. Allowing for use during non-work hours, limited storage, etc., may prove more realistic than an absolute prohibition. *Let the employees solve the problem.* As is often the case, we recommend that responsible employees assist in developing the organizational guidelines. Where this is the case, employees are more likely to support management when dealing with those who violate the policy.

COOKING

"One of our employees has a device at his desk that boils water. He's taken to preparing soup during the day. The odor of chicken or beef stock permeates the area."

An employee's desire to prepare simple lunches or snacks at work is normal and reasonable in most workplaces. A microwave oven for preparing popcorn has become a common feature of office environments. This being the case, employees may wish to heat up a can of spaghetti, prepare a bowl of soup, or warm up leftovers from the previous night's supper.

The downside to cooking at work usually concerns the dedication of space for small appliances, the responsibility for purchasing and maintaining microwaves, coffee makers, etc., and perhaps most importantly, the upkeep or cleanliness associated with food preparation.

In some office settings, group breakfasts or lunches may prove desirable. In these cases, employees may request some time away from work to prepare or clean up after the group meal.

Conflicts over responsibility, time away from work, cooking odors, and queuing up to use equipment may all present the opportunity for management heartburn.

Approach to Take:

1. If cooking at work has no detrimental effect on employees' work, it should not be an issue. As we've said before, treating employees like grown-ups tends to encourage them to behave like grown-ups.

2. Where cooking collides with productivity or morale, you are stuck with the need to *say what you mean.* You have to talk to the employee or employees who are causing the problem. Be honest about your concerns.

3. You may want to bring up the issue at a *regular staff meeting*. Maybe you're not clear about the problem. In the case of a line forming at the microwave, maybe lunches need to be staggered, or additional space needs to be found for another oven. (Bringing an issue to a *staff meeting* is only effective if there is more than one person causing the problem. Don't get caught singling out one individual in front of the entire office.)

   Assuming this is a problem for the entire group, *let the employees solve the problem*. Ask for volunteers to form a committee to evaluate the situation. Let them come up with suggestions about how to make the kitchen area work better.

4. If there is only one person who is the focal point of the problem, ask him privately to help *solve the problem himself*. Tell him your concerns, and see what he suggests. Remember, you can reserve the right to veto employee suggestions, but you'll get farther solving the problem if you're open to his ideas.

Preventive Measures:

This is yet another case where having good communications with your employees comes in handy. The best preventive measure for a cooking crisis is a workplace where you can discuss problems openly and actively involve employees in the solution. If you think about it, this is not so different from families that have a problem keeping the kitchen clean, or deciding who will cook when. Being able to air your concerns honestly and respectfully always facilitates problem-solving.

Any new employees should be advised of any policies regarding cooking/using the kitchen area at work.

COUNSELING

"One of my employees is angering coworkers with his many demands and chronic failure to acknowledge their value. I want to talk to him about this, but don't know whether I can say anything that will improve the situation."

As any psychologist or social worker will tell you, trying to help an adult human being better understand himself can be a sticky business. Many people resist or defend against any information relating to their weaknesses or deficiencies. It's often contended that even after one hundred flattering remarks, one critical one seems to erase the slate.

Most supervisors and managers are ill-trained and ill-equipped to counsel their fellow humans. Anger, frustration, defensiveness, anxiety, and a host of other discomforts often accompany the manager into a counseling meeting. Many of us produce imaginary dramas prior to a meeting. "I'll say this, then she'll say that, then I'll tell her this. . . ." Different scenarios and permutations lead the manager to certain expectations for that meeting that may be more relevant to her fantasies than to an employee's reality.

Despite all of this baggage, employee counseling is a fundamental aspect of management. Employees deserve to know how they're doing and what's not going well. Often courts and other third parties demand to know what information was provided to an employee concerning his performance or conduct *prior* to any action being taken. Moreover, counseling may prove more effective than many managers fear. Bringing a problem or concern to the employee's attention may be all that's required to solve it.

While there are many training firms offering seminars in how to counsel employees, as well as numerous videotapes, perhaps the best resource available to a manager is an employee assistance program (EAP) counselor. These individuals are trained and experienced in resolving workplace problems.

While some organizations view an employee counseling service as an entity to which employees should be sent, the staff of such services may also be used as resources concerning how to approach employees, how to focus conversations, and how to avoid mistakes.

Approach to Take:

Counseling those upon whom you depend every day comes naturally to maybe one manager in one hundred. Each of us must work at developing an approach and style that suits our personality and our needs. There are a few rules of the road that may help.

1. *Define the problem.* Put it in writing. Be as specific as you can.
2. Determine whether the problem you've defined is related to employee inability or incompetence (performance), or to irresponsibility or immaturity (discipline).
3. a. If either of the above is the case, consider it a personnel problem. Work with the employee to acknowledge the problem and define steps for resolving it.
   b. If the problem doesn't relate to conduct or performance, consider it an organizational or system prob-

lem. Work with the employee and/or others to provide the needed training, communication, coordination, etc. to alter the situation.

Let's look at an example of each:

Personnel problems may include things like excessive time away from the job, bullying coworkers, misuse of the organization's facilities, failure to complete assignments on time, or a high volume of personal phone calls.

Examples of system problems include nonfunctioning equipment, antiquated procedures, unclear policy, or unrealistic time frames.

c. In defining steps to resolution, define what you see as the ideal behavior or performance, and consider what you're willing or able to do to facilitate the change. Then sit down with the employee and *say what you mean.* Review the plan. If you get employee agreement on the plan, set up a time line for improvement. Put it on your calendar and monitor the progress.

If the employee disagrees with the plan, consider *letting the employee solve the problem.* See what she can come up with that satisfies your need to see a behavior or performance change and does not compromise what the employee feels is reasonable.

Preventive Measures:

Develop a mechanism for upward evaluation that lets employees feel like criticism is a two-way street. It's important for employees to feel that they're not trapped in the nightmare of bad management at the same time that they are fair game for supervisory criticism.

DAY CARE, ELDER/CHILD

"One of my employees takes time off to care for his son in lieu of taking a vacation. Most of the time away is unscheduled and relates to the boy's health or issues that arise at the day-care center. It would be easier for me not to suffer the disruptions associated with child care and it might be better for him and his family to use the vacation time for recreation."

In more and more families, both parents work full-time outside the home. What's more, many children live in single-parent families where the father or mother works full-time. From this situation has sprung the booming industry of child care, also known as day care. While leaving a child at a day-care center or with a sitter frees a parent to work outside the home, child-rearing issues continue, oftentimes not waiting until the work-day is over.

In addition to child care, elderly members of families often require a working child to assist in their day-to-day needs. Most children of infirm or aged parents find it impossible to quit work, yet are still required to participate in day-to-day decisions concerning their care.

From the employer's vantage point, child- and elder-care issues often disrupt and distract employees from their job duties. Phone calls concerning a child's behavior, emergencies concerning a parent's illness or injury, or attendance at meetings or doctor's appointments are a few of the many requirements placed on workers in this predicament.

While it's easy to advise an employee to "find someone" who can manage such situations in their absence, many people lack the resources to do so and are obligated to choose between coming to or continuing work and attending to their loved one. Moreover, employees who face child- and elder-care issues may feel unfairly treated based on their family needs or parental status. Single parents may see a lack of promotion opportunity based on their inability to work late, spouses who share child-care duties may believe their performance ratings are more reflective of their parental status than their achievements, and children of aged parents may feel similarly disadvantaged.

Approach to Take:

1. Where such care issues distract employees (repeated phone calls, interruptions during meetings, reluctance to travel, etc.), managers must balance their needs for productivity and commitment against the employee's personal needs and healthy home life. In many cases, the use of an EAP or community counseling service is most appropriate. Where an organization has an in-house or contracted EAP, we suggest you make the initial contact with a professional counselor to better understand your options, how to discuss the matter, and what issues the employee may be facing.

   In other cases, a conversation concerning anticipated needs from both sides (employer and employee) is what's most in order. *Say what you mean.* It's perfectly reasonable to ask an employee what can be expected over the coming weeks, months, and years concerning time away from work, personal phone calls, preoccupation, and similar issues.

2. *Let the employee solve the problem.* As we recommend in other matters, such counseling may prove most productive if you as a manager simply outline the situation and your concerns and then look to the affected employee for possible solutions. While scolding or reprimanding a person over sensitive family matters is inadvisable, so is an overly sympathetic posture. The fact is both of you are there to work. If that process is being adversely affected, some adjustment is required.

3. Some large employers have found it in their interest to provide on-site day care or to make special provisions with licensed facilities for their employees. The reasons for doing so are many. *Consider the costs vs. the benefits.* Principal among them are cost-sharing or savings, reduced

time away from work, and improved morale through better, more reliable contact and care with dependent family members.

4. *Get another opinion.* You may want to schedule a visit to an organization in your area that has developed an in-house program. Seeing parents and children together at lunchtime may be enough to show you the benefit of such a program.

   Many employers who have day-care programs for their employees also provide community slots. That way neighbors can bring children to the center, and the employer is viewed as a model citizen.

5. Where telephone access is a difficult issue (blue-collar workers, cashiers, drivers, etc.), contact with dependent children or parents may become an even stickier issue. Parents often require "latchkey children" to contact them upon returning home safely from school. Similarly, children of aging or infirm parents may need to contact a father or mother to assure that medication is taken or certain household safety issues are attended to. We urge employers to make every effort in accommodating employees in these situations. Issues of family care may prove more passionate than a manager immediately recognizes. The morale of such employees may need to be balanced against losing their services altogether.

6. If and where you find it in the organization's interest to participate in child- or elder-care issues and options, we urge you to do so deliberately. Rely on those employees who are currently affected by the issue to gather information concerning availability, costs, quality, and certifications. You may wish to consider contacting municipal, state, or other public agencies that concern themselves with child, family, and health issues.

Preventive Measures:

The best way to prevent problems with day care is to be armed with objective information. As we've just said, this can be a very disruptive problem. By talking to other supervisors and business owners, you can get good ideas about creative alternatives.

In addition, by talking to day-care providers (of both child and elder care), city or county agencies that provide such care, and counselors who are trained in addressing family care issues, you will be in a position to provide more effective assistance for your employees, and be more understanding of the issues yourself.

DEATH IN THE FAMILY

"The mother and sole surviving parent of one of my employees died over the weekend. The employee tells me she'll be out for 'at least a week' taking care of the funeral and going through her mother's personal effects. Her unscheduled absence will seriously affect operations, especially if she's out longer than a week."

As with an employee who becomes sick or injured, the death of family members, even if expected, is unpredictable. Likewise, even where we are "prepared," grief may prove profound and utterly overwhelming.

While large organizations often have personnel policies concerning funeral or bereavement time off the job (often with pay), smaller organizations tend to play each situation by ear. A manager must deal not only with the unanticipated absence of an employee, but also with the ongoing trauma resulting from a loss. Grieving employees may display ongoing symptoms, be subject to fits of sadness, or seem outwardly fine while suffering tremendous inner turmoil.

There's no formula for making assumptions about relationships, durations, etc. As with many other situations described in this book, good judgment on the part of the manager is the most important guide.

Approach to Take:

1. If your organization has no policy or past practice concerning absences of this nature, we suggest consulting an attorney or personnel consultant to see if there are any legal obligations in your state.

2. As for moral or ethical obligations, we think the death of an immediate family member warrants the official sympathy of an employer. This would include at least three days of paid time off, in addition to any vacation or sick time available to and required by the employee.

   In essence, the traumas associated with a death in the family should be likened to the unexpected incapacitation experienced by illness or injury.

3. When referring to the "family," we believe in applying a definition that is broad yet sensible. *Follow the Golden Rule.* Remember, it's your job as a manager to create an environment that's conducive to productivity. Employees who know they'll be given a break in a time of crisis are employees who will be more likely to return the favor.

   Members of the employee's household and immediate family come to mind first. We also include grandparents, and encourage managers to make allowances for special circumstances such as an uncle who lived on the same block, or a cousin who acted as a parent for a period of time, etc.

4. In the absence of legal requirements, where paid time off for bereavement seems inappropriate, you may wish to approve unpaid time off or allow an employee to use vacation and/or sick days.

5. In larger organizations, the personnel/human resource office should advise managers concerning any paid or unpaid time away from work for bereavement.

6. As for the issue of job performance after an employee returns to work, managers must balance sympathy against clear expectations. Workers should be given time to heal, yet be advised that job performance cannot be compro-

mised over the long term. For those of you who want to know whether two months, six months, or a year is a long enough period for healing, we can tell you from our own experience that it really depends on the individual. What is a relatively easy transition for some is absolute hell for others.

If performance continues to be a problem, professional counseling should be urged for the employee. Many hospitals, hospices, and clinics have bereavement services available.

In all these situations, let common sense and clear communications with the employee be your guide.

Preventive Measures:

The only effective measure you can take is to develop a policy about paid bereavement/funeral leave. Even with a clearly defined policy, you'll still have to be prepared to be flexible.

DECOR

"One of my employees decided to decorate the machine he operates with photographs from *Sports Illustrated*'s swimsuit issue. Two women in the shop are offended. They find the photos to be in poor taste."

The fact that employees wish to personalize what might be a sterile work environment seems normal and reasonable. Photos of family members, posters reflecting hobbies or places visited, indoor plants, etc., are common features in the work environment.

As with all matters of taste, the line between acceptable and excessive is difficult to define and hard to enforce. Employees with green thumbs may fill their office space with grow lights, fertilizer, and watering apparatus in addition to the many plants they nurture. A corkboard may become a gallery of cartoons, quotations, or news stories that are updated daily and demand coworker attention.

Where employees have created a work space that feels personal and comfortable to them, they may prove more productive and committed. Allowing an employee to hang her cross-stitching on the partitions that define a cubicle serves to humanize what would otherwise be a sterile office environment.

Similarly, allowing a mail-delivery clerk to affix his favorite team's logo to the cart he pushes may prove more valuable than detrimental to the productive effort.

Other examples include the artistic efforts of children and family members, training and academic certificates, decorative notions involving fabric, knickknacks, lighting, etc., or trophies.

The freedom to create a nest of one's own may be tempered by the effect it has on customers and coworkers. Moderation is more important for employees with customer contact than for those tucked away from public areas.

Approach to Take:

1. How employees visually garnish their surroundings should require no management action unless someone is offended, distracted, or otherwise concerned as a result. Treat every employee concern (as well as your own) as valid or reasonable. *Be consistent.* You may think a concern is frivolous, but you must respond equally to all complaints.
2. Whether the issue is one of taste, time consumption, encroachment, or something else, stick to that issue alone. Don't get hung up in discussing work habits, telephone use, or other problems when discussing office decoration (unless they are particularly relevant to the problem at hand).
3. *Let the employees solve the problem.* Ask for two or three volunteers to establish a policy or plan to handle the immediate problem. Don't look for a comprehensive policy. The offending employee may wish to be on the commit-

tee. If they're unable to reach conclusions, make it clear you'll impose your own.

Preventive Measures:

It's perfectly reasonable to explain to employees that the office has to able to be cleaned relatively easily. Obstacle courses are greatly to be discouraged. In addition, employees should be told not to bring items of value to work, because you don't want to be held responsible for losses.

DESK AUDITS

"I've been evaluating employees based on results of their efforts. I feel I should be monitoring or observing them as they work to fully appreciate their job performance."

In order for a manager to fully understand and appreciate an employee's job and work life, periodic observations may prove worthwhile. These job or desk audits usually consist of fifteen minutes to two hours of attention paid to an employee's work habits or to better understanding the flow of work the employee experiences.

Depending on the purpose, desk audits may involve sampling the contents of in or out baskets, asking employees what they're working on, why, and what's required of them, sitting in on interviews, or discussions with customers, etc.

The purposes of desk audits differ depending on circumstances and organizations. Some managers randomly schedule audits to ascertain the level of an individual's job performance. Others may wish to learn more about their employees and the way in which work is accomplished. Another use would be for determining the appropriate pay or compensation level for a position. Finally, desk audits, when not judgmental, may prove an excellent form of public relations—demonstrating management's desire to better understand the realities of the work-place.

When desk audits are an exceptional event, they can prove nerve-wracking for employees. One often feels investigated and may experience embarrassment over having a personal maga-zine out on the desk or being interrupted by a family member's phone call. Scheduled, periodic visits, written in your calendar (as you would a doctor's appointment), give employees a chance to acclimate to your visits. They may even welcome the chance to explain what they're doing and how they're serving the organization.

Working for a good boss is often akin to feeling as if someone is in your corner. While there are many employees who prefer to be left alone, studies show that a majority of workers feel as if management pays too little attention to their efforts. Job or desk audits can provide a structured system for interacting with and better understanding an organization's staff.

The key is to follow through frequently so that employees become more comfortable with your presence and observation. The second most important factor is your willingness to learn what's on their mind and to have them question you.

Approach to Take:

1. Decide what you want to gain from the session. *Think it over.* What do you want to learn? You may suspect the person is making horrendous errors and other people are covering up for him. By going through his out basket to-gether, you can find out.

2. Put it on your calendar. Tell the employee. *Follow the Golden Rule*—be sensitive to deadlines and emergencies. If trying to schedule a desk audit becomes difficult, you may realize one problem you have in supervising your employees.

3. Focus on the fact you're there to gain information and learn. Be curious—ask questions. This is not the time to argue or debate. You can ask clarifying questions, but this is not a forum for criticism.

4. Before terminating the audit, ask the employee if there's anything else she would like to bring up or discuss as long as you're there. In large part, it's up to you whether or not she believes she can really tell you things. If she thinks you'll use information against her, you're not likely to get anything useful.

Preventive Measures:

A desk audit is in itself a preventive measure in that it facilitates communication and an open flow of information.

DISABILITIES

"I recently advertised a job vacancy. From looking at one of the applicants' resumes, I've come to the conclusion that she appears to be deaf. I'm not sure if I have to hire her or whether my hiring someone else will land me in court."

Disabled and handicapped people are just one of several groups protected by law from discrimination. From a manager's perspective, you can safely assume that every employee (or potential employee) can sue for discrimination—most in several categories. The bottom line is that discrimination against the disabled is illegal.

When it comes to disabilities, three areas warrant particular consideration:

The first is visibly handicapped workers. These are people whose handicap would be obvious to anyone with whom they interacted for an hour or more. Examples are too numerous to list, but might include speech impediments, paralysis, blindness, dwarfism, etc.

Second are those with less visible impairments. Among many examples are depression, hernias, AIDS, etc.

Last there are those employees who are at first fully functional, but develop handicapping conditions during their tenure on the job. In some cases, the onset of disability is employment-related, in others not.

While each of these possibilities represents different concerns for the employer as well as for customers, if an employee's physical or mental condition substantially limits one or more life activities, he is considered to be disabled under the law. The legal definition of disability can be found in the ADA. Copies can be obtained from the Equal Employment Opportunity Commission (EEOC), a local library, or any of various state and local agencies.

The key to understanding an employer's obligation to disabled workers lies in the legal term "reasonable accommodation." It should be noted that the ADA only applies to organizations with fifteen or more employees. Although we believe it's good business to develop and maintain a diverse workforce, in small organizations hiring the disabled is not legally required.

The law requires employers to accommodate disabled workers in any number of ways, as long as they're not cost-prohibitive. While the line between reasonable and unreasonable accommodation is a matter of judicial case law, it's management's obligation to determine what physical or policy changes would be required to allow an impaired individual to work productively. If such accommodation(s) causes an organization "undue hardship," then a decision not to hire, or to terminate employment, is not considered illegal.

A requirement to travel on the job may help illustrate these three cases:

When hiring for a job that requires travel, a manager may find herself confronted with an applicant in a wheelchair, one who had to leave a previous job because of problems related to schizophrenia, or in the third case, an otherwise able employee who recently suffered an auto accident and has been given strict medical limitations relating to bending, sitting, and lifting.

In each case, the employer's obligation is not to make assumptions. Employees or applicants should be advised of the job requirement for travel (auto, airplane, overnight, etc.) and asked in what way, if any, they are prevented from or limited in performing such job duties. Don't be surprised if the answer is "No problem." Disabled people have found ways to accomplish job tasks that otherwise able folks might never have considered.

Keep in mind, this is a rough guide to discrimination, not the final word on the subject. If you have specific questions regarding disabled workers or applicants, check with the EEOC, and talk with an attorney who is versed in employment and discrimination law.

Approach to Take:

1. There are few cases where temporary disability or impairment require a manager to consider the employee handicapped or disabled under the law. If recovery to full duties is expected, then an employee should be considered sick, not disabled.
2. If the employee's impairment appears to be indefinite or permanent, the employer's obligation to reasonable accommodation revolves around whether suggestions made by the employee or a physician are considered "reasonable" or whether they present "an undue hardship." This is a matter best left to an attorney versed in employment law.
3. *Let the employee solve the problem.* If you're unclear whether the employee can carry out the function required of her job, ask her. Accept her response as honest unless shown to be otherwise.
4. When hiring new employees, we recommend having a job description that accurately represents the major duties of the position, any physical requirements, and any unusual working conditions. Applicants should be allowed time to read this job description and then asked it they would have any difficulty performing.

Preventive Measures:

ADA has a profound impact on employers. Although these issues must be reviewed on a case-by-case basis, you should develop and review policies with an attorney.

Several firms provide training in ADA. Many public agencies also provide training. Video training is available as well.

NOTE: The ADA applies not only to people and activities within the organization, but also to its clientele. Most issues of accessibility relate to wheelchair access. However, other disabilities and handicaps (blindness and deafness are two obvious examples) may require reasonable accommodation as well.

DISCRIMINATION COMPLAINTS

"One of my employees alleges she was not selected for a weekend of overtime work because of her race. I want to make sure I address her concerns without getting in trouble."

Whether your forebears came to this country on the *Mayflower* or a fishing boat, discrimination has probably been an issue for your people. Sadly, people have been persecuted in many ways due to their religion, race, sex, color, disability, national origin, age, sexual orientation, and gender. In many cases, discrimination took place at work.

Throughout history discrimination at the workplace occurred less by malicious design than by widely held misconceptions. Proscriptions concerning entire populations (women, Jews, paraplegics, etc.) led to management decisions based more on the person's identity than competence.

Because most managers are unaware of the prejudices we have carried from childhood, complaints of discrimination appear to be unfair and unfounded. There are little things each of us does, however, during the course of a day, month, or year that reveal our preconceptions to those who don't share them.

At one time in New York City and Boston, signs reading "Help Wanted—No Irish Need Apply" were commonplace. There are federal and state statutes designed to protect the rights of the aforementioned groups in the workplace. Allegations of employment discrimination are now common, and commissions chartered to resolve these complaints are established in the federal government and most states.

Allegations or complaints concerning discrimination have two parts: an issue and a basis. The issue concerns an employment decision (promotion, training, performance evaluation, etc.) that has adversely affected or disadvantaged the employee. The basis is one or more of the protected groups listed above. For a complaint to be valid, there must be *prima facie* evidence the individual was treated differently than others outside of his group. The burden on managers is to show a "legitimate business reason" for having made the decision at issue.

Approach to Take:

1. If an employee approaches you alleging discrimination against himself or others, take it seriously. Schedule a time to get together, privately, to discuss it.
2. Because such allegations often escalate into lawsuits, it is advisable to *get another opinion* before proceeding with the discussion. You may want to call your organization's attorney. However, quite often such advice discourages open and sincere discussion due to fear that you'll say something that might be used against you. Therefore, you may wish to solicit less adversarial guidance from the Equal Employment Opportunity Commission (EEOC) at the federal level, or your state or municipal civil or human rights commission.
3. Listen carefully to what the employee is saying. Those of us who are not Hispanic, Muslim, deaf, etc., cannot easily understand the perceptions and realities of the other person. Take notes during the meeting and ask only clarifying

questions. As with a grievance, taking notes not only serves to remind you what was said, but also gives the employee the impression that what's being said is important to you and the organization. Do not argue or debate specifics during this discussion.

4. *Think it over.* Don't respond or decide on anything during this meeting. You will need time, and may require legal advice before answering the employee.

5. Review your notes with an appropriate staff advisor or attorney to get a more detached view of the situation. *Try* not to defend your actions, yourself, or your organization, but rather try to understand how others perceive the matter.

6. If there's a likelihood an outsider would perceive discrimination, explore every and all possibilities for satisfying the employee. Remember, if a federal court finds against you, up to $300,000 could be added to a remedy you currently view as too costly or impractical.

7. If you are convinced the employee is wrong (either misjudging the situation or contriving the complaint), try to avoid a summary rejection of her allegations. At the very least, as a means of prevention, commit yourself to ensuring discrimination doesn't enter into future training/discussions.

8. Never attempt to intimidate or inhibit an employee from raising allegations of discrimination. Even if you foresee the possibility of unreasonable time and costs, a perception of restraint or inhibition will only make things worse.

9. After you've met with the employee and gotten outside advice, meet with the employee again. Whether your response is verbal or written will depend on the guidance you've received.

If there's a perception you may have discriminated, give the employee everything you can. Promise to give him additional training, provide counseling to assist in future advancement, provide him with cross-training, and then follow through on your promise.

Preventive Measures:

Learn more about employment discrimination. Read a book or attend a seminar to become better informed concerning the realities of an important and potentially costly issue.

Learn to acknowledge your own biases. Each of us has misconceptions about other people. The more sophisticated we become in this area, the less likely we are to unintentionally offend or disadvantage others.

Consider addressing issues related to "diversity" with your staff. Where managers are actively engaged with their employees in addressing these issues, discrimination complaints are far less likely. Find out from an attorney the potential costs associated with inadvertent discrimination. As with issues like safety and health, ounces of prevention will likely prove worth the expense.

DOCUMENTATION

"An employee in our organization has been involved in several disruptive arguments with coworkers. When I contacted our human resources office, they wanted to know how many such incidents had occurred and when they took place. The only records I have are incomplete memories."

When attempting to deal with personnel problems, the issue of documentation becomes more important as matters become more serious. When management wants to take disciplinary action regarding performance or behavior concerns, employee reactions (in the form of grievances, discrimination complaints, lawsuits, etc.) may require evidence or proof.

While many managers sense the need for extensive personnel documentation in the event of challenges to decisions, others are reluctant to "count beans" or keep "black books." Thus the need for a paper trail must be tempered by concerns regarding the time and effort required and potential for morale problems.

One thing is certain. Where management actions are challenged, naked (undocumented) assertions may not prove convincing. Therefore, we suggest managers act upon a certain "sixth sense" and document, particularly when it seems as if confrontation and/or action may be forthcoming. The only alternative to trusting your instincts would be documenting any and every personnel problem to be sure subsequent decisions can be justified.

Approach to Take:

1. Your first order of business is to consider where you would keep or maintain documentation regarding personnel matters—good, bad, and indifferent. Some managers prefer a separate notebook. Others a wallet-sized memo pad. And still others, an accordion or drop file set up by the individual.

2. In any case, employees and/or unions may wish to access or review a supervisor's documentation. Where your notes are maintained by some personal identifier (name, Social Security number, etc.), employees may have a legal right to see such personnel records in accordance with state and/or federal regulations. When notes are maintained chronologically and data regarding different employees is interspersed, access may be much more limited.

3. For purposes of evidence or proof, credence is often given to the earliest documentation of an event, as memories fade or may be influenced over time. Accordingly, the most important advice we can give when documentation is considered appropriate is, "Do it and do it now." Whether you write a note on the back of an envelope or an appropriate personnel form is less important than when you wrote it.

4. The credibility of your observations or version of events may be questioned. Provide a copy to your boss, someone in the personnel office, a peer, etc., for purposes of vali-

dating when and why you committed your memory to writing. Such maneuvering is often referred to as CYA or "cover your ass." Even better might be to provide the employee with a copy in an effort to "play your cards face up."

5. At a minimum, documentation should show the date and time it was written and a factual recounting of the events(s) that led you to write it down. If it's typed, we suggest identifying it with your signature or the equivalent. Any recommendations, conclusions, or opinions should be left out of factual documentation. These can be included in a forwarding memo or separate notation. All such writings could be labeled as "memorandum to file" and never leave your desk drawer or filing cabinet.

6. We strongly recommend that employees have access to documentation concerning their performance or conduct. Where an organization maintains closed files that may affect personnel decisions, over time employee morale and confidence in management may suffer. In other words, you may win the battle but lose the war. What's more, sharing your documentation with the affected employee may prove more effective in solving the problem you're experiencing than would building a case against him.

Preventive Measures:

Documenting events of importance is in and of itself a preventive measure. How to do it and what will suffice within your organization, however, are separate matters. We recommend you discuss and/or receive samples of appropriate personnel documentation from your human resources office or attorney. In addition, you may wish to ask a peer within management how she documents such events. In this area, internal guidance may prove the most useful to you.

DRESS CODES

"I feel people should come to work in proper business attire. I shouldn't have to tell men not to wear earrings or women blue jeans."

A generation ago it was expected in office environments that men would wear suits and ties, and women would wear dresses. Times have changed. Many large corporations allow employees to dress informally when not dealing directly with customers.

The problems associated with changing fashions and liberalized dress codes is knowing where lines should be drawn. An imposed code describing acceptable and unacceptable apparel and appearance should normally be a last resort where hints and persuasion have failed to make an impression. You may not like it that men wear earrings and women wear jeans, but we urge you to consider whether the attire employees wear to work really affects productivity, customer service, or morale.

As with many such issues, the manager's role is to balance employee desires, comfort, and flexibility with organizational needs for efficiency and customer satisfaction. In addition, the manager/decision-maker must consider the need for uniformity across the company versus different needs for different departments. How much autonomy will you allow "department heads" in making decisions about employee attire?

Approach to Take:

1. *Be consistent.* If you decide the women in customer service won't be allowed to wear jeans, that means *none* of them will be allowed to wear jeans—especially including the manager/supervisor.
2. If you have a problem with a specific employee, meet with that person individually and discuss the problem. *Say what you mean.* Be very definite in describing the problem. If you have had customer complaints, restate them.

If you have had complaints from other employees, be careful not to reveal the sources of the concern.

3. Follow up with a clear, written notice. In the memo, reiterate reasons in terms of productivity, customer relations, office morale, etc. You must be able to show a legitimate business reason for your concerns.

4. Bring up issues at your *regular staff meeting. Let the employees come up with suggestions.* Give them input regarding the need for a policy or guidelines, and let them come up with a first draft. This is *only* appropriate if the problem is relatively widespread. If there's only one or two "offenders," deal with them individually.

5. If the offense continues, begin progressive disciplinary sanctions (letter of reprimand, suspension without pay, and on to removal for repeat offenses).

Preventive Measures:

If necessary, develop a policy regarding appropriate workplace attire. As we mentioned above, we believe this should be the last resort in defining acceptable physical attire. Begin by *defining the problem.* Consider the impact on morale before implementing a dress code.

EMBEZZLEMENT/THEFT

"I have discovered one of my employees has been stealing from me."

In ancient times, theft and embezzlement were not suffered lightly, as many amputees of those times could attest. In the workplace there is a presumed "bond of trust" between employers and employees. The means of exchange in this setting is wages for labor. When employees are believed or found to have stolen, nine out of ten managers wish first to fire them, if not have them arrested and jailed.

Although we feel there are several ways to handle this problem, it should be noted that embezzlement and theft are among the few disciplinary matters where firing or removal is presumed to be appropriate unless other circumstances are significant.

Approach to Take:

1. *Define the problem.* The distinctions between "petty" and "grand" larceny have always been arbitrary. However, we believe amounts totaling $100 or less can be viewed differently than sums of $100 or more. If an employee has stolen $100 to take his child to the dentist, your response may be different than if he has been taking $1,000 a year in inventory.

2. If you have discovered employee theft or embezzlement, you should consult an attorney to assess the civil and criminal ramifications of the situation.

3. *Consider the costs vs. the benefits* of firing vs. retaining the employee.

   Think about the position the person occupies. Is this a position of special trust—that is, does this person touch the organization's purse strings on a regular basis? People in these positions know they are responsible for safeguarding the assets of the organization. These include cashiers, bookkeepers, supervisors, procurement agents, etc. If this is a special-trust relationship, termination is often appropriate, since few employers are willing to risk a recurrence.

   If the employee does not occupy a position of special trust, consider his explanation, the amount in question, past work record in terms of tenure and job performance, and any history of misconduct.

4. It is expensive to hire and train new employees. A person who is caught, repentant, and willing to pay a price for her mistakes may prove to be of greater value to you and the organization than one who is fired.

5. *Let the employee solve the problem.* If you want to retain the employee, but need to have your faith restored, consider asking what he would do if he were in your shoes. Obviously, the final decision is yours. Restitution of the stolen items (or their value) should be strenuously pursued in all cases.

6. If you decide to fire the employee, do so for reasons of "unauthorized possession of" rather than "theft of" company property, equipment, money, etc. Using the word "theft" has particular legal implications that you can easily avoid. If there are criminal charges involved, remember the police department is not responsible for terminating employment—you are.

   In a large company, notify your human resources department. Be sure to ask them what other actions you need to take. Also ask whether there is any latitude you are given to solve the problem. Many organizations have policies in this area.

Preventive Measures:

Some organizations inform employees at hiring that termination is automatic for theft. This is one issue that really deserves a well-defined company policy. If security is a major issue in your organization, you may wish to contact a consultant who can assist you in periodic lie-detector testing. Periodic physical inventories or audits of sensitive areas are less threatening options.

EMERGENCY PREPAREDNESS

"The other day I was watching the evening news. A local business had experienced a fire and burned to the ground. It occurred to me that I could wake up in the morning and find there was no office to return to."

Preparing for the unexpected shows not only concern for the well-being of others, but also smart business sense. Being prepared (to the extent one can be) for a flood, fire, power outage, etc., may lessen the impact on both workers and customers if disaster strikes. While planning won't stop a hurricane or convince a bomber that she's in the wrong lobby, it does facilitate an orderly response in a time of utter disorder.

Emergencies generally fall into two categories: natural disasters (earthquakes, hurricanes, tornadoes, blizzards, etc.) and their man-made equivalents (fires, chemical spills, heating/cooling-system failures, explosions, etc.). Emergency management requires employers to plan for emergencies of any size at any time. Planning and preparing for these possibilities is a smart business practice. It shows concern for employees whose lives would be seriously disrupted should an emergency affect your organization's ability to do business. It's also in management's interest to plan for emergencies, in that it minimizes financial losses and liabilities.

Keep in mind, people are your most valuable asset. Their health and safety are paramount. Your failure to consider and address the unexpected may result in their harm and the possibility of lawsuits. Intangible assets include computer data, and the services of key personnel. Planning for the unexpected loss of these is worth whatever time and expense is involved. One last note about assets. Make sure you have a *current* inventory of all fixed assets—furniture, computers, artworks, etc. Put a copy of the inventory in a safe place. Consider giving a copy to your insurance agent to file with your policy.

Approach to Take:

1. Like building a successful organization, preparing for emergencies requires a solid foundation of skill and planning. *Let the employees solve the problem.* We recommend you begin by assigning someone to serve as emergency planning coordinator. Next form a preparedness committee, consisting of managers and workers from key areas in the organization.

The emergency planning team should begin by reviewing any existing plans or procedures. These may include documents created and maintained within your organization, as well as public plans maintained at the city or county level. The committee should then brainstorm and establish priorities for areas of concern—from most to least important. We recommend the team meet monthly to address these priorities until they feel quarterly meetings will suffice.

2. While the committee does its work, you, as a manager, may want to consider emergencies in a different sense. You may wish to contact your insurer concerning the unexpected loss of key personnel or the unanticipated interruption of business due to an emergency. Many business insurers have policies that can provide such coverage. *Consider the costs vs. the benefits.* You may also want to consider an alternate storage site for files, computer backup, and other important documents. If the sprinkler system came on unexpectedly after hours and flooded everything, off-site storage may have you back in business much more quickly.

   In assessing the organization's response in the event of differing emergencies, the committee you assign may explore areas and develop ideas that improve safety, increase security, and save money. For this reason, we suggest the committee continue to meet after contingency planning is completed. If the group were to meet for just two to three hours every month or two, the continued focus might yield new and better ideas. It will also continue the dialogue so that plans don't become buried or gather dust after they're created.

3. Emergency planning requires more time, thought, and training than cash outlays. Two types of supplies we recommend buying are fire extinguishers and first-aid kits. While extinguishers may be required by local ordinance, we feel you can't have too many. What's more, employees should all know how to use them. Your local fire department can help demonstrate at no charge.

Committee recommendations may include battery-powered lighting, fire extinguishers, earthquake kits, and drills. While these may seem costly at first, they could save your business if needed and used. Similarly, fireproofing file-storage areas or requiring off-site storage of computer data are ideas that don't normally come up in the rush to get work done.

We recommend you purchase several first-aid kits and let employees know where they are and how their contents can be used. Contact your local Red Cross for advice as to which kits are most appropriate for what areas. Having yards of gauze when someone needs an eyewash kit may prove more than just an embarrassment.

4. Your taxes and charitable contributions support any number of organizations that focus on emergencies and disaster response. Among these are the police and fire departments, the Red Cross, emergency medical services, and local emergency management offices. We strongly recommend you take advantage of their services. Having a fire inspector tour your facility and make recommendations could save your life and the lives of others. Likewise, maintaining a Red Cross-approved earthquake-preparedness kit may sustain you and others should The Big One hit during working hours.

EMOTIONAL PROBLEMS

"One of the most valuable employees in our organization is subject to bouts of depression. At first these periods were brief and seemed controlled by medication. Lately, however, it seems as if his melancholy is affecting both his work and the rest of us more severely."

Despite the many comforts and conveniences we have attained, emotional distress seems to be increasing, not declining. While emotional distress is widely reported in reference to home and community life, the workplace is far from immune.

Many managers react to emotional problems among employees with a sense of frustration and a belief that the cause may be as much related to self-absorption as genuine distress. Debating causes and societal ills will not improve the situation at hand. Behaviors that at first seemed odd, eccentric, or curious may eventually become disruptive, contentious, and counter-productive. While offers of counseling assistance are obviously in order, emotionally ill people do not necessarily respond to treatment or therapy.

The line between emotional distress and disability may seem clearer to an employer than to a physician or therapist. The difficulties associated with supervising such employees can become exhausting long before professionals might consider the condition uncontrollable. The Social Security Administration, the Department of Veterans Affairs, the EEOC, and other authorities accept the fact that emotional illnesses may be classified as disabilities. As is the case with other controllable illnesses or short-term incapacitation, managers should not bank on undramatic cases qualifying for disability retirement.

The ADA presents another concern. Employees suffering emotional problems must, as with all other disabling conditions, be "reasonably accommodated." Of course if the employee insists there is no illness or disability, then he is merely accountable for his behavior—as are the rest of us. If he does allege an illness or emotional problem, management must obtain information to assess the possibility of accommodating to the situation. One difficulty is getting qualified opinions concerning the employee's condition.

Therapeutic remedies (oftentimes associated with prescribed medication) are often gauged in terms of years rather than weeks or months. Therefore, not only is the disruption more evident than if the employee had broken a foot or suffered pneumonia, but the time frames for change and recovery may seem exorbitant.

Most mental disorders are less dramatic than outright schizophrenia, incapacitating depression, or delusionary paranoia. More common workplace symptoms include employees who become easily agitated with customers and coworkers, forget or misinterpret directions, are indifferent to the efforts of those around them, or alternate between enthusiasm and despair.

It might be easier if an employee swore there were kangaroos on her desk, alleged others were plotting to kill her, or began talking in tongues. The day-to-day management not only of the affected individual but coworkers and clients quickly exhausts the patience and understanding of even the most benevolent manager.

Approach to Take:

1. Confront the employee concerning her behavior. *Say what you mean.* Make it clear that, regardless of the attendant circumstances, she is responsible for her demeanor and actions. Ask her if there is any personal problem that would contribute to or explain the difficulties she presents at work.

2. If the employee denies any personal problems or emotional distress, treat her as you would anyone else whose conduct is unacceptable. *Be consistent.* We recommend disciplinary action. (See Chapter 4 for more on Discipline.) Employees who freely act in ways that violate accepted workplace rules and behavior must suffer the consequences.

3. If the employee does acknowledge an emotional problem, you may wish to refer her to EA counseling. See EMPLOYEE ASSISTANCE PROGRAMS (EAPs). If she contends counseling or treatment is already under way, prepare to ask written questions of her physician or therapist. Consider asking for information such as: the diagnosis, symptoms, prognosis, medications prescribed (if any) and side effects, potential adverse effects on the job (you may wish to include a copy of the job description as a reference), safety precautions, etc.

   A questionnaire such as that described above should not be sent directly to the practitioner, as that would jeopardize commonly accepted practices of confidentiality. Rather it should be given to the employee with an explanation as to the benefits associated with having such information at hand. The employee should be informed in writing that returning the questionnaire promptly may assist in accommodating his emotional disability. By the same token, failure to insure prompt return of the questions and answers may result in his being held strictly accountable for any and all of his actions.

4. Where a manager attempts to intervene in matters relating to an emotionally charged or disturbed employee, caution is obviously in order. Our experience tells us that reasoning with individuals in these circumstances is at best counterproductive and at worst incendiary. In essence, people who are feeling nuts don't easily follow logical discourse. Rather, it might prove more effective to insist the employee is not himself and needs to talk to an expert EAP counselor or other mental health professional. While some employees may find such comments offensive, if they are honest, such comments may be preferable to attempts to reason with someone who is not fully rational.

Preventive Measures:

If your organization can justify the expense, develop an EAP to deal with such problems. If your organization can't justify the expense, develop a contact at the United Way so you'll know which agencies you can call on in a crisis.

EMPLOYEE ASSISTANCE PROGRAMS (EAPs)

"One of the employees in our organization calls in sick with suspicious regularity. Mondays are a pretty good bet. She claims to have allergies and an ulcer. However, I've begun to suspect there's something more than illness going on."

Most of the entries in this book refer to personnel or people problems like embezzling, fighting, and leave abuse. An alarming percentage of these "problems" may actually be symptoms resulting from personal difficulties the employee is experiencing away from work. EAPs are intended to provide counseling to employees and their families regarding matters which, while not specifically job-related, may adversely impact job performance or behavior.

Such counseling services may be provided by public agencies (vocational rehabilitation services, mental health centers, etc.), or by in-house counselors or facilitators, or contracted from professionals specializing in this field.

The employee assistance industry has grown dramatically over the past twenty years, mainly because such programs show a positive impact on an organization's bottom line. The contractual or in-house expense must be compared to the costs associated with: insurance, including workers' compensation; unscheduled days off for sickness and other "emergencies"; losing trained employees; etc.

We feel very strongly that everyone should have an employee assistance program, and everyone who has one should use it.

EAPs began with the notion of helping alcoholics. Employers quickly learned that alcohol is a drug and abuse of other drugs—both legal and illegal—might also require counseling services. EAPs have expanded their scope over the years to include financial, emotional, family, and other professional counseling services as well.

Most counseling services provide a few free visits by employees for evaluation, assessment, and sometimes limited treatment. Most problems that are ripe for employee assistance, however, require referrals to specialized services—ranging from United Way agencies to Alcoholics Anonymous to individual practitioners. This specialized counseling is offered or recommended. As with any employee medical appointment, the expense and time off from work are borne by the employee.

Approach to Take:

1. If your organization doesn't provide an EAP option, it's time you investigated. You can begin with state vocational rehabilitation services, or the Yellow Pages. If an EAP already exists in your office, it should be well publicized. Management and employees should be trained concerning how it works.

Most problems with EAPs can be attributed to one of two failings: an unwillingness on the part of managers to confront employees and recommend the program; or a lack of confidentiality surrounding referrals for assistance.

If either of these is a concern in your organization, or if you need advice on referring an employee, call an EAP counselor and seek her advice.

Preventive Measures:

Having a viable employee assistance program can prevent numerous problems addressed in this book.

EMPLOYMENT AT WILL

"Last week an employee committed an offense that required me to fire him on the spot. While not disapproving of my action, two employees have asked whether a two-week notice is required prior to termination."

The legal doctrine known as employment at will existed in most states until recently. In essence, it assumes that employees may resign at any time for any reason without notice and, therefore, employers may terminate or lay off employees "at will." To learn whether your state operates under this tenet, consult an attorney or your state labor department.

In those states which still honor employment at will, the precept may be undone or modified based on employee handbooks, contracts, or other requirements. For instance, if an employee is assured, upon being hired, that she will not be terminated without "just cause," management has created an obligation. In the absence of evidence to the contrary, the employee can assume that job security exists.

Employment at will can only be maintained by neither stating nor implying any "employer-employee rights" regarding separations.

State and federal policies have also influenced employment at will. Employees have legal rights to report injuries, demand enforcement of the Fair Labor Standards Act, point out instances of discrimination and/or sexual harassment, etc. For instance, if an employee is terminated shortly after reporting a job-related injury, the employer may be called upon to show just cause—even under circumstances that retain employment at will.

Approach to Take:

Whenever a terminated employee alleges wrongful removal, a manager should contact the organization's attorney immediately. Whatever is said or done in subsequent meetings, correspondence, or conversations should be done upon the advice of counsel.

Preventive Measures:

We believe that managers should have some kind of evidence for a discharge (firing) decision. Evidence can come in several forms. Among these are: supervisory notes, written as incidents occur; summaries of counseling sessions or warnings executed during or shortly after each meeting; written notices and disciplinary letters that were delivered to the employee; documented performance reviews or physical evidence such as written complaints, wasted materials, damaged equipment, etc. Remember always to sign and date documentation.

In larger organizations, many are led to believe that stacks of such documentation must exist before an employee can be terminated. "Just cause," however, requires only a legitimate business reason. These are not criminal matters, and employers need not feel burdened to prove "beyond the shadow of a doubt" that discharge was warranted.

Where possible, we suggest consulting with an attorney before firing an employee. In more and more cases, employees are suing for their jobs and/or damages and employment at will is under increased assault.

EQUIPMENT FOR PERSONAL USE

"An employee in our office makes two copies of the daily crossword each morning upon arriving at work. He then mails each of them to friends out of town, using the organization's envelopes and stamps."

Clearly an organization's equipment and supplies are intended for business use only. By the same token, employees commonly make use of such items for personal business and/or home use. The most commonly abused equipment include copy machines, faxes, vehicles, and postage machines. In blue-collar environments, home projects are often worked on during lunch or break periods.

Most organizations tend to overlook small-scale use of material and equipment, yet want to act on more obvious or costly abuse. Where to draw the line always becomes an issue. An employee who rethreads a damaged faucet valve may be overlooked, while one who overhauls an outboard motor might require active discouragement or discipline. Where employees are positively prohibited from any such practices, the temptation to sneak a copy of a recipe may lead to confrontations that are unnecessary and counter-productive.

Approach to Take:

1. In order for an organization's policy to be understood, it must first have one. Any such policy should be flexible enough to allow a manager discretion in acting on cases of abuse.

   We suggest the policy require management permission when converting supplies or equipment to personal use. In this way, those who are found in violation will be judged as having transgressed an information or courtesy requirement rather than considered as thieves. The most important thing is to *be consistent*.

2. When introducing the policy or explaining it to new employees, you as a manager should make clear any areas where permission may not be required—such as occasional photocopying or recharging one's own battery.

3. For employees caught abusing such a policy, consider either restitution (buying a roll of stamps from personal funds), or disciplinary action (an official letter threatening removal in the case of recurrence). Any such action should be proportionate to the cost to the organization and should be focused on three things: the consistent enforcement of the policy; the morale of employees who abide by the policy; and the correction of unacceptable behavior. If the abuse is widespread (and only if it's widespread), *let the employees solve the problem.* Let the employees form a committee to come up with suggestions.

4. Your organization's policy, and any briefing regarding that policy, should clearly distinguish between using such resources on the job and taking them home. We recommend that whenever an employee takes home equipment (whether it be a stapler, a drill, or a laptop computer), permission be required in writing. For those employees who have regular permission to use such equipment, documentation to this effect should be retained by the manager.

Preventive Measures:

An employee handbook covering such workplace policies should include the personal use of equipment and supplies. The handbook standing alone, however, will soon be forgotten. We recommend periodic reviews (usually done annually) that would remind each employee the policy exists.

Another step that should be obvious but also must be mentioned is to lead by example. Where a manager converts supplies and equipment to personal use, employees are sure to follow.

EXPRESS MAIL, UNNECESSARY

"Several employees have gotten in the habit of sending anything and everything via overnight mail. It appears as if most of these documents could have been sent by fax or slower delivery systems without affecting customer relations."

With the proliferation of overnight delivery, and with the emphasis many organizations place on customer service, the costs for postage and delivery may become exorbitant. Items of little necessity and low priority may be sent in the most expensive manner simply out of habit. While the need for same-day or overnight delivery may be obvious in some cases, in others the costs simply don't justify the convenience.

Approach to Take:

1. The manager should become aware of the organization's expenses in the areas of postage and delivery. Likewise she should examine her own practices and decision-making processes in this regard.
2. After doing this, a first discussion may be initiated with the postal or delivery service that handles such items.

There may be room to negotiate preferable rates based on the volume and/or frequency involved.

3. If this approach proves insufficient, we suggest discussing the matter with a small but representative group of employees. *Say what you mean.* Inform them as to the organizational cost and a few specific instances of unnecessary expenses. *Let the employees solve the problem.* Ask the group to assess the extent of the problem and the most reasonable options for action.

4. Another alternative might be to track such costs within different organizational components and make the information available to employees. Graphic display of rising or (hopefully) falling costs may have a tacit impact on mailing practices.

5. In any event, we discourage formal policies that involve higher-level approval or rigid criteria. Individual employees should retain the discretion to serve customers in whatever manner is most cost-effective for your mission.

Preventive Measures:

Ask your long-distance carrier for information comparing fax and E-mail costs to those involving physical delivery. While overnight services will prove advantageous in many cases, you and those you manage should be aware of the costs of different options.

You may also wish to explore the legality of using faxes and/or electronic mail in place of paper originals.

FALSIFICATION OF DOCUMENTS

"One of my employees certified on a time sheet that she worked eight hours over the weekend. I just learned from another source this was not true—she was out of town the whole weekend."

In most employment circumstances, falsification of organizational reports, documents, and records is considered a firing offense. This has less to do with the severity of the crime than with the breach of trust that results.

While it's often difficult if not impossible to demonstrate whether the employee was willful in his actions, the best barometer is your own response in terms of your future trust in him. In some cases, this breach of trust can be mended. A disciplinary action need be no worse than administrative reprimand. In others, however, the "bond of trust" between employee and employer may be irreparably broken.

Factors to consider are any personal gain to the employee, the employee's response upon being confronted, workload and similar pressures, and the importance of the document in question.

Approach to Take:

1. *Think it over and define the problem.* Confront the employee. If her explanation seems inadequate or evasive, adjourn the meeting. Consider what she's said. Develop follow-up questions for a similar discussion the next day. In this way, you can voice all your questions, concerns, and misgivings with less pressure to come up with "the right questions." You may want to discuss the matter with an attorney versed in employment law. Particularly in the case of a significant discrepancy, there may be an issue of fraud.
2. Consider disciplinary action up to and including termination in every case where the employee cannot be exonerated. Don't decide on a disciplinary sanction without taking time to *think it over.* Assess the level of trust and regard you retain for the employee. Keep in mind you need to make decisions based on the good of the organization. Losing trust can be a legitimate business reason for terminating an employee. In all cases, be sure to maintain documentation of the event.
3. *Consider the costs vs. the benefits.* If you keep the employee around, you have to be sure you feel you can trust

him in the future. If you decide to fire him, *consider the costs vs. the benefits* of finding and training a replacement. In the end, we recommend you pay attention to your gut feeling.

Preventive Measures:

We suggest a firm *written* policy advising employees that falsification or misrepresentation of facts in any matter related to their employment may (not necessarily will) result in termination. Please also bear in mind that employees willing to take short cuts or to lie in writing often hold their employer in very low regard. Few people are willing to lie in matters relating to an employer they respect.

FAMILY MEDICAL LEAVE ACT (FMLA)

"One of my employees has been dealing with her son's chronic ear infections for the last two years. Now he's going to have surgery, and she wants three weeks off to take care of him. I don't know whether or not I have to give it to her, and if so, if I have to pay her for the time."

The Family and Medical Leave Act (FMLA) requires employers (with fifty or more employees) to give up to twelve weeks of unpaid, job-protected leave during a twelve-month period for birth or adoption of a child, care of a spouse, child, or parent with a serious health condition, or the serious health condition of an employee. Again, for organizations with fewer than fifty employees, we believe it's just good business to be flexible in working with employees who have friends or family with a serious illness.

FMLA requires employers to continue to pay health-care benefits during the leave, in the same proportion they are paid when the employee is present. (If the employee contributes to his health insurance, he must continue to do so at the same rate while on FMLA leave.) FMLA also requires the employer to provide an equivalent job at the end of the leave. Likewise any other benefits—pension, seniority, etc.—will not be lost during the leave. That is, the employee retains those benefits and returns at the same level at which she left. In addition, the leave can be paid or unpaid and taken in conjunction with or in addition to other paid leave (vacation, sick pay, etc.).

Approach to Take:

1. Before you consider an extended leave policy, talk with an attorney or a human resource professional versed in both ADA and FMLA. These are very sensitive issues, and the potential for making mistakes is high. Things to consider before you make decisions are:

   Whether or not employees can mix and match FMLA and sick leave.

   If you will allow employees to accumulate sick leave and if there will be a cap on the total number of days.

   If workers will be allowed to give sick leave to others. In some large organizations, employees are allowed to give sick days to coworkers. It's a very humane policy, and it can also create considerable expense for the employer.

   How do you define "family"—as always, we recommend erring on the side of a liberal definition. An aunt or niece or other relative may be just as much immediate family for some employees as a father or son are for you.

2. In the case of the employee who needs a relatively short leave, *follow the Golden Rule.* FMLA dictates you give the employee the leave, but your own policies make the determination whether the leave is paid or not. Consider how you would feel if your child or parent were ill. We recommend giving strong consideration to allowing employees to use sick and/or vacation pay for these leaves. In the long run, we find morale and productivity are enhanced where employees know there are humane leave rules.

   Also see the section on ILLNESS, EXTENDED.

Preventive Measures:

The best way to deal with FMLA and other leave issues is to consider the problem before it comes up. Meet with a human resource professional and/or attorney to devise policies that best reflect the needs of your organization and your employees.

FEUDS

"Our two technicians feel as if the engineers are arrogant and disrespectful. By the same token, the engineers resent the technicians for being uncooperative and for overstepping their jobs."

Feuds within an organization often carry on for years. What began as a minor resentment or slight evolves into something resembling the Thirty Years' War. Individual employees may avoid one another—communicating only in writing or through a coworker.

Similarly, employees in different parts of an organization or different job classifications may build up lasting resentments, robbing each other of efficiency and satisfaction. This organizational phenomenon (as opposed to individual feuds) is usually characterized by "we/they" language, implying two separate species.

To say that feuds are counter-productive is an understatement. Not only do they affect the work habits of the individuals involved, but everyone on the sidelines is affected in terms of morale. They are often pressured into taking sides or perceived as preferring one party or another.

While this organizational distress may initially reflect the juvenile behavior of Hatfields and McCoys, it eventually turns toward management. Failure to decisively intervene and resolve such matters leads most employees to believe there is an absence of effective management and they must fend for themselves rather than work with each other.

Approach to Take:

1. *Define the problem.* Either by interviewing feuding employees or observing their specific behaviors, determine whether the feud involves personal differences or job-related issues. Each will require a different course of action.

   In some cases, what began as job-related matters has evolved into personal dislikes or characterizations. "He won't let me use his computer when he's out of the office" turns into "He doesn't trust me." Where this is the case, follow the course of action below for personal differences.
2. For personal feuds, we advise you to contact a mediation service. If your organization has an EAP through a contract, that service may have access to trained mediators. Otherwise, contact the Federal Mediation and Conciliation Service located in Washington, D.C., and several major cities, a local mental health facility, the American Bar Association, the United Way, or some other similar clearinghouse.

   Although mediators are not licensed, and certifications vary from one locale to another, their training is aimed at dispute resolution through improved understanding and exploring realistic options. *Consider the costs vs. the benefits.* Not all mediators are expensive (many double as social workers, personnel specialists, guidance counselors, etc.), and their fees are usually far lower than the costs the feud represents in terms of organizational productivity.

   We suggest your organization provide for both the time and costs of such intervention. We also recommend you require some written report from the mediator concerning the outcome of his efforts, especially where you're not a participant in the dispute resolution process.
3. Where the feud is focused on work issues only, you may wish to explore the issue yourself to determine what pro-

cess requires adjustment. Interview individual employees, asking specific and job-related questions only. "How soon before the deadline do you receive reports?" "Could the pipe assembly be welded before you inspect it?" "How much training would you need to enter the data your-self?"

As the picture becomes clearer to you, so should the points of friction. These can actually be charted or drawn in terms of a flow chart or diagram. Once the analysis is complete, turn the problem over to the feuding employ-ees themselves. *Let the employees solve the problem.* Ask them to recommend options rather than make decisions. From their recommendations, decide on a course of ac-tion that will minimize the temptation to feud. Explain to all affected employees why you chose the course you did.

4. *Get another opinion.* Alternatively you may wish to have an internal or external consultant analyze the territorial aspects of accomplishing work and recommend how bar-riers might be eliminated. Her analysis should focus on the individual or territorial issues resulting from the pres-ent system. Whatever findings are made should be put in the hands of affected employees for comment. Once this is done, you as the manager should decide on a course of action and explain your rationale to those same employ-ees.

While all this effort may seem unnecessary or excessive, its costs are usually exceeded by the benefits. Feuds more commonly escalate than diminish. Their effects on even the smallest of organizations (a dentist's office, gas station, or convenience store) may prove exorbitant in terms of lost customer confidence and internal morale.

Preventive Measures:

While history tells us that feuds and bitterness are inevitable, measures can be taken to minimize the frequency and risk. Managers should consider team-building exercises long before feuds and territorial issues come to the fore. Likewise, many successful managers preclude such disputes by checking in with employees on a regular basis and learning where friction is occurring earlier rather than later.

In larger organizations, allowing for peer appraisal or multi-rater assessments may also prove useful. Evaluation questions designed to assess inter-personal relationships and teamwork may be used to detect feuds early.

FIGHTING, PHYSICAL CONTACT

"One of my employees has struck a coworker. What should I do?"

Over time it becomes virtually impossible to avoid anger (toward a boss, subordinate, coworker, or customer) at work. Enraged employees, like all of us, have several options for venting frustrations. Physical violence is the one option that is, without exception, inappropriate.

The root cause of workplace violence may lie in an employee's upbringing, psychological imbalance, or drug/alcohol use. In any event, it must be dealt with swiftly and taken seriously, to ensure that any similar incident is prevented. Workplace violence is increasing, as is the media coverage of it. To keep things together, and ensure your employees feel they are working in a safe environment, a quick response is vital.

Many of those who exhibit violent characteristics at work have given no consideration to the consequences. Therefore, penalties and sanctions, short of removal, may prove ineffective.

Approach to Take:

1. Assuming violence in the workplace constitutes serious misconduct, do not react or respond with physical force

unless absolutely necessary for the protection of the victim.

2. Call the authorities. In a small business, this may mean calling either the police or building security officials. Many large businesses have security personnel or staff.

3. After the parties are separated and tempers have cooled, it's time to decide what action to take. Begin by getting information to help *define the problem:*

    a. Interview everyone involved in or witnessing the incident—individually.

    b. Ask only what happened, and reject any editorial opinions or advice.

    c. Initiate some form of disciplinary action against any physical aggressor. (Assume that justification for an act of physical harm is extremely rare.)

       Disciplinary actions include: a formal letter to the employee; suspension from work without pay; reassignment or demotion to different duties; or firing. (Talk to your attorney about firing an employee who's been physically aggressive. You want to make sure you're covered in the event of reprisals.)

    d. Consider a serious penalty/sanction—not only as a show of concern for people's safety, but also as an acknowledgment of the likelihood that this person might do it again.

Preventive Measures:

1. Use an employee assistance program (EAP) for referring people who seem abnormally aggravated or aggressive.

2. Develop a policy about physical violence, make it known to all employees, and make it clear there will be *no tolerance* of violence in the workplace.

    Reference: Anfuso, Dawn, "Deflecting Workplace Violence," *Personnel Journal,* October 1994, p. 66.

FLIRTATIONS

"A new employee in our organization is young and very attractive. It seems as if men from every corner of the building find time to linger at her desk and engage her in conversations. The effects on her performance and others' attitudes are beginning to show."

While flirtation in an office can come from and toward either sex, the majority of organizational problems in this area involve men trying to attract the attention of eligible, or even ineligible, women. Some flirt just for ego gratification or attention, while others are in search of true romance. Any and every case holds the potential for disruption.

A manager's job need not involve the active discouragement of love and sexual attraction. In large and small organizations, coworkers may fall in love, have affairs, or whatever. Where this is done discreetly and does not disrupt the work flow, a manager may simply chalk one up to birds, bees, and hormones.

Ensuring appropriate workplace behavior is, however, a necessary aspect of management and supervision. The problem is always where to draw the line. The fact that two employees are attracted to one another and others take note of it may not require intervention. On the other hand, private conversations during working hours, love letters through the E-mail, unnecessary efforts to cross each other's path, and similar behaviors must be discouraged.

In many documented cases, it's the manager's own flirtatious behavior that sets the tone. Many have lost their job or been demoted for creating a "hostile work environment" as a result of their flirtatious behavior. (See the section on SEXUAL HARASSMENT.) We suggest if your own behavior may need adjustment, you contact an EAP counselor as soon as possible.

Approach to Take:

1. When employees begin displaying their attraction or affection for others in ways that disrupt work, swift action is appropriate and necessary. You should make a point of verifying the effect or impact of office romantics—even documenting your observations.

2. Those who flirt to a fault (with or without invitation) should be advised their conduct is unacceptable. *Say what you mean.* Those involved should be counseled individually. Where one is preying on the other, without any apparent encouragement, only the offending employee should be confronted.

3. If the situation persists, offenders should be informed in writing that termination may result if a change in behavior isn't made. You may also wish to investigate similar court cases that have resulted in findings of sexual harassment. Advise the employee(s) that open flirtation could jeopardize your standing as a manager if allowed to continue. Offers of employee assistance or similar counseling should be made to demonstrate the magnitude of the problem, as well as resolve any deeper emotional situation.

4. Finally, if you have the misfortune to manage a pathological Romeo or Juliet, they should be advised their flirtations are absolutely unacceptable in your organization and may be grounds for dismissal. If they are working during a probationary period, we strongly encourage you to terminate employment rather than gamble on some dramatic personality change.

5. As in any situation that may result in a finding of sexual harassment or sex discrimination, management documentation is absolutely essential. What's more, allowing unwelcome flirtations to persist may put you as a manager in jeopardy for having tolerated or perpetuated a work environment that feels "hostile" to members of a given sex.

Preventive Measures:

Short of hormone therapy, we know of no measures that can prevent workplace flirtation and/or romance. Good clear training on sexual harassment may discourage unwanted flirtations and make what is in and out of bounds clearer to the flirt.

FOOD

"Our office always has the faint odor of popcorn; our employees joke about how coming to work is like going to the movies. They're always poking fun at the one employee who brings a sack of popcorn to work every day, and then munches on it through much of the day."

"Brown bagging" and lunch boxes are as much a part of work as copy machines and time clocks. While the contents of an employee's lunch are none of your business, when and where she eats are. As a manager, you should be concerned about the image your organization presents to customers, the possibility of equipment damage, and efficiency. In some settings, an employee munching on popcorn throughout the day may be perfectly agreeable to everyone. However, in others, action may be required to limit where and when (or under what conditions) employees may eat or drink on the job.

Some organizations provide space and facilities for employee meals and snacks. The principal issue concerning "break rooms" involves the cleanliness of the facility and/or misuse of the equipment. Such items as designated refrigerator space, who cleans the microwave, running out of coffee, etc., can preoccupy individuals whose time and thought would be better devoted to their work.

Approach to Take:

1. If an employee's eating habits have no detrimental effect on her work or that of others, they should not be an issue. As we've said before, treating employees like grown-ups tends to encourage them to behave like grown-ups.
2. Where an employee's habits clearly differ from the norm (in your office), you are stuck with the need to *say what you mean.* You have to talk to her and be honest about the problem. Be sure you set aside time to talk to her in private. Tell her what the problem is—whether it's odors, noises, time away from work, etc.
3. Rather than develop a policy for everyone, you may ask the one who is the focal point *to solve the problem himself.*

    Employees may have health-related reasons for needing to eat on a more frequent basis. If one of your employees has such a need, it's reasonable to: a) request documentation (from a doctor or clinic); b) have *the employee solve the problem* if his eating interrupts others; or c) consider discussing it openly at a *staff meeting.* Remember, you can only take it up "in public" if you've received permission from the employee involved.
4. Where a policy is warranted, solicit volunteers to draft one. Circulate the draft for comment before finalizing. You may also wish to propose food and drinks as an agenda item for an upcoming *staff meeting.*

Preventive Measures:

When new employees come on board, they should be advised of any policies relating to food and drink on the job.

GAMBLING

"Four of the employees in our office spend lunch together playing poker. Although the stakes are never high, tensions between winners and losers have been mounting."

In recent years, gambling has become less the province of Mafiosi and more that of the government. Most states have lotteries, and many augment these with horse/dog racing, off-track betting, and/or casino games. Whether you personally find gambling to be enjoyable or sinful has little to do with employee habits on the job. It's only when gambling interferes with productivity and teamwork that you should take notice.

While most of us think of gambling as frivolous or entertaining, many people are addicted to gaming. For them, it's a significant distraction from both work and home life. Quite often, compulsive gamblers must seek credit from loan sharks, who may disrupt their work lives or preoccupy them with threats.

Another habit common to compulsive gamblers is a desire for betting in settings where it would otherwise be inappropriate—like the workplace. Coworkers may be approached and coerced into betting on matters or events in which they would otherwise have little interest. Betting pools in the office concerning baseball, basketball, and football games may start out innocently enough, but can escalate into skirmishes over both time and money.

Approach to Take:

1. If employees are gambling at work, confront them and put an end to it. Make it clear that any gaming during working hours may result in disciplinary action.
2. *Ask someone else.* Where employees demonstrate addictive behaviors in this regard, contact your local hospital or mental health center concerning Gamblers Anonymous or other similar programs. Ask someone associated with

the program how they recommend you confront the employee. If you have an EAP, use it!

Preventive Measures:

If your organization has personnel policies, an employee handbook, or new-employee orientation, be sure to mention that gambling while at work is strictly prohibited. *Say what you mean,* but also make sure you mean what you say. A ban on gambling means you are also precluded from entering a football pool at work.

GAYS AND LESBIANS

"Last night I noticed one of our long-term employees entering a gay nightclub while holding hands with another man. I had no idea he is homosexual, and worry what will happen if others find out."

Discussing issues regarding same sex relationships, sexual orientation is always precarious. Some believe that such personal behavior is an abomination in the eyes of God and/or criminal in the eyes of the law. Others, ourselves included, believe that gay and lesbian relationships are normal and altogether acceptable.

What should be clear to any reader is that the decision of gay men and women to identify themselves as such ("come out of the closet") is often determined by the anticipated reaction of family members and employers. Without laws to protect them from the abuses coworkers and managers might inflict, gay and lesbian employees are reluctant to speak of their personal relationships.

Where an employee suffers at the hands of others at work because of his religious beliefs, handicap, age, color, etc., specific laws provide workplace protection. With the exception of a few municipalities, this is not the case for those who love members of the same sex. The absence of laws, however, does not preclude organizational policies or individual management controls to prevent discrimination due to sexual orientation.

Where gay and/or lesbian employees flirt, harass, or otherwise actively disrupt the workplace environment, they should be subject to the approaches outlined under those headings just as any other employee. Likewise, where the political or social beliefs of gay/lesbian workers infringe on the ability of others to accomplish their work free of disruption, management intervention is appropriate and may be necessary.

In sum, although it may be difficult for some heterosexual managers to put themselves in the place of a minority, handicapped, or gay employee, the Golden Rule should apply.

Approach to Take:

1. Managing a diverse workforce is a task more demanding than most books, training sessions, or policy statements imply. A manager's attitudes toward women and minorities (including sexual minorities) are shaped by upbringing and experience. The first step, therefore, involves acknowledging and understanding the prejudices you harbor.

2. Whether your concerns involve your own opinions and feelings or those of others in the organization, we suggest discussing issues surrounding gays and lesbians with an employee assistance program or other counselor. In larger communities, there may be gay/lesbian organizations that can provide you with information (not propaganda) that will help you in managing fears and concerns. Dealing with such deep-seated fears, concerns, beliefs, and/or prejudices demands guidance and support from a professional.

3. In the end, it is your obligation to manage employees and problems based on job performance and work-related behaviors. Being gay or lesbian is irrelevant in this context.

Preventive Measures:

The best preventive measure in this area is ongoing diversity training. Learning not only to accept differences but also to value and celebrate them is a long-term project. Virtually every organization that has accepted and acted on this course has benefited in terms of both economics and quality of work life.

While there are many private and public organizations that provide seminars concerning such issues, we recommend a long-term and sustained program of meetings, reading, and instruction designed by managers and employees together. Tolerance and acceptance require a lifetime of learning.

GIFTS

"Everyone had drawn the name of a coworker for the Christmas party. Each person was to buy a gift. The present Theresa bought obviously cost less than those purchased by others. Her embarrassment dampened the entire affair."

Certainly the spirit behind gift-giving can elevate morale within an organization. Acknowledging birthdays, year-end holidays, marriage/baby showers, retirements, etc., is something management should savor, not discourage. Any workplace in which a sense of celebration comes naturally or has been cultivated is one in which employees are more likely to stay and provide extra effort on the job.

The difficulties around gift-giving have to do with money, status, and influence. Many organizations and/or work groups find it more convenient to set a dollar limit on gifts. In this way those with less inclination to spend or who have greater financial burdens need not feel embarrassed or ashamed. It's difficult for such people when the more lavish spenders set the limits or the tone within the organization.

Another area of concern surrounding gifts is who gets them

and who doesn't. If every expectant and/or retiree is celebrated, this is not a worry. But if only certain people receive gifts while others in similar circumstances don't, management should be concerned. Likewise, the size of the gift(s) should be relatively consistent.

A final caution regarding gift-giving concerns the possibility of misunderstandings and favoritism. The giving of gifts to one's manager or supervisor may be viewed as a form of tribute or "brown-nosing." When the occasion warrants giving a gift to a superior, care should be taken to have the financial burdens shared equally and to ensure that it's from the entire group, not just one individual.

In order to succeed (in enhancing teamwork and elevating morale), the giving of gifts should be voluntary. Pressuring those who are not so inclined only creates tension and resentment. If one person chooses not to participate, adjustments must be made to continue the event without him, without shame, humiliation, or ill will.

Approach to Take:

1. *Let the employees solve the problem.* Managers should allow employees to celebrate events as they please. It may, however, be useful to agree on certain guidelines within an organization or work group. If any of the concerns discussed above relate to your workforce, we recommend a committee of employees develop the necessary guidelines.

   Let them develop a set of criteria, and then circulate the suggestions to all employees for (confidential) comment. As always, we encourage you to involve the employees in the decision making, and be open to comments—both pro and con—regarding new policies. Once guidelines have been developed, they should be put to coworkers (and the union if appropriate) for comments and/or objections. They should then be finalized and distributed.

   In voicing your own concerns, you should reassure employees that on-the-job celebrations and the giving of nominally valued gifts are encouraged. The framework in which giving takes place should only be designed to ensure that it's not destructive to morale and team building.

GLASS CEILING

"In our line of work, business is often negotiated on golf courses and in saunas. While some of the women who work here may be otherwise qualified for executive positions, they, along with some of the less athletic men, may be detrimental to business."

The term "glass ceiling" relates to the fact that women and minorities can rise only so far in many organizations despite professed equal employment opportunity. Statistical studies have shown that, depending on the organization, advancing women and people of color usually "top out" at a certain level or "hit the glass ceiling."

This is often because the organization can only visualize a male and/or European American occupying the next level. While the organization may believe in equal opportunity, leaders are not yet ready to break ranks with tradition.

Although the term "glass ceiling" was originally used by women's groups and former Secretary of Labor Lynn Martin to describe the problem women face at higher organizational levels, glass ceilings may also apply to the handicapped, those who speak with accents, or people who were never taught certain habits of dress or social habits common to the wealthy.

The difference between a glass ceiling and other forms of discrimination is the almost complete lack of awareness as well as of malice. In these cases, an organization's leadership cannot see the very barriers it imposes. Discrimination, however, need not be intentional in order to be illegal. Organizational factors that result in disadvantaging women and minorities must be shown as both legitimate and job-related. Golfing, beer-drinking, country-clubbing, fishing, etc., may fail the test.

Approach to Take:

1. Managers within the organization should be trained as to the nature and complexity of glass-ceiling issues. Such training could be done in a classroom or seminar, from viewing videotaped presentations, or by reading articles and books. Training can build a base of awareness, and awareness may result in the interest or will to act.

2. Survey your own organization as to the barriers that confront individuals as they rise in the organization. Such a survey should be administered confidentially by an outside source to ensure the most honest and complete information is gathered.

3. *Get another opinion.* Management may also wish to learn how other organizations have acknowledged and dealt with their glass ceilings. This can be done by going to the library and asking to have the national periodicals index searched for the term "glass ceiling." The resulting array of articles will point you in the direction of appropriate organizations to call or write.

   You may also wish to talk to colleagues in other organizations to see how they've addressed this issue. We believe the more open you become to seeing through the glass ceiling, the more likely it is to break.

4. *Let the employees participate in solving the problem.* Allow women and minorities to participate in any action planning regarding glass-ceiling issues. Since they are the ones most likely to be able to see the barriers, their participation will add credibility to any efforts taken.

5. The most important commitment, however, must come from the very highest echelon(s) of your organization. Where everyone but "them" acknowledges and/or understands these sensitive issues in this area, the necessary changes still cannot be made.

Preventive Measures:

As you recruit for higher-level positions in which women and/or minorities are "under-represented," you may wish to have your selection criteria reviewed by individuals who are aware of glass-ceiling issues. Their input may help you and the organization become more aware of the barriers that are invisible to you but not to those different from you.

Gossip

"I don't really mind it when employees talk behind my back—but damn it, lately one of them has been tying up productive time gabbing with anyone within listening distance."

Organizational gossip is normal, natural, and sometimes even productive. Every work setting with at least a handful of people develops a "grapevine" over which information is shared. Managers should learn to tolerate a "normal level" of gossip (verbal or electronic, on or off the clock) since attempts to control it often prove futile.

Gossip can, however, become counter-productive. It can: distract people from their work; adversely affect teamwork; undermine authority; and lead to hurt feelings. When and why gossip crosses the line involves management judgment, awareness, and discretion.

Although you really can't control gossip, one of your biggest concerns should be ensuring your own actions don't generate topics for the grapevine. The more open you are with employees—particularly about things which impact them—the less fodder you provide for the gossip mill. If you are thinking about layoffs, keep your work force informed on an ongoing basis.

Approach to Take:

1. *Define the problem.* The first consideration a manager should make in these cases is whether to intervene at all. Criteria upon which to make a decision include: productive time lost, effect on teamwork and morale, customer (internal and external) perceptions, and maintenance of order and respect. If you feel that things have gotten out of hand, they probably have.

2. If you choose to confront an employee, our suggestions are:

   a. *Get another opinion.* Ask your colleagues what they have done to defuse office gossip. Keep in mind *you* are the one who will have to implement their suggestions. Feel free to modify others' ideas.

   b. *Think it over.* What is it that's really causing the trouble? Look through the criteria listed above, and be very clear what effect the gossip is having in the workplace. Once you have clarified for yourself what the problem is,

   c. Confront the employee and *say what you mean.* (Don't confuse stating the problem with airing your frustrations. It's okay to say, "I'm frustrated because I think these rumors of layoffs are cutting into productive time." It's not okay to say, "You're wasting time gossiping about layoffs.")

   d. Don't debate. If the employee becomes defensive ("I'm sure I don't know what you're talking about, it's not really like that, you're blowing this completely out of proportion, etc."), then *let the employee solve the problem.* Tell her you would like to give her an opportunity to prove to you you're wrong. Give her a time line for getting back to you, and be sure to note the date on your calendar.

Preventive Measures:

Allow employees opportunities to evaluate each other—anonymously. If this is impossible or might breed more anxiety than benefit, consider a job satisfaction survey—anonymous as well. Be sure to ask specifically whether gossip, rumor, and/or extraneous conversation has proven disruptive.

There may not be a need to name names or point fingers. Reporting coworker feedback or publicizing the results of a survey may prove a corrective measure in and of itself.

HOLIDAYS

"A new employee was shocked and dismayed to learn that birthdays are not considered holidays in our organization. Since we already give employees eight paid days off from work, I'm reluctant to concede this issue."

There are no laws or other requirements about private employers observing holidays. Employees and customers, however, expect an employer to close on certain days, and most provide employees with a paid day off. Certain holidays are considered standard in the United States. Among these are New Year's Day, Memorial Day, Fourth of July, Labor Day, Thanksgiving, and Christmas. While millions are required to work on these days, it's customary to pay double time or some other form of premium pay to them.

Other holidays observed on a national basis are Martin Luther King, Jr., Day, Presidents' Day, Columbus Day, and Veterans Day. Federal government employees are afforded the six standard days off, along with these four, for a total of ten. As the Federal Reserve Banks close on these days, other banks follow suit, and so have many private employers.

Statistics show that blue-collar employees in the U.S. average about nine holidays per year, and white-collar about ten. On the average, state workers get eleven days off, mainly because states have their own unique holidays. For example, in Louisiana and Alabama, Mardi Gras is a state holiday. In Utah, it's Pioneer Day, and in Alaska Seward's and Alaska Days are added to the list.

Because some holidays have particular significance to only a portion of the workforce, many employers have allowed employees to have "floating" holidays. This approach is similar to flexible work hours and compressed work weeks. Employees may be given specific holidays where the office or plant is closed, and others to choose as they wish. Some employees choose religious holidays such as Yom Kippur or Good Friday. Others prefer birthdays and other personal occasions as holidays. And a certain portion of the workforce will simply add floating holidays to extend vacation time.

Approach to Take:

1. Determine the requirements of your business. Retailers are different than twenty-four-hour plumbers, who are different from a symphony orchestra. Your policy regarding holidays should match the realities of the work being performed. Some operations require a complement of employees every day of the year. Hospitals and utilities are obvious examples. In these cases, holidays are more likely to represent premium pay than days off.

2. *Let the employees solve the problem.* If you already have a policy designating certain holidays, see if it suits the employees. They need not take more time off work with pay, but may wish to adjust the holiday schedule or use floating days in lieu of fixed ones.

3. If you require employees to work on a designated holiday, the norm in most areas is to pay twice the hourly rate. Even with such a premium, some employees would prefer to be with their families, or may already have made special plans. We suggest you try to plan for such work as far in advance as possible, and look for volunteers whenever you can. Forcing someone to work on a holiday when

she would rather not may, in the long run, cost you more than you gained during that day.

4. In some cases, people's religious beliefs require them not to work on certain days. For Muslims and Jews, these days are scattered throughout the year. For others, it may be a weekly Sabbath. Requiring someone to work on a religious holiday may constitute discrimination based on religion. By the same token, there's no requirement to pay people for religious holidays requiring their absence from work. In most cases, employees will use vacation days on such holidays and you, as a manager, can manage without them during those times. Where you must work an employee on such a day, consult your attorney first.

ILLNESS, EXTENDED

"We have only one computer programmer. Her services will be needed intensively during the next three to four months. However, a serious illness will prevent her from coming to work for the next two to three months. After that, her full recovery may still require additional time. To accomplish the programming workload we face, I would like to replace her immediately."

Employees in organizations of fifty or more who require extensive leaves of absence due to illness are guaranteed up to twelve weeks time away from work while retaining full job security. Such leave may be fully or partially paid or unpaid, depending on your policies and their leave accumulation.

The twelve-week requirement is contained in the Family and Medical Leave Act (FMLA) of 1993. This federal law is designed to retain job security for employees who contract a serious illness. While "serious" is a matter that will be left to interpretation by courts, we believe you should err on the side of caution or contact an attorney regarding the circumstances at hand.

Of course the FMLA does not require that all twelve weeks be used. That time frame is the maximum unless state laws or your organization's policies allow for greater employee benefits. An employee who may require intermittent time off due to a serious medical condition may also be entitled to accumulate twelve weeks off.

The easiest way to understand provisions contained in the FMLA is to reacquaint yourself with the Golden Rule. Imagine yourself being involved in a serious auto accident requiring months away from work and other aspects of your daily life. Consider the pain, disappointment, and financial consequences you would face. Now imagine your organization fires you for your inability to report for work. In essence, the law mandates the compassion we would expect for ourselves.

Approach to Take:

1. Most lengthy absences due to illness occur with little or no warning. Such events seriously test the old axiom that no one is indispensable. The first and most obvious response is the need to adjust workload to minimize the immediate impact. In some cases, this may involve bringing a temporary employee on board.
2. As mentioned above, do not allow the workplace difficulties you face to obscure your own sense of concern and compassion. *Follow the Golden Rule.* Contact the employee and/or family. Be sure that any medical insurance questions are answered by your carrier. Keep coworkers informed regarding the individual's condition and progress, etc.
3. If called upon to explain how paid and/or unpaid leave will continue during the absence, be sure to contact your legal or human resource function if appropriate. In essence, your job is to balance the employee's hardship with your own and that of coworkers.
4. In small organizations where the FMLA doesn't apply, or where the twelve-week limit is exceeded, management must make its own call. In doing so, the first thing to

consider is the expectation of the employee's full recovery. If she is not expected to regain the capacity for full-time work, then consider her to be disabled. Information concerning disability benefits is available from your local Social Security office.

5. If the FMLA is not a consideration, base your decision on whichever of the following factors you consider to be relevant: the potential for full or partial recovery, any written personnel policies or past practices, the employee's years of service, his performance record, the adequacy of temporary replacement, whether you intend to treat future cases in a similar fashion, and the effect of your decision on employee morale.

Consider the costs vs. the benefits of different alternatives. Keep in mind that whatever you decide (outside of FMLA) will reflect on the rest of your workforce. No one expects you to ruin your business for the sake of one ill employee, but your ability to be compassionate and caring will be observed by those around you.

Preventive Measures:

If you have a policy that allows employees to accumulate sick leave, you may at least facilitate the process in the case of an extended illness. If employees can carry their unused sick leave from year to year, if and when they need it, they can legitimately take leave time with pay. (See the section on SICK DAYS.)

In addition, you may want to consider developing a policy that allows employees to donate accumulated sick leave to others.

INJURY COMPENSATION

"My office manager has been complaining about his elbow hurting. It worries me, because I don't know whether or not the pain is work-related, or if I'll have to pay for medical care if it is."

In the last ten years, there has been a lot of media coverage on huge settlements in employee injury cases. It's often difficult to separate the hype from the reality—and it's enough to put employers on notice about the seriousness of workplace injuries. Since workers' compensation insurance covers only work-related illness or injury, a lot of the confusion comes in defining what is and what is not related to work.

Workers' comp laws are state laws, and coverage, rates, and benefits vary by state. All programs have a couple things in common. They are all "no fault" laws. In most cases this means, with claims that are accepted, neither the employee nor the employer admits fault for the illness or injury. (There are exceptions such as intoxication of the employee, self-inflicted injury, and where an injury results from a fight in which the employee was the aggressor.)

In addition, all programs provide employees with payment of medical bills, and varying cash payments (depending on the state, the level of disability, and the kind of insurance) in exchange for employees giving up the right to sue employers. In essence, employers give up their right to reject claims in exchange for protection against lawsuits for negligence.

Both the benefits and the insurance coverage are governed by the states. In most states, there are maximum benefit levels and minimum coverage levels. Depending on the state, an employer may/must insure through a state-run insurance program, purchase insurance in the private market, or self-insure. There is a stringent financial standard that must be met for self-insuring, so only large employers are able to entertain this option.

In all states, there are essentially the same kinds of claims: medical-only claims; temporary total disability; temporary partial disability; permanent partial disability; permanent total disability; and death claims. All of these claims presume problems that come about in the course of employment. This can be a very complicated issue, and is the stuff of most lawsuits.

Medical-only claims are the most common type. This is the illness or injury that requires little or no time off the job. Because the employee is able to continue working, there's no requirement for income-maintenance cash benefits. Temporary total disability refers to an illness or injury of an indeterminate length of time, but with the expectation an employee will recover fully and return to work.

Temporary partial disability implies work restrictions. The employee doesn't require time off work, but probably does require either temporary reassignment or, at least, a temporary change in job duties. Permanent partial disability is perhaps the trickiest claim, and the one that engenders the most litigation. In this type of claim, the employee may be able to work again someday, but likely will have diminished capabilities of some kind. The disagreement comes over whether or not the person will be able to work, to what degree future wages have been effected, whether the illness or injury was truly job-related, etc.

Death claims are relatively rare. Most states have a complicated schedule for determining death-claim benefits. Again the issue here is whether or not the death was work-related. The terms of death claims are generally clearly spelled out within each state system, and have minimum and maximum amounts and time limits.

Premiums are charged on the gross payroll total. Most states allow for the exemption of corporate officers and owners. Rates vary widely not only from state to state, but also across industries. Higher-risk sectors like construction require higher premiums than relatively sedentary occupations like architecture or other office work.

Approach to Take:

1. If you have employees and you're not already paying premiums for workers' compensation insurance, you should

be. Look in the Government section of your telephone directory under state offices to find the number for your state office. (It may be listed under Workers' Compensation, Industrial Insurance, or under your state labor department.) Call and find out the requirements for your state.

If you have a choice between state-provided and private carrier-provided insurance, *consider the costs vs. the benefits* of each alternative. Compare the benefits to make sure you're getting the same coverage for the same dollars.

2. If you receive a claim that you're unsure about, start by getting more information. Talk to the supervisor and to the injured employee. Document the information you receive. In the case of a trauma (as opposed to a less visible illness or long-term injury like carpal tunnel syndrome), find out if there were witnesses. Gather factual information from them. Keep clear, dated notes which include the name of the witness as well as the information provided.

3. If you work in a large organization, check with your HR department about your options for rejecting a claim. There are likely to be well-developed procedures for what to do in these cases.

In a small organization, where you believe a claim is for an injury or illness that is not work-related, talk to an attorney who's versed in workers' comp cases. It's in your best interests to be fair to your employees, but it's also important not to accept claims you truly feel are not justified. You must balance the effect on morale of declining a claim versus the impact on your insurance rate of accepting a marginal claim.

Preventive Measures:

There are many things you can do to decrease the likelihood of illness or injury in your workplace. The most obvious is a program to train all employees in the proper use of all necessary tools and equipment. In addition, do an audit of your workplace to see if there are hazards waiting for accidents to happen. Look around for electric cords that run across traffic-flow areas, supplies stacked dangerously high, and other easily fixed physical hazards.

Beyond that, there are physical and occupational therapists and physicians who specialize in workplace issues. For employees who are required to perform repetitive tasks, there may be different, less stressful ways to do the same job with less probability of injury. For people who are sitting all day, there may be easily performed exercises that can make the difference between back trouble and physical comfort.

There are also companies that will evaluate the air in your workplace and check for any unseen hazards. It may be that there are either parts of your operation or other situations within the building that are putting employees at risk. While "sick building syndrome" may have been overplayed in the last few years, it can be a very serious problem if not addressed in a timely manner.

Also see the section on PHYSICAL FITNESS.

References: For additional information, see *Workers' Compensation Handbook: A Guide to Job-Related Health Problems,* Robert D. Power, M.D., and Frederick Y. Fund, M.D., KW Publications, San Diego, 1994; *The Handbook of Employee Benefits, Design, Funding, and Administration,* Volume I, Third Edition, edited by Jerry S. Rosenbloom, Business One Irwin, Homewood, IL, 1992; and *J. K. Lasser's Employee Benefits for Small Business,* Jane White and Bruce Pyenson, Prentice Hall, New York, 1993.

JOB DESCRIPTIONS

"One of my employees insists on having a job description. I don't know how to write one, or what I'm supposed to include."

Job descriptions are often considered useless investments in paper, ink, and time. If read at all, they are subsequently entombed in the darkest recesses of desks and file cabinets. On the other hand, an employee who is not clear about his job responsibilities may appear incompetent and disinterested. Supervisors often assume that employees know what they are supposed to be doing, whether they have been told or not.

A job description can eliminate confusion by defining responsibilities, boundaries, organizational flow, and specific job tasks. Job descriptions should be reviewed from time to time to ensure they continue to reflect the job as it grows and changes.

Approach to Take:

1. Talk to the employee about what she actually *does* in her job. Ask her to make a list of duties and responsibilities. Then sit down and make your own list of what you think the job entails.
2. Get back together and compare your lists. Be prepared to listen to the employee's input. Make no mistake about it, you have the final say in this discussion. However, respect for her opinions concerning her job can do a lot to improve performance, saving you time and frustration.
3. Remember to *follow the Golden Rule.* Have you ever been confused as to what your boss wanted from you?
4. *Let the employee solve the problem.* Allow the employee to write his own job description. Agree to a trial period of three to six months. At the end of the stated period, meet with the employee to discuss his performance during this period. If you are satisfied, his job description remains as written. If not, you get to change it.

   In large organizations, the human resources department likes to oversee the writing of job descriptions. While their perspective and experience may prove valuable, remember that you and the affected employee are the ones who really understand what is required on the job.

Preventive Measures:

Always develop a job description before you hire someone to fill a vacancy. If you interview, show it to applicants and ask them for comments and concerns.

> ### JOB SHARING
>
> "Two employees have approached me asking if they can 'share a job.' The current incumbent has a child with special needs and would prefer working part-time. Her 'job partner' retired three years ago and is looking for part-time work himself."

Job sharing challenges the assumption that an employee is a single individual working approximately forty hours a week. Similar to the example shown above, four individuals could occupy three full-time positions simply by sharing time at and away from work. Such arrangements present both advantages and disadvantages.

The good news involves reliability. Where two or more individuals enter into job-sharing agreements, reliability is usually enhanced. For example, when one feels sick, rather than call in sick, he may call his coworker, who is able to fill in. Similarly, when one takes a vacation, the desk or job need not be vacant for a period of weeks.

Another advantage is the organization's ability to retain the services of conscientious and skilled people who are unable to work full-time. It's unfortunate when an employer's need for a full-time worker forces an individual to either stay or leave the organization.

One of the difficulties associated with job sharing involves benefits. Many organizations avoid full benefits packages through the use of part-time employees. Where two people occupy a single job, or three people a pair of jobs, the cost of benefits may increase. In some cases (where spouses already have full-time employee benefits or where retirement benefits are already in effect), there may be room for negotiating around this concern.

Another drawback to job sharing involves the security of knowing who is on the job. Neither the manager nor coworkers may feel comfortable where a desk or work bench is occupied by a different person at different times. Likewise the number of hours per week may, in some arrangements, vary. For example, while Ed is away visiting his grandchildren, Lisa may work forty hours per week. Upon his return, each of them goes back to working twenty hours.

One issue of which you need to be aware is training. If you provide training—in new systems, regarding new procedures, or in new products or services—you must be sure to include all partners who are sharing a job.

In addition, you should acknowledge that it may be difficult to conduct performance evaluations for a position that is shared. In coming to an agreement about how and whether to allow job sharing, you must consider this issue.

Approach to Take:

1. In most cases, a manager's job is to consider and/or facilitate employees' needs in this area. While job sharing may prove useful, we see little need to promote it where it hasn't been requested or needed. When you are approached, keep an open mind on the subject.
2. When you are approached, it may be best for you to determine your own needs in terms of expenses, coverage, performance continuity, etc. *Define the problem.* Consider whether or not your customers will be adversely affected by job sharing.

   Let the employees solve the problem. Leave the hours, space sharing, and other agreements up to the employees who want to share. Do, however, insist on some written work plan to be developed by the employees sharing the job.

3. If you're unsure as to the long-term viability of a proposed arrangement, see if the employees will agree to a six-month or one-year trial and an understanding that the plan could be terminated at the end of the trial.

JURY DUTY

"One of our project engineers has been summoned for jury duty. He's in the final phase of a very important job. It would be the worst time for him to be gone."

Essential to the foundation of the U.S. government is the concept of trial by jury. The Constitution allows each of us who might be charged with a criminal offense the right to have a group of our "peers" determine our innocence or guilt. As it takes six or twelve peers for any one accused, jury duty is a very important feature of U.S. citizenship.

The specifics, however, are never as easy. Jury duty can result in short- or long-term disruption and significant organizational costs. An employer's instinct is to desire to have an employee excused from jury duty in order to maintain smooth, cost-efficient operations. Where business operations may be seriously hampered, this can be requested of the court in question (federal, state, county, or municipal). Excuses are granted on a case-by-case basis.

Whether an employee will be paid by the organization for the time spent in service of the court is a management call. Many believe allowing participation in the jury system is part of the cost of doing business in this country. Each court pays a token daily fee to anyone appearing for jury duty. Employers who maintain workers on payroll during such periods often pay the difference between salary and the fee, or simply ask the employee to sign jury checks over to the organization.

Many employers are willing to bear the costs of jury duty for a certain period of time and no longer—say, one month. Where this is the case, the employee should be well aware of the policy and should make her decision about jury participation based on that information.

Terminating an employee for jury duty is illegal in most jurisdictions. Some employers who don't wish to bear the financial or organizational burden of jury duty among employees simply refuse to pay any salary or wage for the time the employee serves. In this way, the employee's job security is insured, but the likelihood of serving for any length of time is slim. Clerks of court commonly excuse prospective jurors for reasons of economic hardship.

Approach to Take:

1. The vast majority of medium and large employers pay full salaries and benefits to employees who are selected for jury duty. While we don't want to raise the flag or hum the "Star-Spangled Banner" in your direction, subsidizing jury duty is simply the right thing to do. Only in cases of severe and obvious economic hardship would we advise otherwise.

2. Some internal procedures regarding jury duty are in order for any business or not-for-profit, as the likelihood of an employee being summoned is high. Employees should know how to report the receipt of a jury summons. We recommend a single point of contact in the organization be notified within one work day of receipt.

   Secondly, your policy regarding service and request for excuse should be made known to all employees. Only the clerk of the court can grant an excuse, but the organization can set a policy about why and when to ask.

   Finally, your policy regarding court fees to jurors and payroll procedures for employees in service to the court should be in writing and available to affected employees. If juror-fee checks are to be signed back to the organization, timeliness and an appropriate point of contact should be determined.

3. If you're the proprietor or director of a small organization, and are called to jury duty yourself, an excuse is presumed

in most jurisdictions. Explain your position to the clerk of court by phone or in writing—as specified in the summons itself.

> ### KEYS TO THE OFFICE
>
> "One of my employees arrives at work earlier than the rest. She has asked me for a key to the building rather than having to wait for me or my assistant to arrive."

Whether or not to provide employees with keys to the workplace or spaces therein is simply an issue of trust. Some employers prefer that each employee entrusted with a key sign a statement as to its appropriate use and safeguarding. Others prefer polygraph testing, while a third group simply trust employees to handle the organization's keys as if they were their own.

Certainly access to locked workplaces should only be considered for those with a demonstrated need. Rather than assume what that need is, it's better to ask the employee why she's requesting access and how she plans to use and safeguard the organization's keys.

Approach to Take:

1. We subscribe to the belief that trust of employees is an essential ingredient to productivity, profit, and morale. Allowing employees to carry keys to the workplace is advisable when two basic conditions are met:

   a. The employee should have a demonstrated need for access.

   b. The employee should be willing to sign an agreement concerning the use and safeguarding (including loaning and copying) of keys.

      Many locks can be keyed so that it takes a specific authorization to make copies.

2. *Consider the costs vs. the benefits.* In some ways, the answer to this question depends on the kind of business you're in, the configuration of your office/facility, and the classification of employees requesting keys. If you are in an industry, like fashion design, where trade secrets are a valuable asset, you should adopt a different policy about keys than if you're in the freight-hauling business.

   Another issue to consider in the cost/benefit analysis is the question of time. If not having keys means an employee must wait for you or other authorized personnel to open the office, or can't work late without having someone else stay to lock up, consider the lost or wasted time. Such efficiency issues may argue for more keys, or may indicate a flaw in the way work flows through your office.

3. If security is an issue in your organization, you may want to consider consulting a security specialist and/or an insurance agent. If your workplace has an alarm system, be sure to notify the appropriate agencies regarding clearance for employees with keys. Also be sure to train all personnel in the use of the system.

Preventive Measures:

This is an issue where prudence and planning can prevent problems in the future. If you're uncomfortable about giving keys to employees, talk it over with key personnel and develop a policy that makes sense for your organization.

As we've said before, you may also want to consider your hiring practices. If trust is an issue, think about redesigning your screening process. In a workplace where security is a concern, always be sure to check references.

KNOW-IT-ALLS

"Every time anyone in our office has a question, one employee has all the answers. It doesn't matter what the subject is, she's always there with an answer. By Friday afternoon, everyone around her is ready to scream. While it's great having a self-assured employee, her insistence is very annoying."

When most of us attempt to describe an individual who is truly wise and knowing, we usually conjure up an image of a person who also exhibits high levels of modesty and/or humility. Not so with the know-it-all. Her problem is the perceived understanding of problems and solutions beyond that of the "mere mortals" with whom she works.

This (usually unconscious) arrogance, while aggravating to coworkers, is especially difficult for a manager. After all, if anyone is charged with having all the answers, it's you. Know-it-alls commonly second-guess management reasoning and decision making.

As most such individuals are blissfully unaware of their own behavior, so they fail to recognize the consternation they cause within the organization. Often they fail to see or understand the anger they engender, which is more a result of their inability to stop and think than of any given response itself.

Staff meetings become more difficult as other employees may become more reticent in expressing their needs and concerns. After all, why should one express a doubt or concern when the answer will be on his lips within seconds.

One of the hardest aspects of dealing with know-it-alls is that their idea, answer, or alternative may actually be preferable. Because they seem to perceive themselves as more competent than others, few others want to accept their input. In sum, the problems presented by such individuals have more to do with style than substance. Their competence and ability to explore appropriate solutions may be truly enviable.

Approach to Take:

1. The most important thing to consider when dealing with a know-it-all is patient (and perhaps repeated) confrontation. *Say what you mean.* The individual should be privately counseled in an atmosphere that feels as agreeable as possible (over lunch, after the successful completion of a job or project, or after acknowledging one of her better ideas/suggestions).

2. The most important factor in successfully confronting the know-it-all is your own attitude. The less aggravated the better. *Think it over.* You may wish to have a written list of clever ideas and helpful offerings from the individual which will remind you of her value. After all, the idea is to change future behavior rather than dwell on past mistakes.

3. Explain that his ideas and suggestions may be discounted or rejected merely on the basis of how they are being presented. Offer a specific example or two that illustrate your preferred model for behavior (suggesting rather than telling, listening rather than talking, asking rather than assuming, etc.). Explain that the employee's value to you and others will grow if and as the offensive side of his behavior diminishes. Be sure to *say it again.* Make sure you get him to summarize what you've told him to make sure he's gotten it right.

4. Some managers find success in asking such an employee if this subject has ever come up before—in other jobs or in his personal life. If the know-it-all can acknowledge you're not the first to identify what must be a lifelong problem, it can make your job of correcting his behavior that much easier.

5. Most know-it-alls really do possess a certain gift for understanding, evaluating, and responding quickly. Many have the ability to solve problems more creatively than you and/or others. This ability can prove very useful and should be acknowledged during your conversation. In doing so, you may wish to remind the individual that others

need to be acknowledged for their strengths and abilities too.

6. Depending on whether you have access to an EAP and the expertise it offers, you may wish to seek the guidance of a counselor whose services you're already paying for. Counselors may have ideas that are more specific to you, the individual in question, and the organization for which you both work.

Preventive Measures:

In organizations that use peer evaluations or 360 appraisals, the know-it-all would receive candid information from coworkers on a regular basis. Such feedback is usually provided anonymously and is intended for developmental purposes.

LATE COMPLETION OF WORK

"This morning I assigned a project and told the employee I need a report in two weeks. Upon returning to my office, I realized he seldom completes projects on time. I'm anticipating scolding him two weeks from now."

The fact is some of us are faster and others slower at getting a job done. Sometimes being slow or late is in the eyes of the beholder. For instance, when we're in a hurry to catch a train or make a traffic light, everyone seems to move at a snail's pace.

When the tables are turned, we wonder why the other person is in such a rush and how it's affecting his blood pressure. Where one employee simply doesn't organize her work sensibly or take time frames seriously, intervention may be required.

Remember that in many cases getting a pedantic person to make quick decisions, a slow writer to whip out a report, or a cautious mechanic to hurry up a repair, may be an exercise in futility.

From the employee's vantage point, it often seems management wants to have it both ways—professing attention to detail and quality, while enforcing strict time constraints. Usually, if work is to be completed faster or sooner than you're now experiencing, addressing work habits is more successful than imposing stricter time frames and sanctions.

Approach to Take:

1. *Define the problem.* If someone simply takes too long to get started or works too slowly, a manager should first confront her honestly. (Keep in mind that some employees really are just irresponsible, but most people who appear to work slowly really are just slow.)

   After you've talked with the employee, begin to impose time frames that challenge the employee without overwhelming him or her. When you do so, the employee should be advised that excuses for delinquency may not be accepted. (The old "My dog ate it" won't work with grown-ups.) Disciplinary sanctions may be imposed if work is late.

2. It's a different case when employees appear to be working diligently, yet their work still isn't complete on time. In these cases, a manager should take the time to observe and/ or discuss the employee's work habits or processes so that both parties can understand how and where they lose time.

   Some employees may be overly cautious, others overly obsessed with quality. In many cases, employees are simply ill-trained in how to do their work efficiently.

3. Finally, a responsible manager must look at the part she plays. Where work environments are particularly competitive, demands for both quality and timeliness of work can become unrealistic. Furthermore, a manager's assumption that "he should know how to get the job done on time" and "that's what I pay him for" may be altogether off base. Just as managers may gain new insights regarding their own responsibilities between the covers of this book, so employees often require greater knowledge, understanding, and training concerning their jobs.

Many people have a difficult time saying, "I'm not sure I understand how to do this," for fear they'll be judged incompetent or burdensome. In an environment where individual managers can admit their own needs for improvement, employees may be more likely to follow suit.

LAYOFFS

"We added a new group of employees a couple years ago as we geared up to market a new product. The market never really took off. Unless business picks up soon, I'll have to lay them off."

Nobody likes the idea of firing employees. Whether it's for insubordination, because of changing market conditions, or because of a move to another location, letting people go is a drag.

There are several issues to consider when confronting layoff decisions. One overarching item is the morale of employees who are left. While it may be impossible to avoid cutting the size of the workforce, nobody wants to work in a morgue. In the rush to "save" the company, many managers forget the necessity of thinking long-term. What does the organization look like six months from now when all the changes have been made?

Another thing to review in planning for layoffs is what your legal and financial obligations are to terminated employees. Employers, especially in large organizations, must be certain to review employee protection legislation to make sure all bases have been covered. If you employ more than one hundred workers, and plan mass layoffs or plant closings, you'll likely be affected by the Worker Adjustment and Retraining Notification Act (WARN). This Act requires you to give sixty days notice to all affected employees, or show cause why you can't.

If you have a work force greater than twenty, you may well be affected by the Consolidated Omnibus Budget Reconciliation Act (COBRA). Essentially COBRA gives terminated and retired workers the right to continued access to their group health insurance coverage.

Finally, the Employee Retirement Income Security Act (ERISA) may come into play if you have a pension plan, or if you plan to give terminated employees a severance payout over time. All of this legislation is complex and time-consuming, and can be expensive for your organization if you don't comply. When getting ready to lay off employees, be sure to contact your accountant and an attorney versed in employment law.

One practical note: Whether you're considering layoffs, or just terminating one employee, remember your obligation to provide a final W-2. If the employee requests it, you must provide it within thirty days of the final work day. Otherwise, it will be due to the employee by the end of the following January, along with all your current W-2s.

Approach to Take:

1. *Consider the costs vs. the benefits* of laying off employees. It may be possible for you to have the same number of employees work fewer hours, and still be able to retain them. Check with your state unemployment insurance office to see whether the employees may be able to get part-time unemployment insurance and still work part-time for you. Many states consider it preferable to having to pay full benefits.

2. *Let the employees solve the problem.* There are two questions you can ask the employees. One is to help come up with other options—like ways to increase the market or sell more to existing customers, job sharing, or maybe even joint venture opportunities you hadn't considered.

   The other question is what kinds of help you can give them if you do need to go through with the layoffs. You have a moral, and possibly in some cases a legal, obligation to help employees be more employable. This doesn't mean you should put your organization at risk trying to help those who are leaving—it just means you need to consider ways you can help them keep working. Many community colleges have retraining programs, and some state unemployment offices also have options available to private employers.

3. Although the economic evaluation is important in this decision, there's more than just economics at stake. *Follow the Golden Rule.* Think about how those remaining are going to feel after the deed is done. Will you still have credibility with them when you say yours is an organization that's concerned about its employees?

Two ways to ensure continued productive relationships with remaining employees: be as open and honest as you possibly can about why the layoffs are taking place, and what the situation will be afterwards; consider opening the books to employees so they know firsthand what's going on and what they can expect.

As we've said many times, the more involved your employees are in decisions which affect them, the more committed they'll be to implementation. If they don't believe one round of layoffs will be enough, you'll have a very difficult time winning back their trust.

4. Finally, consider providing career counseling for all employees—those leaving *and* those staying. It will help employees clarify their goals and their role in the organization, it will foster credibility that you care about them, and it may even uncover hidden talents among your existing employees.

Preventive Measures:

Although you can't control economic changes in the market, you may have more control than you think over your response to those changes. A good marketing team, and a good strategic planning process that builds in flexibility, can go a long way toward using economic downturns to your advantage.

We can't stress too much the value of open communication with your employees. If you practice this on a regular basis, when you do have a crisis that calls for drastic action, you're less likely to lose the commitment of your workers.

Reference: Joinson, Carla, "Easing the Pain of Layoffs," *HR Magazine,* February 1995, p. 68.

LEAVE ABUSE, VACATION AND PERSONAL DAYS

"One of my employees called in this morning to say he'd be late. This time the excuse was a leaking pipe. He calls in so often with so many different emergencies, you'd think he keeps a list by the phone."

Virtually all employers provide employees with paid time off for rest, relaxation, personal business, and/or vacation. In most cases, how the worker chooses to use this time is entirely up to him. Some prefer one- or two-week outings, others a day here and there, while a few may even forgo the benefit altogether, being happier just to come to work.

When an employee schedules a vacation or just a day off to go fishing or shopping, you as a manager have the opportunity to plan, adjust, or even ask the employee to reschedule her time off. Unscheduled emergency, or call-in leave, allows a manager little flexibility. Any adjustments must be made immediately.

The difficulty comes when employees take time unexpectedly, resulting in repeated consternation at work. Excessive unscheduled call-ins may be merely a symptom of a larger problem—substance abuse, family problems, emotional distress, or just irresponsibility. The employee who leaves a message before you arrive, or who has a chronically ill child, may really have an emergency—once or twice. Managers who suffer these habits often find initial sympathetic responses turning to suspicion and frustration.

If, under the Fair Labor Standards Act (FLSA), you manage "exempt" employees, one note of caution is in order. If an exempt employee requests time off without pay, make sure it is only granted in full-day increments. Granting "leave without pay" in hourly or shorter increments may leave you with an unintended liability for overtime compensation. The liability could extend back for months if not years. If you have questions about this, contact your accountant. (See OVERTIME, FAIR LABOR STANDARDS ACT.)

Approach to Take:

1. Granting or denying paid vacation for unscheduled days off should be a matter of supervisory discretion. Under normal circumstances, we suggest you *follow the Golden Rule.* Try to accommodate the needs of employees when such problems occur in their personal lives. After all, how would you feel if a boss failed to acknowledge a crisis you experienced, and then denied you paid time off which you'd already earned?

2. With an employee whose life involves perpetual crisis, you may wish to take action. When suspicion runs high and patience runs low, we suggest you advise the employee that any future excuses for unscheduled time off may prove unacceptable, regardless of their apparent legitimacy.

   In cases where an individual instance or absence leads you to suspect abuse, request acceptable documentation from the employee—from the highway department, the auto repair shop, or the day care center—prior to approving paid time off.

3. There are also many cases of employees whose lives really are more unpredictable than our own. Difficulties with family members, finances, housing, etc., may prove both legitimate and disruptive. In those cases, we recommend contacting public and/or private counseling services. A simple call to the United Way or a county hospital may reveal services available to the employee that could preclude future instances of absence.

   In cases where counseling services or the use of a larger organization's EAP seem appropriate, we recommend the employee make the call or the visit at your suggestion or direction.

   Even in cases where the problems are completely legitimate, employees need to understand you're relying on them to come to work—or to schedule absences far enough in advance that you can schedule replacements if necessary.

Preventive Measures:

Managers should maintain a leave record for each employee. Records should be reviewed quarterly to detect overuse, current balances, excessive accumulations, etc. Managers should be particularly aware of patterns that might imply abuse, such as emergencies on Mondays only.

Vacation abuse is often a symptom of a personal problem. Making arrangements with an EAP and advising employees of confidential counseling opportunities may prevent the problem from ever occurring.

We also encourage organizations to have absence or leave policies. These should spell out when and under what circumstances employees should notify the organization concerning such absences. It may also state that insufficient reason(s) or excuse(s) may result in a non-pay status for the day(s) of absence, and/or disciplinary action.

LUNCH BREAKS

"An employee just left my office complaining that she keeps her lunch breaks to the prescribed thirty minutes but some coworkers are taking forty-five minutes to an hour before getting back to work."

In most parts of the country, employees are entitled to lunch or meal breaks if they work a full shift of eight hours or more. In most cases, such breaks are unpaid. This assumes the employee is released from the workplace, if he so chooses, and from performing work during that period.

Most organizations allow thirty to sixty minutes away from work for lunch.

Meal breaks are paid or "on the clock" in cases where employees are restricted from leaving the work site, or are required to perform work during the prescribed time frame. (Please note: An employee who eats lunch at the job site and picks up a ringing telephone is only on a paid lunch break if she is *required* to serve in that capacity.)

Approach to Take

1. Unless there's a compelling reason to keep people at work throughout their shift, we recommend unpaid meal breaks on any shift. Whether an employee is an engineer or a janitor, productive work requires enough concentration of effort to make a mid-shift time-out beneficial.

2. Lunch policies are also useful. *Let the employees solve the problem*—whether an organization decides on a prescribed time frame and limitations should be decided in conjunction with employee desires. If staggered lunches suit the employees and you have no objections, try it. If one employee prefers thirty minutes, while another requests a full hour, consider whether the difference will affect morale or productivity before deciding. Whatever a manager decides should be realistic and enforced within reason.

   When coming up with a policy about meal breaks, we remind you that whatever you come up with needs to be easily monitored. Although it enhances morale to be flexible about these things, don't embrace flexibility at the cost of your sanity.

3. Organizations whose policies dictate a half hour for lunch, but in reality allow considerably more, should consider amending the policy, lest other requirements be considered "flexible" as well.

4. When an employee habitually overstays her lunch break, it's the manager's job to enforce the rule. *Say what you mean.* You must clearly state the policy and your observation of the employee's infractions. Counsel the employee regarding her options. If there is not improvement, take disciplinary action.

Preventive Measures:

One way to establish trust and also maintain a consistent policy regarding lunch breaks is to bring it up in a *regular staff meeting*. Talk to the group about whether they think the current policy is fair. In the absence of a policy, discuss what seems reasonable in defining a new policy.

In addition, you must be sure to live by your own rules. If you've established a forty-five-minute lunch break for employees, don't expect them to live by that rule if you consistently take an hour and a half.

Lying

"An employee with absenteeism problems called in yesterday alleging car trouble. She said that AAA had been called and the car was to be towed to a garage. I told her to bring in a statement or receipt verifying these events. However, she didn't do so, alleging today that she simply forgot to ask for them. I don't believe her."

At some time or other, everybody lies. The supposition that we grow more honest with age is no more credible than some of the people with whom we work. Most common in the workplace are fabrications motivated by the embarrassment that would be suffered if the truth were known. Regardless of the motivation, however, liars don't change their habits easily. When caught and confronted, they often lie again. If the need for honesty has not become obvious to them upon reaching adulthood, it's doubtful you'll change the equation.

"I can't believe a word she says" is a common lament among managers. If this is so, your working relationship has been disrupted, perhaps beyond repair. Accepting untruths as a way of doing business is a bit like allowing those who wish to cheat on their taxes to do so while the rest of us pay the difference. Such a double standard cannot be maintained over time.

Approach to Take:

1. Wait to confront a liar until you have evidence or documentation that calls his credibility into serious question. The example that opens this entry would certainly suffice.
2. *Say what you mean.* Let the individual know that the lie or cover-up is of greater concern than the misdeed. Mistakes can always be corrected but once you've lost faith in a person's credibility, restoring it is a long and uphill battle.
3. *Let the employee solve the problem.* While most employees will not recommend administrative action against themselves, it may be worthwhile to put less pernicious lies in front of the employee—asking him for an appropriate resolution. At a minimum, any resolution should include an acknowledgment of the fabrication, and a means of preventing recurrence.

Preventive Measures:

Perhaps more important than whether an individual has lied is why. In an atmosphere where employees perceive reprisal for telling the truth, management should expect less than honest behavior.

Where trust and honesty already exist and one person's truthfulness is undermining that rapport, aggressive action may prove beneficial. Other employees may require reassurance that honesty is indeed the best policy. Visible consequences for lying (up to and including removal) may solidify rather than undermine overall levels of trust.

See also FALSIFICATION OF DOCUMENTS.

MATERNITY

"My assistant manager was promoted to the job four months ago. Thus far her performance in the new job has been excellent. She has just informed me, however, that she's pregnant and will require 'at least two months' of maternity leave during our busiest season."

Most readers assume the supervisor in the example above is a man. This is only a safe guess because more managers are men than are women. The productive difficulties surrounding a leave of absence for childbirth raise concerns among managers, regardless of gender.

Federal and most state statutes require employers to treat pregnancy as they would any other temporary disability (a medical condition which prevents an employee from coming to work for a period that is neither indefinite nor permanent). Consider an employee who requires an organ transplant, or one laid up for weeks after a serious auto accident. The only differences between these temporary disabilities and pregnancy are that pregnancy only happens to women, and pregnancy allows for advanced preparation.

Approach to Take:

1. In all cases of maternity leave, the manager must bear the burden associated with the employee's absence. While the Family and Medical Leave Act of 1993 requires employers of fifty or more employees to allow up to twelve weeks of unpaid maternity leave, this requirement does not apply to new hires.

   With new hires, particularly those still in an introductory probationary period, or "temps," employer discretion is called for. While allowing a temporary employee a brief, unpaid leave may improve overall morale and employee loyalty, it is not required. Before denying her the leave of absence and moving to replace her, we urge you to *follow the Golden Rule.* Would you do the same if she required a kidney transplant?

2. In the case where an employee is unsure whether or not she will return to work after childbirth, the manager should begin by letting her know you appreciate the difficulty and magnitude of that decision. Deciding between greater income or closer parenting is not a picnic. *Let the employee solve the problem.* Tell her you don't know what to do and give her the opportunity to come up with a solution. Be sure to give her a time line for recruitment purposes.

3. If you have an employee on a special assignment, or one who's been advised by her doctor not to work during pregnancy, you will have to provide managerial backup for her, just as you would if she were a man being treated for prostate cancer.

Preventive Measures:

If it were legal to prevent pregnancies, you might not be here.

NEGATIVE ATTITUDE

"I supervise an employee who appears to have been 'born to complain.' No matter how positive things seem, he sees the glass as half empty."

The pessimist, the pouter, the cynic, the critic, the persecuted. Each can not only cast a pall over an otherwise tolerable workplace, but also may negatively affect your bottom line. What's more, the expression "one rotten apple . . ." too often rings true.

If left unchallenged, negative attitudes may take on a life of their own—usurping the credibility of management and undermining efforts to improve the organization. An employee who has no problem telling your customers about internal or-

ganizational matters can prove to be a source of embarrassment. The employee who rolls her eyes every time you make
a suggestion is annoying, but can also threaten your ability to
get things done.

Approach to Take:

1. Document complaints in writing. A few instances are all
   you need to bring home the point.
2. Set up a meeting alone with the employee and ask him
   what's going on. *Say what you mean.* This is no time to
   be coy. Say, "I think there's something going on, and I'd
   like to know what it is." Don't accuse, don't loose your
   temper. Acknowledge that whatever is going on is driving
   you crazy.

   Most negative employees will attempt to have you focus
   on the situations alluded to in your documentation, rather
   than on their personal behavior. Your focus on the *problem* (rather than an interpretation of events) will help to
   counter diversionary moves or games.

   LISTEN to what comes back. Don't interrupt, don't
   make faces, don't disagree. Listen to what the employee
   has to say.
3. *Get another opinion.* Ask fellow managers or friends what
   they've done that's proven effective with negative employees.
4. *Let the employee solve the problem.* Ask him to propose
   a solution. Make sure you get one that will ensure you
   don't have to suffer anymore. Make it clear what you
   think the solution must include. Having the employee
   come up with the solution will facilitate implementation/
   enforcement, but remember, you don't have to capitulate
   to anarchy.
5. Get the suggestion back from the employee, and try to
   review it calmly and rationally. This is the time to come
   to an agreement, but don't agree to something just for
   the sake of compromise. Don't accept a solution you can't
   live with. If an employee's suggestion is unacceptable, you

have to tell him why it's unacceptable. (You are not the mom. You do not get to say, "Because I said so.")

6. In some cases, you may need to *consider the costs vs. the benefits* of hiring outside mediation/conciliation services. At those times when agreement seems impossible, the cost of a professional mediator may be much less than the cost of ongoing conflict.

7. Be prepared for the possibility that nothing will work. Some people are just negative and there's nothing you, the manager, can do to change his behavior. What you can do, however, is make it clear this behavior won't be tolerated. It's difficult to think about firing someone for being impossibly grumpy, but you don't have to be held hostage by your employees.

Preventive Measures:

The better your rapport with your employees, the more defused they'll be. An armchair hour or so each month with each employee talking about work in general (not a specific matter) can make a big difference.

Consider the possibility of anonymous, upward appraisal, where employees get the opportunity to evaluate their boss. Upward appraisal is a great tool for getting a sense of how employees feel about management and how the organization is being run.

NEPOTISM

"The son of one of our more senior employees has applied for a job vacancy. He's well qualified and, if his parents are any reflection, would fit into our organization nicely. However, I'm concerned about the relationship he might have with his mother so nearby at work and whether others will think he was hired because he has 'connections.'"

While some organizations proudly acknowledge the generations of family members who have worked there, others worry regarding the consequences of bringing family to the workplace. Most of these concerns fall into two areas: favoritism and the ability to separate work and family lives.

In many cases, a husband and wife, father and daughter, or some other combination of family members actually run the organization. Such traditions go back to ancient times. The effectiveness of these models, however, is often dependent on the owner or manager's ability to see, evaluate, and treat family members in a manner consistent with others. Where employees perceive disparate or unfair treatment (in hiring, promoting, rewarding, etc.), morale may suffer and with it productivity and customer service.

Where family members work closely with one another or especially when they're in a superior/subordinate relationship, concerns regarding their ability to separate work life from home life abound. Such anxieties are experienced not only by the individuals themselves, but also by those who must work with and around them. If they disagree regarding an issue at work, that might be a reflection of a dispute they're experiencing during their off hours.

One final concern regarding nepotism is the related matter of couples who have a romantic involvement away from work. In such cases, we urge you to read the entry titled ROMANCE.

Approach to Take:

1. Most organizations don't anticipate issues concerning nepotism until they arise. Where policies already exist, you should review them and determine whether they are still useful and reflective of the organization. Where no policies exist, the first consideration should be whether to have one. There are innumerable instances of family relationships at work that pose few problems and are highly productive.

2. Openness and honesty are imperative in dealing with nepotism issues. *Let the employees help solve the problem.*

Confront the family members and brainstorm the concerns, misgivings, and perceptions that should be anticipated and addressed. You may also wish to discuss the matter with others in the organization confidentially to ensure that real and potential anxieties are aired before any such problems are encountered. Once this is done you may wish to establish a written policy, formal agreements with the individuals involved, and/or a "wait and see" posture.

3. If your organization is large and relationships within it complex, you may wish to prohibit certain working relationships among household or close family members. The most likely area to be targeted would be supervisor/subordinate. However, other areas such as promotion review panels, bonus committee members, grievance officials, etc., also warrant attention. Several large organizations have developed absolute prohibitions concerning family members working at any level in the same organizational component.

Preventive Measures:

While nepotism concerns and realities can't be avoided altogether, the place to begin is in the hiring process. You may want to ask any candidate whether he has a relative or household member working in your organization before making any selection.

ORGANIZATION CHARTS

"We have plans to serve a new category of customers beginning next year. Additional personnel will be required to handle the workload. We're uncertain as to which division should be assigned the task and allowed to recruit the additional personnel."

An organization chart may resemble a family tree to those who have never seen one. It's an attempt to diagram both the structure of your organization and the functions performed by each component. Some charts may become extremely complex, attempting to portray graphically the relationships that exist among different components.

The value of an organization chart is usually realized when size has increased to the point where confusion exists as to who does what. Without clearly defined roles, overlap and redundancy may adversely impact an organization's productivity and the relationships among personnel.

A structural organization chart is usually composed of boxes and tiers used to represent organizational components and levels of authority. A single box at the top may represent the chief executive with lines downward to departments, divisions, or similarly titled work groups. These might then lead to branches, sections, teams, or similarly titled components, and so forth.

Alternatively you may have a hub-and-spoke organization chart. If many functions are tied to one administrative officer or department, this design may be more representative of your organization.

A functional organization chart breaks down each box on the structural grid and attempts to define its responsibilities or reasons for existence. For instance, the box labeled "Finance" might functionally be described in terms of budget, accounting, auditing, forecasting, etc. Maintaining such a chart may assist in determining where growth or shrinkage should occur as well as assessing strategic changes and how they will be accommodated. It may also help new employees understand who does what. For instance, what is the difference between the Sales and Marketing departments.

The problem with a one-page description of this subject is that it can't possibly address all the issues that go into designing organizations. Often organization charts can facilitate the planning process, just because you can draw a picture which reflects your thinking. It's often easier to discuss and critique ideas when you can see them. While the following approach will help you get started if you're feeling that your organization has no structure, a strategic planning session is probably in order.

Approach to Take:

1. Figure out how work flows through your organization currently. Who reports to whom, who has responsibility for what, etc. If you have a small organization that's growing quickly, list the functions needing to be filled. You may have been writing all the paychecks yourself. That was easy when there were three of you, but once there are more, you may want to establish an accounting function. Putting it all on paper can help you begin to get organized.

   In addition, *let the employees solve the problem*. Ask your employees where they think their job fits in the organization. You may be surprised to find the product-development person you thought reported to marketing is really working for sales. Draw a picture of how it looks now. Keep your customers in mind as you review your current practices. Knowing where and how they fit can facilitate improved customer service.

2. The trickiest part of developing an organization chart is getting clear about how you and your staff want the organization to look. In an existing organization, you may be resistant to change—even if you realize the existing picture is murky. In a growing organization, you may feel overwhelmed by the new tasks that need to be fulfilled.

   This is where strategic planning comes in. You may want to hire an "Organizational Development" (OD) consultant, or buy a book on strategic planning and have at it on your own. Regardless of the method you use, we urge you to take this task seriously. Although trite, the metaphor of building a house without a foundation is particularly relevant to this problem.

3. Once you have a general idea of how you want the organization to function, you can develop the chart. Where no organization chart has existed before, we suggest two

approaches: consult a business librarian at your public library or the business section of your local bookstore to find a text that will include organization charts; and shop for software to help you develop a chart. (Obviously, if you're working with a consultant, an organization chart is one of the products you can expect her to deliver.) There's no sense starting from scratch when perfectly good models already exist.

Software is available for both Mac and PC and averages about $150. An hour in the library (or by modem) researching the periodicals index can save you time and money and aggravation in the process.

Where you have had an organization chart, but feel it's hopelessly out of date, the process is the same. Don't be afraid to consider new possibilities for your organization.

4. Once you have come up with a new chart, circulate it among key employees for their observations, criticisms, and suggestions. Particularly if you are redesigning an organization, remember that morale and productivity may well be affected by how you handle the process. The more involved the employees are, the more likely they are to feel ownership.

Reference: Brooks, Susan Sonnesyn, "Managing a Horizontal Revolution," *HR Magazine*, June 1995, p. 52.

OVERQUALIFIED EMPLOYEES

"I recently hired a person with a master's degree in psychology to perform a basic interviewing job. Although we discussed the routine nature and lack of latitude associated with the job, it's become clear after six months she's bored."

Many school systems have developed separate programs to accommodate the academically gifted as well as those for whom school is a difficult challenge. While the need to focus attention on slower learners was obvious from the start, the problems associated with exceptional learners may be just as significant. So it is at work.

Overqualifications for a job are not necessarily found on resumes. Many people possess knowledge, skills, and abilities which exceed job requirements to such an extent they become bored, rebellious, meddling, etc. One obvious example is the secretary who has more executive talent than the boss he serves.

The difficulty for the manager is that the organization cannot challenge every individual's potential. By the same token, employees who can work circles around their peers or who can complete a day's work in five hours often prove disruptive to teamwork and morale. They may find themselves with idle hours spent looking out the window, writing letters, reading books, or distracting coworkers in conversation.

Often an overqualified employee feels compelled to second-guess or advise management. Their suggestions and ideas for improvement are generated at a pace that cannot be accommodated. In time, they take on the persona of a know-it-all, busybody, pain in the neck, and so forth. (See the section on KNOW-IT-ALLS.)

Approach to Take:

1. While it's easy to say the wrong person was selected for the job, it's difficult to squelch the talents of the overqualified. Only when the situation has carried on too long will a manager feel as if a less qualified or less creative person would prove preferable. Accommodating the overqualified person, however, demands time and energy.

   To begin with, the individual should be counseled regarding the problems she creates. *Say what you mean.* It must be acknowledged that her job duties are essential to the organization's mission, else why would the job exist. While it's okay to note that the individual's talents are not being fully utilized, it's also necessary to have her acknowledge the need to perform her duties. If she believes the job itself is trivial or unnecessary, the problem has more to do with her attitude (concerning organizational integrity) than with abilities that exceed the job description.

2. Once agreement has been reached concerning the need for the job itself, then the employee must decide if he wishes to continue to perform in it. *Let the employee solve the problem.* You should point out that money and job security are not the only considerations in this regard. There may be no guarantee of future promotions or job changes. Therefore, happiness, peace of mind, and a sense of belonging must also enter into his consideration regarding his future in the position.

3. If the employee chooses to remain in the job, the two of you must agree that those everyday tasks are her primary concern. While she need not love her job, she must also avoid showing any resentment. Beyond that, allow the employee to suggest what other challenges she might wish to add in addition to the day-to-day duties. Clearly these additional responsibilities must not interfere or detract from the primary focus discussed above.

4. It should be made clear the additional contribution is tied to the employee's peace of mind and fulfillment, not to compensation. If he resents accomplishing more than others for the same salary, steer him back to the decision regarding whether to stay in the job or find more fulfilling work elsewhere.

5. The key ingredients for success when dealing with the overqualified worker focus on the acknowledgment of his knowledge, skill, and ability; the insistence that his primary function in the organization is to perform the duties of his job; and the recognition that contributions beyond those duties will be welcomed and appreciated but not necessarily rewarded by elevating him to a higher level.

6. In some cases, the overqualified employee will neither leave nor accept the limitations of her situation. In those cases, administrative or disciplinary action may be required concerning the problems she poses—wasting time, distracting others, etc.

Preventive Measures:

The best preventive measure is to avoid hiring the overqualified employee in the first place. If your instinct tells you you're interviewing someone who is overqualified for a position, you're probably right. If you think there's some chance of advancement relatively soon, go ahead and do it. But if your intuition is that the interviewee will be miserable in the job, you're probably right.

Because the '90s job market is tight, you're more likely than ever to run into this problem. Keep in mind the long-term needs of both you and the employees, and don't be sweet-talked into hiring the wrong person.

OVERTIME, FAIR LABOR STANDARDS ACT

"As business picks up, I'll either have to hire a new person or start paying overtime to the three folks I supervise. I'm not sure if the systems analyst on our staff qualifies for overtime."

The Fair Labor Standards Act of 1937 institutionalized the eight-hour day and forty-hour work week . . . but not for everyone. The Act divided employees into two categories—exempt and non-exempt. For non-exempt employees, work beyond forty hours in a week requires compensation at a premium rate of one and a half times the normal pay.

There have been numerous interpretations of the Act, both by the U.S. Department of Labor and federal courts. Their decisions have put most technical questions beyond the reach of anyone not expert in pay matters.

Two areas are of special note. Where exempt or salaried employees are given unpaid time off work (whether at their request or your suggestion), it must be accounted for as entire days—not hourly. You should check your policies and practices to insure you're in compliance. The other provision is that the forty-hour work week refers only to hours worked. Therefore, if a non-exempt employee has a paid holiday on Monday and works thirty-six hours during the remaining four days of her work week, no overtime is required.

Approach to Take:

1. The FLSA is enforced by the Department of Labor's Wage and Hour Division, as well as any state department with a similar mission. These entities have a right to inspect your payroll accounts to ensure compliance. We suggest you work with a certified accountant when setting up your payroll, and that he check your system on a periodic basis.
2. A question that most managers eventually confront is when to pay overtime on a continuing basis, and when to hire a new employee. Some employees prefer longer work weeks and greater compensation. Others tire of overtime and find the additional earnings less of an incentive. We suggest you keep in touch with your employees. As long as they are both happy with the additional pay and alert on the job, overtime may prove less costly than hiring a new employee and keeping him busy forty hours a week.

PARKING

"At one time we could provide parking spaces for every employee who drove to work. Complaints from customers concerning a lack of parking has forced us to eliminate half of these spaces in order better to serve the public. The question is, who keeps and who loses."

For many organizations, especially those in more urban areas, the cost of employee parking spaces can prove exorbitant. In some cases, prospective employees decide whether or not to take a job based on the availability and cost of a place to put the car. Because of this many organizations can only provide parking for a few employees.

The decision as to who gets space and how convenient its location is is one that could be debated without resolution. Older employees often advocate seniority as a basis for determination. Executives assume job rank or organizational status should be the determining factor. The more democratic and usually less senior or ranking argue for a lottery system. And, of course, the early risers believe parking should be allocated on a first-come, first-served basis.

In the end, where parking is limited or proximity to the workplace is an important issue, some will be happy with your system and others disgruntled. The best you can hope for is to minimize resentment by attempting a process that is both fair and realistic.

Approach to Take:

1. In accordance with local and state law, as well as your own public concern, priority for parking should be given to those with physical handicaps first. Most state motor vehicle or licensing departments have regulations for determining qualifications for handicapped parking.

2. Priority may also be given to car pools and people who must use their own vehicle during working hours to conduct the business of the organization. Other common criteria include the level or status of the individual, and employees of the month or quarter.

3. Many organizations that are trying to move away from hierarchical structures and status symbols allocate parking on a random or on a first-come, first-served basis. In these cases, a president or executive director may have to compete for space with a clerk or maintenance person. Where a system of RHIP (rank has its privileges) has existed for some time, any such parking scheme may have a more disruptive than beneficial result.

4. Where a lottery is implemented, drawings should be held again on a periodic (six-month or one-year) basis. Management must also be prepared for those who lose and will not find space for the private vehicle they drive to work. Where a first-come, first-served system is used, there must be sufficient spaces to accommodate everyone. No organization can afford to have employees miss time on the job while they cruise for alternative spaces because they arrived too late to find a vacancy.

5. Less traditional alternatives involve allowances for private parking, free or discounted public transportation passes, secure indoor storage for bicycles, and telecommuting. You may wish to contact a state or local transportation or mass transit office for additional ideas. Another possibility is to poll employers in similar circumstances to your own regarding their practices. As always, we believe that whatever solution you agree upon, employees will be more likely to accept it if they were involved in its formulation.

PARTIES

"A man who had worked in our office for over thirty years retired recently. We threw him a big party in the conference room that began at lunch and ended after 2:30. After things were cleaned up, I let everybody go home for the rest of the day. Now other office managers are telling me their staffs are upset with us for taking an afternoon off with pay."

In an organization that promotes teamwork and camaraderie, people will eventually suggest luncheons, dinners, and less structured parties—either in or outside of the office. Even in more traditional work settings, employees want to celebrate occasions such as showers, retirements, birthdays, holidays, etc. For the most part, there's nothing but good news associated with such amusements. Office parties, however, can also exacerbate tensions and behaviors that would otherwise be less conspicuous.

Among the issues a manager must consider are: time off work to prepare and/or celebrate; costs and cost sharing; consumption of alcohol; invitees and those excluded; the involvement of spouses and family members; distractions and resentments.

There are basically two kinds of parties organized at the workplace—those generated by employees and those initiated by management. A common example of the former would be a wedding or baby shower, while the latter is often exemplified by a summer picnic or winter holiday party. Unfortunately, it's often the case that management assumes little involvement in the planning or execution of either category.

In cases where celebrations have the greatest positive impact on an organization's cohesiveness, a large number of people are involved and committed to enjoying themselves. Delegating responsibilities for planning or execution, especially to women and lower-level employees, eventually sends the wrong message—namely that the rest of us are too busy to consider having fun.

Approach to Take:

1. If you believe it's true that the family that plays together stays together, so it should be in your organization. One simple thing you can do is use your calendar to remind you of birthdays and other significant events well in advance so that you as a manager can initiate parties and acknowledgments. Your active participation in or initiation of celebrations will set an example for others.

2. If you already have parties relating to holidays, consider ways they might be improved or made more enjoyable. Begin planning them early; make informed decisions regarding cost and funding; and try to involve people in ways that will employ their talents and maximize their participation. In short, make parties a priority.

3. While parties can enhance teamwork in your area, they can also have a detrimental effect where others outside your group feel excluded from your celebrations. If this

is the case, consider joint or cross-functional events.

If you have individuals within your own area who are reluctant to participate, or even dampen the efforts of coworkers, talk to them. *Say what you mean.* Explain why parties and acknowledgments are important, and learn how such events can be made more enjoyable for them. Avoiding the issue and allowing them to excuse themselves will, over time, undermine the very spirit you and others are trying to develop.

4. Other internal issues, including financial ability to contribute, the availability of time for after-hours get-togethers, feelings surrounding the involvement of family members in office parties, etc., are bound to present themselves. One idea that may help address these issues is an informal questionnaire concerning office celebrations.

   If you're interested in this option, we recommend the questionnaires be developed internally, but distributed and compiled by someone outside of your work unit. (If you're in a small office, you should be able to talk about these questions. If you can't, it may mean you need more informal gatherings with your staff!) Consider that some people will only be comfortable if the answers are confidential.

PERFECTIONISTS

"Our team has a difficult time reaching consensus principally due to one individual's need to ensure that every decision is complete and unambiguous. While his striving for perfection is admirable, it's also frustrating for most of us who need to finish and move on."

Management worldwide is in the midst of a quality revolution. Total Quality Management, statistical process controls, customer service, and quality improvement teams all lead managers and workers toward "doing it right the first time." But there's a point where quality becomes cost-prohibitive in terms of the time devoted to any given work item. Striking a balance between an organization's commitment to quality and the need to get things done is perhaps the most significant management dilemma of the 1990s.

While in theory individuals who seek perfection in their work are to be admired, they also present many problems. Although a manager taps his desk or paces the floor waiting for an assignment to be completed, the perfectionist's retort, "You want it done right, don't you?" seems irrefutable. As with all things in life, compromises (in this case between quality and timeliness) must be made and the perfectionist must learn to accept the reality of time constraints, profitability, and scheduling requirements.

A less common form of perfectionism concerns an individual who's intolerant of others' mistakes. While she may allege that "there is no excuse for sloppy work," such an attitude doesn't allow for normal human behavior. Over time they become known as nitpickers—willing to spend more time critiquing errors than acknowledging successes.

Approach to Take:

1. The agenda for dealing with perfectionists is no less than trying to alter a lifetime of behaviors and beliefs. Just as it's difficult to get some individuals to stop and check their work, it may be more challenging to have a perfectionist submit work knowing it may contain an error or mistake.

2. As is often the case, the first item of business is to come clean with the perfectionist. *Say what you mean.* Let him know his pursuit of excellence has attendant costs and a balance must be struck in order to improve his performance. Because perfectionism is a lifelong problem, you may wish to ask if the individual has ever been counseled like this in the past and/or whether he has made attempts to strike a more productive balance before. Assess the success or failure of previous efforts to accept mistakes.

If the employee denies knowledge of this attribute/flaw in her work habits, suggest she ask coworkers and/or family members about the possibility that her commitment to quality may exceed practical limits. In other words, you won't solve this problem until or unless the perfectionist recognizes it herself.

3. If you and the individual in question can agree the problem exists, the technique by which his work habits might be changed will necessarily involve his own ideas and perhaps those of a professional counselor. If your organization has an EAP available to it, both you and the employee should seek the advice of a counselor regarding how or where such input can be obtained. If you don't have an EAP, call your community mental health center and ask them for a referral. This is not to imply perfectionists are insane, but rather their work habits are deeply embedded.

Preventive Measures:

Multi-rater or 360-degree feedback mechanisms may prove valuable in correcting perfectionists. The assessments of coworkers, customers, and/or subordinates help to validate your managerial impressions and apply a certain degree of peer pressure on the employee. Using such evaluation tools on an ongoing basis will help you and the employee detect and begin action on the problem sooner rather than later.

PERFORMANCE EVALUATION

"In our organization, we're supposed to conduct annual performance reviews, and have a form for doing so. Both managers and employees seem to be uncomfortable with the evaluation process. In some areas, it simply never takes place."

We believe it's the manager's job to establish the limits of performance evaluation. The more involved you are, the more likely you are to get the results you want. People all want attention—one way to give it to them is through the evaluation process. Most employees would appreciate knowing how they're doing and where they stand. Most employees resent mangers who they perceive are too busy or not well enough informed (or too scared) to communicate that information.

To avoid confrontation, a lot of managers will ask the employee to evaluate her own work. While managers sometimes see this as progressive or benevolent, employees resent it because it puts them on the spot. Motivated productive employees tend to downplay their performance. (We call this the "aw shucks" effect.) Marginal or incompetent employees tend to inflate their efforts or value to the organization. (You could call this the "you could never live without me" effect.) There are new systems for performance appraisals which include the employee's self-evaluation among evaluations from many others. While 360-degree feedback is catching on in many organizations, there is still a need for supervisor input into the evaluation.

Performance appraisals should focus on three primary functions:

1. acknowledging superior efforts and competence;
2. identifying deficiencies and liabilities; and
3. improving work habits or efforts by identifying areas where changes may be beneficial.

When performance evaluations represent nothing more than completing a form or judging employees after the fact, they may do more harm than good. Where evaluations involve planning, problem identification, goal setting, and/or agreements for improvement, they may prove to be a valuable management tool.

In most organizations, pay is to a greater or lesser degree tied to performance. Annual performance evaluations may result in bonuses or ongoing salary increases. In most cases, the amounts of these one-time or ongoing monetary benefits depend on the individual's performance rating.

Where pay for performance is used to compensate or reward employees, managers feel the added stress associated with appraisal. They also feel more vulnerable where pay determinations are being based on inadequate information and subjective impressions. The best antidote for this uneasiness is to have periodic performance reviews throughout the year—at least quarterly. As in school, when most of us had three report cards before the final grade, so quarterly (or even more frequent) reviews may prove the old saying "The best surprise is no surprise." (See also RAISES, ANNUAL and AWARDS AND BONUSES.)

Approach to Take:

1. *Define the problem.* Decide what you want to evaluate. Are you interested in assessing the employee's performance, the job itself, or different aspects of the job? In order to get useful information out of the process, you must determine what you want to know.

   Performance evaluations, when possible, should be used as developmental tools rather than mere rating schemes.

2. What do you want the employee to accomplish in each aspect of the job? Many managers think it's up to the employee to figure out job expectations and how to meet them—then they're disappointed when it doesn't happen. Therefore, you need to *say what you mean*.

   Clearly state your expectations. If attendance at all training functions is a required part of the job, make sure the employee understands that. If filing an extra copy of every report is expected, let him know that. Don't make employees guess what you want from them.

3. Because they are unable or unwilling, managers seldom take the time to plan for more effective employee performance. They spend more time on daily damage control, and then manage their employees after the fact.

Performance management and evaluation is an area where planning in advance really pays off.

Managers should consider their own needs, along with employee strengths and weaknesses, and devise a *plan* on an annual or semi-annual basis. For some jobs, this may be a work plan written in terms of projects and time lines. For others, the plan may set goals and objectives designed to challenge the employee to deliver results—hopefully realistic ones.

For most employees in most organizations, we recommend this approach. During the year, a manager should maintain a log or inventory of problems attributable to employee job performance. At the end of the year, sit down and discuss these areas with the employee. *Let the employee solve the problem.* Solicit suggestions from the employee. Together agree on improved work habits that will prevent similar problems in the future.

Preventive Measures:

The best way to make the performance-evaluation process work better is to use it more often. Managers and supervisors who sit down with employees on a quarterly basis are much better informed—and more able to be a resource for their subordinates—than those who drag out the dusty file once a year.

PERSONALITY CLASHES

"One of the employees I manage drives me nuts. Others get along with him well, finding him talented, witty, and entertaining. I, on the other hand, find him insincere and lazy. Time after time he seems to get the best of me, so that confronting him on these issues accomplishes nothing more than making me look foolish."

While most personality clashes are presumed to be among sub-ordinate employees, the example shown above illustrates we're all susceptible to this particular difficulty. Many of us find ourselves liking or disliking other people within moments of meeting them. Although none of us wishes to acknowledge we're oil or water, eventually we find ourselves working around someone with whom we just don't mix.

Where personality clashes exist within the workplace, co-workers are almost invariably aware of it. We can read the body language, sense the anger, and are often openly called upon to take sides. A single conflict between individuals of any level within the organization can have the effect of factionalizing the entire group. Questions of right or wrong and good or bad are soon eclipsed by the issue of "What do I do now?"

One possible cause of personality clashes is prejudice. Racism, sexism, and other forms of discrimination have been with us longer than memory and often precipitate what on the surface appear to be personal differences. Common examples are "pushy" women, "uppity" minorities, and "blatant" homosexuals. These problems result in some of the same symptoms on the job. Recognizing them may be easier than seeing some other personality clashes, but resolving them is a more difficult matter.

None of us is immune—it's bound to happen—and it affects everyone.

Approach to Take:

1. In some cases, conflict on the job is the result of a specific event or recurring abrasion. In others, it's a more instinctual dislike that has less to do with work than with who the individuals are and how they perceive the world. This implies while you may be able to find a root cause for some disputes, others can be traced to no issue or event—just a visceral response.

   Given this, *let the employees help solve the problem.* Begin by interviewing the employees separately. Persist in asking why they present recurring conflict. Asking, "What don't you like about her?" is perfectly appropriate.

Say it again. In this case, don't assume you've understood what the employee has told you. Document each employee's answers, putting such responses in front of them to ensure the list you've created is complete. ("Is this everything, or is there more?")

2. If the lists thus created seem anchored in vague generalizations and/or recriminations, you're probably managing a case involving "oil and water." In these matters, professional mediators or conciliators are the most likely sources for resolving the conflict.

   Where the lists point to specific job behaviors and/or incidents, you may be able to resolve the matter yourself. Look to the work processes that bring the employees together in ways that spawn disagreement and see how they can be modified. Perhaps the employees themselves can propose process changes that will go a long way toward resolving their own problems. Proposed solutions need not be panaceas. Asking each employee, "Can you live with this?" and, "Will this help?" may be the best you can do for now.

   In outlining these approaches, we're challenging the long-held assumption that employees present problems which management is called upon to solve. Personality clashes are a perfect example of a problem over which you have little, if any, control. In most cases, such disturbances can only be solved by the employees involved and your role is merely that of a facilitator.

3. *Be consistent.* If you yourself are involved in a personality clash, we suggest you seek outside facilitation as well. This could be accomplished through an EAP, a human resources professional, a professional mediator, or a more senior manager. Many organizations frown upon any manager who admits to a problem she herself can't solve. While we're sympathetic to the dilemma this may pose, in the end we believe it's most productive and profitable to dig in and solve the problem at hand. Waiting and/or gritting your teeth seldom accomplishes more than lost time and dental bills.

Preventive Measures:

Multi-rater or 360-degree feedback mechanisms may prove valuable in correcting personality clashes. The assessments of coworkers, customers, and/or subordinates help to validate your managerial impressions and apply a certain degree of peer pressure on the employee. Using such evaluation tools on an ongoing basis will help you and the employee detect and begin action on the problem sooner rather than later.

Many organizations use lengthy assessment processes before making hiring decisions. These methods involve several individual interviews and/or group conversations with prospective candidates. If used, such a process should encourage those on board to identify potential personality clashes (of the more instinctive or visceral type) before bringing a new person on staff.

PERSONNEL FILES

"I recently had the unpleasant task of firing an employee for chronic tardiness and absenteeism. Our legal department has just received notice from his attorney that this action will be challenged and requested a review of his personnel records. From what others tell me, the file may be inadequate."

A personnel file is the summary of a person's employment history with your organization. From it a manager or human resource professional can determine the individual's salary history, career progression, benefits history, discipline, and performance records. Some of the history may be in the form of documents and copies; other matters may be summarized on personnel record forms. Quite often the file will also contain documentation concerning training and advisements (concerning hazardous materials, sexual harassment, workers' compensation, etc.).

The reasons for maintaining current and accurate personnel files should be obvious. Absent such documentation, management and the employee are left to reconstruct events and employment history from memory or from a scattered collection of documents. Since such files contain personal and/or private information, access should be limited to the fewest number of people possible. This can be accomplished by maintaining personnel files in a locked cabinet, the key to which is strictly controlled.

Automating a personnel filing system is efficient in terms of cost, space, and the environment. Histories of pay, retirement contributions, and promotion may lend themselves to on-line documentation. You may, however, require original documents, especially where signature verification is an important issue. For example, if you advised an employee of her right to file a workers' compensation claim and she declined in writing, a computer file might prove woefully inadequate if the employee's declination were ever called for. In addition, a computerized system may present additional security problems if not designed with limited access in mind.

Approach to Take:

1. Whether you have one employee or hundreds, a system of personnel filing is appropriate to your organization. If such files do not now exist, it's time to get started. We suggest using a standard manila prong file system. Many employers use the left side for manual record keeping or summary sheets and the right side for original documents.

2. We recommend that informal supervisory notes, records of counseling sessions, and other less official items be filed elsewhere. Some managers maintain a "drop file" by employee name in the office, while the personnel folder is maintained at a central location. In a smaller organization, there is often less need for documentation and, therefore, a single file may be more advantageous.

3. *Follow the Golden Rule.* It's our opinion that employees should have free and open access to their own personnel

files. If maintained in accordance with the guidelines provided above, they should find the contents more official than interesting. Before turning over the file, it's wise to briefly review the contents to ensure that nothing from another person's record has been misfiled in that folder, and that nothing concerning the employee is inappropriate for his review.

4. Given the propensity of legislatures to write retroactive laws, and of individuals to file legal actions against their employers, we recommend you retain personnel files indefinitely. Most employers have separate filing systems for active and inactive folders. It's better to rummage through the basement for records you thought obsolete than to admit you discarded them.

5. There are many software vendors marketing in the area of HRIS (human resource information systems). Many of these are quite elegant in that they generate performance evaluation forms, retirement options and documentation, health-benefits history, etc. Others are much more basic and, of course, less expensive. In larger organizations, such software is fast becoming a business necessity. In smaller ones, it may prove to be more cumbersome than valuable.

PERSONNEL POLICIES

"One of my professional staff recently completed a special project. She worked several evenings and one Saturday to complete the job on time. Now she's asking for compensatory (comp) time in conjunction with vacation days. I'm sympathetic to her request; however, other salaried employees have worked late without reimbursement in terms of vacation or compensation."

As organizations mature, the need for consistent personnel policies becomes more and more apparent. Employees expect consistency and often feel disadvantaged when one person is given latitude or a benefit that they're later denied. Such policies also make management decisions in areas such as leave, hours of work, expenses, bonuses, etc., easier. After all, referring to a manual takes less time and produces fairer results than accessing memory. Policies also ensure consistency among managers in different areas.

The downside of personnel policies is usually reflected in a manager's lack of discretion or latitude. The personnel manual often seems rigid and fails to take individual circumstances into account. Particular provisions may have been written to prevent abuses such as tardiness, expense-account padding, etc. Thus it could be said that many personnel policies are written to the lowest common denominator and prescribe rules in areas where you wish they didn't apply.

In sum, where policies don't exist, managers and employees wish they did, and where they do, the opposite is often true. In addition to a need for overall consistency, management may also wish to reflect on the subtle way in which policies enhance employee morale. The belief that individuals cannot get away with certain liberties and that an overall framework implying fair play exists can preclude decisions that might otherwise be construed as favoritism or discrimination.

It's often management that's most culpable in violating a personnel manual. The desire to treat "my people" or "this particular case" differently may, over time, undermine the entire policy. This has quite often led to an image of human resource management as merely enforcing rather than advisory or consultative.

Any organization's personnel policies should be considered flexible in that they will change along with technology and culture. Moreover, individual events will precipitate the need for new policies that haven't been considered in the past. A manual or booklet should be reviewed periodically to determine the adequacy and current relevance of its provisions.

If yours is a unionized environment, most if not all personnel policies are incorporated into the negotiated agreement or contract. These are considered to be "conditions of employment" and are often the areas of greatest concern to union representatives. Whether you are unionized or not, most management decisions that are perceived as violations of personnel rules are grievable.

Approach to Take:

1. If your organization lacks personnel policies altogether, and you're reading this entry out of necessity rather than curiosity, get moving. We recommend shopping for software programs that make developing a personnel manual simpler and more comprehensive than starting from scratch. *Get another opinion.* You may also wish to review the personnel policies of organizations you know and admire for their management practices.

2. Where personnel policies are already in place, but seem inadequate, a committee comprised of at least one representative from management and employees should conduct a comprehensive review. In such cases, you may also wish to contact organizations you admire or purchase software that would allow for a complete rewrite in a new format.

3. If and where you feel it's in everyone's interest to deviate from a written or established policy, proceed with caution. We suggest you either document why the policy failed to address the particular circumstances you face or have it rewritten in a fashion that will better serve you and others in the future.

   Legally a policy that's been inconsistently interpreted or violated over a period of time may not be enforceable at the time it's needed most. Likewise, where managers or organizational components interpret a rule differently, you can expect employees to rely on the interpretation most favorable to their circumstances.

4. By themselves your personnel policies are nothing more than ink and paper. *Be consistent.* To be effective they must be distributed and employees should be reminded periodically as to their contents. Every new employee

should be given a copy of the guidelines and a brief in-
troduction regarding the contents. If you put annual reminders in your calendar, you'll be more likely to mention
and/or briefly review the policies at a staff meeting or
other appropriate occasion.

Preventive Measures:

Personnel policies in and of themselves can be used as preventive measures. Where employment policies are spelled out
clearly from the beginning, there's much less room for confusion. This doesn't mean your personnel policies need to be
static, just that they need to be used and reviewed on a regular—say, yearly—basis.

PHONE CALLS, PERSONAL

"Every afternoon one of my employees checks in with his
wife and children. By the time he's done, about an hour of
productive time has been lost. Not only that, but he's tying
up one of our phone lines."

When employees steal material or equipment from the job, that
act of theft or misappropriation should be taken very seriously.
(See THEFT.) For better or worse, stealing or misappropri-
ating time (violating the maxim "Eight hours work for eight
hours pay") is considered less heinous a crime. Most of us,
whether labor or management, are afforded a certain amount
of leeway to use phones, copy machines, etc. However, those
with easy access to a business phone (generally white-collar
workers) may test management's good graces.

Quite often coworkers are acutely aware of telephone abuse
long before the manager catches on. Having to serve customers
while a coworker is abusing phone privileges can prove infu-
riating. Such resentment can be expressed in lowered morale,

impaired teamwork, and/or extended abuse (if you can't beat 'em, join 'em).

Approach to Take:

1. Where telephone abuse is known or suspected, you as a manager must confront the employee sooner rather than later. *Say what you mean.* You don't need to be Agatha Christie—you don't need to wait until you have "sufficient evidence"—before confronting the employee. A mere suspicion warrants the beginning of a conversation and putting the employee on notice.

    (As always, the manager's discretion and judgment are paramount in determining the seriousness of the problem. If department morale, teamwork, and productivity are at risk, personal phone calls can get out of hand.)

2 Tell him you suspect he may be tying up time and phone lines for personal reasons. Offer the employee your suggestion(s) as to how much work time may appropriately be used in connection with personal calls.

3. Many employers designate breaks, allowing employees ten to fifteen minutes during the morning and/or afternoon for these purposes. Others with more flexible hours and equipment requirements may ask employees to make up the time at the end of the day.

    We believe parents with latchkey children or children in day care should be allowed five to ten minutes to check in with their kids after school. Of course, true emergencies—be it family, automotive, community, or otherwise—should be handled as they arise.

4. If an employee does not respond to confrontation and counseling, we suggest you prepare formal disciplinary letters (see Chapter 3 on discipline) concerning specific instances of abuse. Where two to four letters have not corrected the behavior, termination should be considered.

5. If your organization encourages employees to do volunteer work, the issue of what's a "personal" phone call may be more difficult to discern. If you allow (or even en-

courage) volunteer work on company time, be sure to *be consistent,* and make sure other employees aren't being unduly burdened by one person's volunteer activities.

Preventive Measures:

Generally speaking, strict policies concerning personal telephone use prove more burdensome than worthwhile. In addition, the manager who calls a *staff meeting* to discuss telephone privileges—when only one or two staff members are abusers—is usually scared of confronting a single employee.

One alternative is to voice your concern regarding *suspected* abuse, and then ask the staff if such suspicion is warranted. Another option is to survey employees confidentially (see QUESTIONNAIRES AND SURVEYS). Include specific questions about personal calls in addition to questions relating to efficiency, teamwork, and job satisfaction. If the employees are unhappy regarding the phone habits of coworkers, *let the employees solve the problem.* Form a committee, or ask them to do so, and let them come up with suggestions to solve the problem.

PHYSICAL FITNESS
"Three employees approached me the other day asking if our organization would contribute to their memberships in a health club. They feel as if we should have a 'wellness' program as it would contribute to their physical and mental health."

There are many employers who believe providing time, equipment, or other incentives to promote physical fitness within the workforce is worth the investment. Many Japanese companies begin their day with ten to thirty minutes of group calisthenics. Some large U.S. companies provide workout facilities in the workplace.

There are good reasons for organizations to be concerned

about the physical fitness of their employees. Healthy employees miss fewer days of work due to illness, require fewer and shorter hospitalizations, incur fewer and less serious on-the-job injuries, and are more productive.

The best companies provide comprehensive programs that include not only the promotion of good health, but also resources to facilitate risk management, and behavior modification, and other preventive measures such as on-site physical therapists and movement analysts. As with so many things in this book, the greatest predictors of success in a wellness/physical fitness program are the support of upper management and the participation of employees in the criteria and program design.

Approach to Take:

1. If you work in a small organization, *consider the costs vs. the benefits* of different fitness options. You may be able to get a group rate at a nearby health club, or you may have extra space in your workplace to provide a workout or aerobics area of your own. Also check with local medical centers in your area to see if they offer programs or seminars that employees could attend. In these days of concern over cost containment for medical expenses, there are many options available through medical service providers.

2. *Let the employees solve the problem.* Employee participation is perhaps the most important ingredient in developing a successful program. Discuss it at a *regular staff meeting.* Solicit employee input, and ask for volunteers to form a committee to develop suggestions.

3. We recommend sending a questionnaire to all employees to get a sense of what's important to them. Suggested topics to include are: smoking-cessation programs; weight management; stress management; cholesterol testing and management; aerobics classes; and other exercise/workout facilities.

4. If you work in a large organization that doesn't have a fitness program, consider taking the risk of suggesting it.

Make an appointment with someone in the human resource department, and also talk it over with an employee assistance counselor. Let them research ways to justify the expense. Particularly in an organization where physical labor predominates, such a program provides a relatively quick payback.

POLITICAL CAMPAIGNING

"This morning an employee in our group was distributing literature concerning a friend of hers who's running for city council. She was also sporting a large campaign button on her blouse. On the one hand, I don't think such activity is appropriate to the workplace. On the other, I applaud her involvement in civic affairs."

While many of us avoid the subject of politics, socially and at work, others become impassioned concerning political campaigns or the morning news. When such passions disrupt the flow of work, lead to discomfort and dissension, or have employees soliciting campaign funds from coworkers, the line between freedom of expression and workplace disruption may have been crossed.

Other concerns may revolve around the candidates themselves. Aspirants to public office may want to visit your organization, pass out literature before or after work, or tour your facility in order to increase their visibility and "press the flesh." This is especially true in local elections, where a few votes can determine the outcome.

Political campaigns often affect larger, private organizations in that corporate or union political action committees (PACs) may have been formed to raise money for a given party or candidate. Solicitation for such funds can prove awkward. Some will resent it as an invasion of their privacy and/or coercion.

In soliciting for a PAC, officials may characterize a particular party or candidate as being more friendly or understanding regarding the needs and success of your organization. In most cases, there are no laws that prohibit this, especially when the target audience is administrative, professional, or managerial employees.

Approach to Take:

1. The personnel policies in many organizations already set limits on political activity at the workplace. Some union contracts also address the issue. If so, take time to review those provisions. If you still have questions, and work in an organization that has a human resource or personnel office, consult with them to determine whether the limits or guidelines are being exceeded.

2. In the absence of guidelines, *let the employees solve the problem*. As political campaigning is reflective of democratic institutions, so it may be best to deal with concerns about politicking by polling employees. When an individual approaches you regarding excessive rhetoric or pressure, or where your own sense of proportion seems challenged, we think the entire issue of partisanship at work warrants discussion. In most cases, the employees themselves will agree to guidelines that limit the amount of activity at the workplace and/or during working hours. If somebody violates the guidelines agreed to, they should be subject to administrative or disciplinary action.

3. Where you yourself have strong political leanings, we suggest you leave them at the entrance to your office. It's only reasonable for subordinate workers to feel intimidated when a boss discusses her political views or advocates a candidate. Since such reactions may work against the person or organization with which you ally, silence may, in this case, prove golden, or at least more valuable than advocacy.

Preventive Measures:

If you are already developing guidelines concerning political activity in the current election season, it's time to incorporate those policies into your overall personnel guidelines or manual.

PRIVACY

"A couple of employees in our organization are suspected of having drinking problems. I believe they bring liquor to work and store it in their lockers. Although we have rules concerning alcoholic beverages at the workplace, I'm not sure whether I can order them to open their lockers and have the contents inspected."

The lines between an employee's right to privacy and an employer's right to know what goes on at the workplace cannot be clearly drawn. From a manager's standpoint, it would seem logical to have rights to search a desk belonging to the organization and located at work, test employees for their honesty or use of controlled substances, or determine whether a prospective employee has a history of emotional problems. From the employee's standpoint, the legitimacy of such actions is questionable.

Federal laws in the area of privacy rights and limits are few and far between. That means that any public laws limiting or defining a manager's rights in such areas are left to state and local discretion, if addressed at all. The existence or absence of statutes, however, does not prohibit an employee from filing legal action against her employer concerning invasions of privacy. Accordingly, some basic guidelines or rules of the road may be in order.

If your organization believes there's a need for surveillance of work areas, or inspection of desks, lockers, briefcases, etc., there must be a legitimate or even compelling *business-related reason* for doing so. For example, why would a day-care center wish to install cameras in an employee break room or an architectural firm require employees to open up their desks for inspection of the contents? On the other hand, if these cases involved a pharmaceutical manufacturer and a mail-order company, such actions may appear more reasonable.

Where the concept of privacy is applied to desks, lockers, briefcases, handbags, etc., employees should be notified in writing as to the employer's intent to periodically search such spaces and items. Periodic reminders (once every year or two) may be necessary to ensure employees understand the limitations on their privacy. Where employees acknowledge or agree to such conditions of employment, and they can easily be construed as business necessities, implementation is usually legal. Consulting an attorney, however, is always a good idea in these matters.

Employees' permission (usually in writing) should also be standard operating procedure before answering inquiries from outside entities concerning their salary, attendance record, years of service, or other personnel matters. Many lenders ask individuals to sign releases before they begin such investigations. Employee permission is also recommended in cases where attorneys or law enforcement officials request data contained in an employee's personnel records. Of course, if a valid search warrant is presented to you, contact your attorney regarding your legal obligation to comply.

Where an employee is requesting a benefit such as time off work to care for a sick family member, you may require him to furnish acceptable documentation that will substantiate his reasons. A similar example would be an employee who takes two weeks of sick time. Asking her to furnish evidence from a physician as to her inability to work during that period may be perfectly acceptable. Note that it becomes the employee's responsibility to obtain such information so as to minimize any invasion of privacy on your part.

There have been numerous court decisions at the state, local, and federal levels concerning the propriety of questions when interviewing candidates for a job. While most managers know not to ask a woman if she's planning to have more children, there are more subtle questions that may also violate an individual's privacy or rights under law. In some jurisdictions, questions regarding matters such as tobacco smoking, prior drug use, or sexual orientation may be considered "over the line." It's our belief that interview questions be limited to assessing the knowledge, skills, and abilities required to perform the job on a day-to-day basis. Where questions to different applicants vary, suspicion as to whether they were intended to reveal personal, private, or prohibited information increases.

The use of mechanical tests such as polygraphs, urinalysis, breathalyzers, metal detectors, etc., are a separate category altogether. In most of these areas, laws and statutory language are much better defined. We recommend you only consider using mechanical testing devices such as these upon the advice of your attorney.

Approach to Take:

1. Privacy is one area of employment law where statutes may exist at several jurisdictional levels and where new case law from courts is published regularly. This is because, by its very nature, issues of privacy at the workplace involve issues sensitive to employees and management alike. Therefore, the best approach to take can be summed up in two words: Don't guess. When these issues arise, call your organization's legal advisor or an attorney who specializes in employment law and practices.

2. Be as open and honest with your employees as you possibly can. If you suspect problems regarding theft, veracity, substance abuse, etc., your candor may work in your behalf. It's not that being open about such concerns and suspicions entitles you to test the limits of employee privacy. Rather, saying that you're concerned about sick-leave abuse, pilferage, consumption of alcohol on the premises, etc., may actually solve the problems you're articulating. That would preclude any need for searches, lie detectors, medical substantiation, etc. In essence, an open

and honest manager is a gift often returned by the employees.

3. If the nature of your organization and the work performed in your area dictate practices that touch on issues of privacy, make every effort to disseminate those conditions of employment. Remind employees frequently of the limitations on their privacy and how, when, and where you intend to use the discretion allowed you. For example, if your organization has military contracts requiring security clearances for employees, let the employees know early and often they may be subject to random urinalysis screening. Go so far as to provide them with details as to the process used, the handling of samples, and the consequences to those whose samples test positive for illegal drugs. After all, the intent is not to catch violators but to prevent violations.

Preventive Measures:

We can't stress enough how important it is to be honest with your employees. There may be rare occasions where you'll be taken advantage of for your candor, but we believe you will be rewarded for straight information.

PROBATIONARY PERIOD

"My partner and I are about to hire our first employee. We have no idea how it'll work out. We're wondering it it's appropriate to have this new person work under a trial or probationary period. If so, what difference would it make?"

Trial or probationary periods are not required of employers when bringing new people on board. Many managers prefer informing new hires that their employment is conditional for periods usually lasting from thirty days to twelve months.

Probationary periods should be viewed as an extension of the decision-making process regarding who to hire. In essence, the employer is informing a candidate that he must prove worthy of hiring, even after several months on the job. If not, then termination during this trial or probationary period is the equivalent of being rejected as an applicant. Whereas termination for cause may be challenged in most states (see EMPLOYMENT AT WILL), rejection during a probationary term is usually regarded as equivalent to rejecting a candidate or applicant for employment.

Employees should also be advised that this period affords them a chance to size up the organization and their job "from the inside." Just as you are free to let an employee go during a probationary period, she is also free to leave. In fairness to employees, this can be a time to evaluate whether or not a job is as promised. A structured review should take place at or just before the completion of the trial period. It should contain all the elements of a performance evaluation.

Approach to Take:

1. If you choose to use probationary periods as a screening tool for new employees, *consider the costs vs. the benefits* in determining both the length of the period and the possibility of letting people go before the trial is completed. "Once they get used to being around here, they'll see the light" may be an honest assumption or it may be a way to avoid confrontation. All new employees should be advised, in writing, that status as a regular employee should not be assumed until this trial period has been successfully completed.

2. Try to be objective about how long it really takes to learn the new job. In the end, this will come down to a question of management judgment. If you are replacing an employee who's leaving (under favorable circumstances), ask her to help you figure out an appropriate time period for probation. (If the position is being vacated under duress,

this is not a good idea. You probably won't want to hear the answer from an employee who's going away mad.)
3. People's habits are formed years before they start working for you. Employees are not going to change appreciably over the course of a probationary period. The new employee who hangs up on a crabby customer is probably not well suited for a customer service position. On the other hand, an employee who misses work on Fridays may be having problems with child care or elder care. The only way to find out is to ask. *Say what you mean.* Be direct in pointing out problems, and ask for more information before making decisions about retaining new employees.
4. Managers should enter review dates in their calendar to assure trial periods do not expire unnoticed.
5. In most cases, benefits such as medical insurance, child care payments, etc., are not available to employees during the probationary period. Sick days and vacation days accrue during this period, but usually employees are not allowed to take them until the probationary period has been completed.
6. This probationary period is your opportunity to evaluate the performance of a new employee before you make a commitment to him—and vice versa. Try to be objective in your evaluation, but remember that new hires need to be able to add to the morale and productivity of the workforce.

Preventive Measures:

Consult an attorney concerning employment at will in your state, and the legal liabilities associated with the trial or probationary period.

Many organizations form personnel committees to help establish hiring policies and procedures. Such a forum ensures consistent treatment of new employees. Be sure to include employees on personnel committees.

PROCRASTINATORS

"We were supposed to have completed this entire book long before getting around to the entry on procrastination. Too many things seemed to come up along the way and distract us. This time we were fortunate enough to get an extension. Our luck may run out in the future."

No organization can survive over time without getting things done. Customers seldom want to hear why goods or services are late. Procrastinators, therefore, have either lost focus on the importance of their work and those who rely on it, or simply lack the ability to maintain focus on any one thing very long. Whether he's looking for distractions or is helpless to prevent them, a procrastinator has a serious detrimental effect on productivity.

Many of those for whom procrastination is a problem are bored. Whether the cause is overqualification or too many years on the job, the day-to-day routines or pressures of the job no longer seem to interest or affect them. They may be thinking about better ways of doing the job, improving the management of your organization, or last night's TV shows. The bottom line is deadlines are jeopardized and schedules are continually moved out.

The other population of procrastinators is occupied by those who have never been able to focus on one thing very long. If a fly were to land on her desk, she'd rather watch than shoo it away. Like children with a learning disability, they require constant reminders as to what they're supposed to be doing.

A third population of procrastinators aren't really putting things off. They simply lack the organization skills necessary to know what to do next. In their own way, they're flailing at their assignments rather than planning and executing. These folks are actually busy but it appears as if they're avoiding logical next steps. That's because they don't know where they're going.

Approach to Take:

1. *Say what you mean.* The easiest way to find out why an employee puts things off is to confront her about the problems you're experiencing. Then ask reasonable questions designed to understand why her work isn't getting done on time. You may want to ask questions like:

    Am I the first to point out that you become easily distracted?

    Are you the kind of person who can read a whole book in one or two sittings?

    Does the work seem to get repetitive and/or boring?

    Is this a job that can hold your interest over months at a time?

    Do you have a plan as to how you'll get things done?

    Do you think you understand your work assignments?

2. If it's becoming clear to you the individual lacks the ability to stay focused, your choices are limited. You may either document performance failings and eventually get him out of the job he now occupies, learn to live with his shortcomings, or explore the possibility of employee assistance counseling.

3. If the employee appears to be overqualified or bored, we suggest you look through the entry titled OVERQUALIFIED EMPLOYEES. You can also try working with him to determine how the job could be made more interesting. If he's creative and interested in staying in the job, the two of you may be able to come up with a way to do the job that would be more stimulating.

    The final option with the bored employee is to be honest and ask him if he really wants to keep the job. *Let the employee solve the problem* He must be willing to help define the options. There may be other options within your organization that would be more suitable. You may be willing to help him find a new position. You have to determine how much it's worth to you to solve the problem.

4. For the disorganized employee, coaching and/or formal training are the order of the day. People who aren't in the habit of developing outlines, using a calendar, or establishing suspense files or time lines, must learn how to change their work habits. In these cases, a clerk or secretary may have techniques to offer the engineer or project leader. Classes in time management or a seminar in planning skills may be offered at your local technical or community college.

Preventive Measures:

When assigning work, especially long-term projects, to a known procrastinator, you should request outlines and/or time lines early on. Such individuals should be asked to show you how the job will be accomplished within the time available. You should also request regular project updates—say, every two weeks—to prevent surprises at the end of the job.

PROMOTIONS

"Ever since one of our service technicians announced she would retire, the behavior of one of my employees has dramatically changed. He's become somewhat like the brown-nosers we despised in school—wanting to be sure I notice everything he does. I'm convinced he's bucking for a promotion, and I'm sure coworkers resent the change in his behavior as much as I do."

Normally promotions are happy occasions for both the employee and the manager. A change in status and pay for loyal and productive employees should, in most circumstances, be celebrated. However, where promotions lead to problems, you as a manager may have more of a challenge than you could have anticipated.

Many employees become competitive when opportunities for promotion arise. Rather than being supportive or congratulatory, they vie to outshine one another. Senior employees may feel "entitled" to promotions. Women, handicapped, and minorities may feel overlooked and neglected. You're often caught in the middle.

In most organizations, a promotion not only rewards the individual selected, but often is perceived as a slap in the face of others who remain in the same positions and pay levels.

Approach to Take:

1. A key to successful promotions is expecting the worst. *Follow the Golden Rule.* If you've ever been passed over for a higher-level job, or watched someone less worthy prove the Peter Principle, you know it can be difficult.
2. Before a selection for a vacancy is made and announced, you should prepare each potential candidate for the possibility they won't be picked. Individuals who are being promoted should be advised as to the potential resentment of their peers, and urged to provide input as to how teamwork and morale can be maintained.
3. If you have an employee you're considering promoting, but are concerned he might prefer to remain in his existing position, *let the employee solve the problem.* Tell him what you're thinking, and get his view of whether or not it's a good idea. He may jump at the chance, or he may be flattered to have been asked and decide it's not a great idea.

Preventive Measures:

We believe the best way to prevent problems with promotions, like so many other issues discussed in this book, is to be as open as you can with your employees. People don't like to be surprised. The more information they have, the more likely they are to behave responsibly.

Also keep in mind that, despite your best efforts, some employees will act out no matter how much information they have. In those cases where behavior is counter-productive, counseling is in order. No amount of long-range planning can eliminate all problems associated with promotions.

QUALITY IMPROVEMENT TEAMS

"At our last staff meeting the employees complained about the performance evaluation system. Many of their concerns are quite valid. Rather than hire a consultant, I would prefer having them propose options and alternatives."

Throughout this book, we've suggested asking the employees to propose solutions that they themselves will have to live with. Such a process has been formalized in many organizations, especially those adopting Total Quality Management (TQM) philosophies. Groups composed of employees, managers, and/or union officials either volunteer or are assigned to analyze a dysfunctional process or program and propose improvements. Common names for these entities include quality improvement teams, process action teams, quality circles, and employee involvement.

The benefits of quality improvement teams should be obvious. Because our own people understand our organization best, they're the most qualified to analyze, evaluate, and propose alternatives. In addition, where improvements are generated from within the rank and file, they're more likely to be viewed favorably. These internal groups also help to share a burden traditionally carried by management alone. Formulating these teams is a way of expressing confidence in the creativity and integrity of employees.

One of the biggest problems associated with quality improvement teams is the time spent away from regular job duties.

Involved employees may be distracted from their work for a number of hours every month. What's more, large or particularly thorny problems may require months of meetings, research, and discussion. While acknowledging that the quality of the teams' decisions may be better than their own, managers are likely to become frustrated with the lengthiness of the process.

Some managers may also become threatened by quality improvement teams. By design, they may come to take over a role traditionally relegated to management officials. In some cases, senior managers may reject the findings or conclusions of the group, which only further exacerbates the issue of "Who's in charge here?" or "Why bother?"

The reason we promote the use of employee involvement has more to do with long-term morale and organizational health than with the quality of any given recommendation or decision. Where employees develop a sense of ownership, their commitment to internal and external customers grows.

Additionally, workers come to understand the difficulties associated with managing an organization. In trying to improve any aspect of the organization, members of the team realize there are many perspectives other than their own which must be considered. Such is also the case with managers. As they work with employees to find solutions or improve work processes, they may narrow the gap between management and employees. Thus both parties mature on the job and become more valuable over time.

Employee input into decisions can become a habit. Managers may become comfortable asking workers to plan an office party, develop a code of ethics, or determine when overnight mail should and should not be used.

Approach to Take:

1. Where quality improvement teams aren't currently the norm, we suggest beginning with smaller matters and working your way toward large or institutional problems. Places to begin might include typing backlogs, covering

for absent employees, scheduling who gets off for the year-end holidays, or any other matter that doesn't require extensive investigation.

2. Consider hiring an expert in organizational development (OD) or a human resources training firm to outline the necessary ingredients of a successful team. Issues such as who chairs meetings, how long they last, how to deal with more and less vocal participants, whether to work for agreement through majority vote or consensus, etc., will inevitably come up. These professionals can make suggestions at the front end of the team's work rather than waiting to deal with them issue by issue.

3. Consider reading up on employee involvement and process action teams yourself. There have been volumes written in the past several years on this subject. Much of it will provide you with a useful orientation as to what you can expect.

4. Request that the team or its leader(s) provide you with plans, time lines, and interim or status reports. Suggest they use you and/or other managers as resources, but not be dependent on your authority. As their work on a problem or issue progresses, do your best to keep your hands off. Although they may take too much time, or head off in a direction you would prefer they hadn't, allow teams to make some mistakes. Just as when you were new to management, quality improvement teams must get their feet wet and learn to make mistakes as they go.

QUESTIONNAIRES AND SURVEYS

"I work in a very large organization. We've been looking at several different ideas for rewarding employee efforts other than the annual salary review. Since we're not sure which ideas are preferable to the employees, we're considering the use of a questionnaire to get their opinions."

The two most basic types of questionnaires or surveys are those used internally to assess employee opinions and those used externally to determine customer satisfaction. Both of these applications are gaining greater favor as managers are less inclined to make decisions without broad input.

The internal survey usually focuses on one or more of the following areas: employee attitudes or satisfaction; personnel policies and practices; and general working conditions. They may be targeted to specific areas of the organization, solicited from a random sample, or distributed to everyone.

In most smaller organizations, employee attitude or opinion surveys may be less desirable. Employees are more accessible and have a greater expectation of personal contact with their bosses. The need for a survey in these organizations raises concern as to the level of communications and whether *staff meetings*, one-on-one informal chats, and/or quality improvement teams are being utilized.

Concerns surrounding internal questionnaires are many. Who will design the survey and write the questions? Who will compile and record the information gathered? Will there be guarantees of anonymity? Will they be done on paper or via a computer network? How will the information be used? Will the findings be reported back to the employees? Will the survey raise expectations to a level that can't be met?

External surveys are intended to provide information from those who use your organization's products or services. These are usually designed in an effort to improve products and/or customer service and gain greater competitive advantage. As external or customer feedback questionnaires are more matters of marketing than internal management, we will not address them further.

Approach to Take:

1. The first thing to decide when considering a questionnaire is why. These instruments involve time and effort and may affect worker expectations. All of this is fine if you understand the value of its use. Questions include: What do

I need to know, why do I need to know it, will a survey provide me with the information I seek, and are there better alternatives?

2. If you believe data collected from employees will be useful to management, you must also decide if it will be distributed to the participants as well. Because employees are aware that questions are being asked, and also believe their answers may lead to changes, we're of the opinion they should have the results. The alternative is to leave them wondering what you learned and how it has affected you. Better to come clean.

3. Next, consider the method by which the questionnaire will be developed. In some cases, such as attitude surveys, the way in which questions are asked is particularly important. Likewise the length, format, and means of delivery are all matters related to design. Your options include hiring a private consultant, delegating design to a particular office such as training or human resource management, developing a special team, relying on commercial software programs, or doing it yourself.

4. Other matters are more administrative in nature. Should the survey be done on paper or on-line? What assurances will you give employees as to the anonymity of their responses? Once completed, how and where will the forms, disks, E-mail, etc., be sent? Who will be assigned (or hired) to compile, analyze, and present the results? How will the data be sliced and diced? What will the time frame be for responses? Will responses be voluntary? While such questions represent more detail work than substance, all of them and more must be considered and planned in advance.

5. All of this work looks onerous at first glance. That shouldn't scare you away from using questionnaires to better understand the needs, desires, and feelings of those you employ. We see tremendous value in the judicious use of this tool, as it generates communication that might otherwise be impossible.

Preventive Measures:

Surveys are a good idea in even the best-managed organizations. We remind you, however, that open, honest, and concerned managers who already rely on feedback from employees may have less need for this option. Most managers contend they know what employees think and how they feel about work. Where this is actually the case (and it often isn't), surveys may only serve to depersonalize close working relationships.

RADIOS/MUSIC

"One of my employees listens to classical music all day. One loves bluegrass. The sound wars are escalating. The rest of us are too distracted to get anything done."

For some people, entertainment and work do not mix. For them it seems simple—either listen to a symphony or distribute the mail, either write a report or listen to the ball game. Others can see nothing wrong in making their work days more enjoyable through aural stimulation.

The issue of radios and music in the workplace provides a reminder that managing employees is more difficult than it may seem. Some people find music a relaxing background, while their coworkers may feel homicidal listening at work.

Approach to Take:

1. *Think it over.* The issue of music or no music is yours to decide. If you feel that audible music interferes with productivity, you should think long and hard before allowing it to continue. On the other hand, maybe you believe music enhances the work environment. Be clear about what *you* want before you talk to employees.

2. *Say what you mean.* If you feel the music has to go, explain your reasons carefully. Allow additional discussion only in writing directed to you. Be prepared to consider new views on the subject, but make it clear that suggestions or comments are just that. No petitions—no votes.
3. If you think music has a place in your office, take the issue to a *staff meeting. Let the employees solve the problem.* Ask every employee to write a brief policy on this subject and submit them anonymously to you. You'll want them to comment on what kind of music, where, when, and how loud. After you have read the employee input, develop a policy and circulate it at a subsequent *staff meeting.*
4. If music is allowed, let the employees be responsible for the equipment and its operation and security. You do not need to get in the business of radio maintenance and protection.
5. *Get another opinion.* Ask people outside how it is handled in other offices. Someone else may have simply moved all the country music fans into the same room.

Preventive Measures:

Whatever the policy is, make sure all existing employees are informed. Include the policy in any information you present to newly hired employees. Make it clear that any violation of the policy will result in some form of disciplinary action.

If you remodel or open a new office, consider a design that prevents coworkers from being distracted by the music of others.

RAISES, ANNUAL

"Our organization is in financial trouble. I've been trying to cut costs wherever possible. While I really can't afford to give any of our six employees an annual raise, I know holding their salaries to current levels will spell trouble and may result in my losing one or two."

All of us anticipate earning more money as living costs increase and as our skills develop and mature. Organizations have commonly performed annual salary reviews and adjustments based on either, and usually both, of these factors.

Cost-of-living adjustments (COLAs) are a common feature of most large organizations and many small ones. The more sophisticated systems are often tied to national or regional economic statistics such as the Consumer Price Index. Throughout our lifetime, experience has shown us that a dollar buys less from one year to the next. Therefore, in order to have wages with at least consistent buying power, periodic adjustments appear necessary.

COLAs only serve to maintain the economic value of a job. Most employees (managers included) look forward to increased earnings over time. There are three ways to do this: get promoted; leave the organization for a job with a "better future"; and, where promotion is not possible and resigning is not desirable, receive annual raises. Accordingly, the annual raise has become a custom. It helps in retaining the knowledge and experience of employees, saves costs related to hiring and training new ones, and helps maintain a more loyal, long-term work force.

Where annual raises are desirable, most organizations begin with COLAs. It's our experience that these are computed and implemented across the board and tied to some statistical or economic analysis. Where higher-ranking employees receive a greater percentage adjustment, their lower-paid counterparts will eventually learn of it and resent the disparity.

Disparities are inevitable when performance raises are employed. These salary increases should be distinguished from one-time bonuses or awards (see AWARDS AND BONUSES). In essence, the annual performance increase is anchored in the employee's additional long-term value. It acknowledges that the employee is not being promoted up the organization's hierarchy, but her ongoing value to the organization merits recognition in terms of her salary. We believe this is fundamentally different from a bonus related to a specific accomplishment or a particularly good year.

Another form of annual raise is the "step" or longevity increase. Such systems provide a small percentage increase in salary based on an additional year (or in some cases two or three years) of service to the organization. The idea behind longevity increases is to pay individuals with organizational knowledge and experience more than junior employees in the hope they will be less likely to take such experience elsewhere. If, after ten years with the organization, an engineer is being paid 10% more that the industry average, she'll be less likely to leave you for a better opportunity.

This compensation strategy doesn't always work. In some organizations, twenty-year employees may be paid far more than more junior counterparts, yet be acknowledged as less productive and less likely to learn new skills and techniques. Longevity increases should not be considered as substitutes for promotion. Where employees are looking to improve their status as well as earnings, longevity raises or step increases may not satisfy their needs.

Performance increases must be tied to some system of performance appraisal. While many organizations perform annual evaluations based on statistical output (including goals, objectives, and written performance standards), others lack such data and must do more qualitative reviews. In essence, despite any theory to the contrary, annual performance evaluations are seen by employees as precursors to annual salary reviews. (See PERFORMANCE EVALUATION.)

The problems with annual raises have to do with management realities butting up against employee expectations. One of a manager's roles in any organization is to maximize productivity while minimizing costs. While employees may be dedicated to these aims, their principal loyalty is usually to family, retirement, and other economic needs. What's more, where employees have grown accustomed to annual raises and/or COLAs, eliminating or deferring those benefits is bound to affect their morale and attitudes.

In hard times, employees may be more understanding when it comes to lowered or curtailed raises. What's more, managers may sense employees have reached salary levels where the threat of them leaving for a higher-paying position is minimal. Nevertheless, it would be wise to anticipate problems when and where annual raises must be cut—even for the most legitimate of business reasons.

Approach to Take:

1. Consider cost-of-living adjustments to be a budget necessity. Just as rent, electricity, postage, and other expenses will inevitably rise over time, so should the wages and salaries of employees. In cases where the employee's attitude or productivity doesn't warrant any kind of raise, either address this in your personnel policies or consider whether the individual's services should be retained at all. An alternative approach is to put that particular employee on a form of probation, which must be successfully completed in order to garner his COLA.

2. In cases where budgets dictate foregoing COLAs, we suggest you first consider the additional costs that might be associated with their curtailment or postponement. In the end, costs associated with denying anticipated adjustments may far outweigh those associated with finding the money to pay them. If such an analysis still leads you to suspend these annual increases, we suggest you approach the employees with open books. They should understand and, to the extent possible, appreciate the organization's predicament and should be told under what circumstances adjustments may be reinstated.

3. If you're considering the use of performance increases to salaries (pay for performance), you're probably headed down a long and treacherous road. The organization's grapevine usually produces comparative data that might anger employees whose annual raise is less than their peers'. Where a manager can produce data that will explain such differences, hard feelings may still linger. When performance reviews and raises are determined

based on impressions and qualitative judgments, resentments are likely to be stronger and more persistent. Employers who lack or mistrust quantitative appraisal data may turn to 360-degree evaluation programs. Most experts, however, recommend these systems not be used to determine pay until they've been in place for at least a year or two, if at all.

While we're not the biggest fans of longevity or seniority raises, they may prove valuable in cases where the cost of bringing on new employees is extremely high. For example, if your organization has invested in significant amounts of training regarding statistical process controls and modern management methods, a new employee, although qualified, may require much time and attention in order to successfully adapt. Longevity raises, therefore, may prove worthwhile in acknowledging the value of loyalty and experience. We recommend such raises not be too dramatic and become less frequently awarded over the course of a career.

4. If these recommendations seem confusing, it's no accident. Compensation policies, especially those related to annual incentives or raises, have always proven difficult. A new notion or strategy takes root every few years, only to be found flawed, and superseded by the next. Our best advice is to beware of salary raises for performance and to consider cost-of-living adjustments as an economic or competitive necessity. If you require more sophisticated information, there are many consulting firms with compensation specialists on their staff.

Preventive Measures:

A clearly stated salary policy, consistently applied, can save you a lot of grief in the long term. In addition, a sensible budgeting process that accounts for salary increases can serve as a guide to help formulate a salary policy.

REIMBURSEMENTS

"An employee from our office was recently sent to a conference in Chicago. On his expense sheet, he noted the standard government allowance for food is $40 per day and, therefore, there was no need to itemize. He remarked that his expenses easily exceeded this amount."

Employees are often called upon to spend money out of pocket to accomplish the work assigned to them. Examples might include travel expenses, gas and upkeep for a company-owned vehicle, unscheduled purchases of office supplies, and entertaining customers. The integrity of workers concerning accurate reporting of expenses is usually not questioned. There is, however, potential for abuse that can put cash in the dishonest employee's pockets.

In many organizations, the "padding" of reimbursement reports is considered more the norm than the exception. Just as some people believe everyone cheats on their taxes, many employees feel the same way about reporting expenses. If and where this is the case, honest employees and meticulous record keepers may feel disadvantaged.

Whether suspicious or not, many managers believe expenses should be monitored, strictly accounted for, and/or audited to prevent cheating. This can be done in every case where reimbursement is requested, or randomly. In either case, the review function should be designed as a deterrent and, therefore, made known to all affected employees.

In some cases, management senses a high degree of trust and believes that verifying reimbursements is a waste of time and money. If it costs fifty dollars to save ten, a manager should consider whether the benefits (in this case, ten dollars cash and the likelihood that others will be deterred) exceed the costs.

Approach to Take:

1. If you don't already have a system for reimbursements, now is the time to develop one. Keep in mind the objective. From time to time employees may have to use their own money for organization expenses, and you want to repay those loans. The tricky part is the documentation. What level is appropriate?

   For small purchases, say under $20, we recommend setting up a petty cash account. This can be maintained by the office manager, or a clerk in the office. Start with $100. Use the cash to reimburse small amounts. The only way to get cash from this fund is to present a receipt. At the end of the week, or the month, or the quarter (depending on the size of your organization), the money and receipts should be balanced. The total of cash and receipts should equal $100.

2. *Let the employees solve the problem.* Discuss the subject with employees, and get their input regarding the best way to keep track of expenses. Ask them to form a committee and come back to you with recommendations. Try to keep an open mind, and remember that, although you have the final veto power, they're the ones who are going to have to use the system.

3. If you're not comfortable asking employees to design the system, *get another opinion.* Find out how colleagues in other organizations take care of reimbursements. Get opinions on what works and what doesn't and why. Then put together your own procedures. For larger expenses, we recommend developing a reimbursement form that takes into account a variety of expenses. That way, you can use the same system for different kinds of expenses—out-of-town travel, client entertainment, office supplies, or whatever.

4. Whatever system you develop, make it clear to employees that cheating will not be tolerated. Mention that you will

be doing regular audits of expense vouchers, and then do them.

Preventive Measures:

Once you have a system in place, be sure to review it thoroughly with new hires. In addition, review the policy with employees from time to time to see how it's working.

RESIGNATIONS

"For months one employee has been driving me (and others) to distraction. Neither counseling nor warnings nor disciplinary letters have solved the problem. She occasionally talks about resigning, but obviously has not followed through. I'd like to encourage her."

Resignations are usually received as bad news—a valued employee is moving on. These occasions may prove disruptive in terms of recruitment, time, locating qualified applicants, and training new hires. There are occasions, however, when a resignation is a welcome event. Many managers are reluctant to fire un- or counter-productive employees, fearing resultant litigation. In such cases, a voluntary resignation may be the most desired outcome for manager and employee alike.

Soliciting or coercing an employee resignation may prove tantamount to firing. An ultimatum of "Resign or be fired" is an example of an *in*voluntary resignation.

The employee and the manager may become increasingly hostile as the dance of suggestion followed by inaction progresses and escalates. Usually if an employee is ready to leave, he will—if he is not, and you want him gone, documentation, progressive discipline, and termination procedures are often the most productive avenue. While some employees may require a suggestion or nudge to make up their mind regarding resignation, persistent efforts to force a decision may prove counter-productive.

Approach to Take:

1. We believe resignations are *voluntary* separations and termination or discharge is involuntary. Therefore, we discourage managers from exploring the murky middle ground without the assistance of an attorney familiar with employment law.

   Consider the costs vs. the benefits. Be clear about what they are before you talk to the attorney. Also be clear about what is your preferred outcome.

2. Voluntary resignations under adverse circumstances are negotiable. In order to make the separation most comfortable for both parties, a manager may wish to negotiate about accrued time off, severance pay, continuation of benefits, etc.—again with the advice of an attorney.

3. Another technique that may prove valuable is mediation. Hiring a professional trained in dispute resolution may help you and the employee assess your respective options. Common ground may be discovered in areas that neither management nor employee thought to explore.

Preventive Measures:

The best preventive measure is a policy regarding how much notice is required for resignations. Be careful, though, because such a policy may affect employment at will. (See EMPLOYMENT AT WILL.) Check with an attorney before establishing this kind of policy.

Another preventive measure is to acknowledge that management is often complicit in allowing negative employment situations to reach the point where resignation is a desired outcome. Dealing early with difficult employees can preclude having to solve this problem.

The common refrain "I've tried everything" should be considered in light of the many tools shown in the beginning and throughout the text of this book.

> **ROMANCE**
>
> "One of our team leaders seems to have fallen head over heels in love. I'm delighted for her. The only problem is that the object of her romance is also a member of her team."

While love may be a many-splendored thing, its outbreak within the confines of an organization may be more cause for concern than celebration. Office romances can affect the demeanor and productivity of coworkers along with the participants.

The first and most obvious concern must be favoritism or some other form of advantage to the members of the couple. Does one supervise the other or travel among those who do? Is one of the lovers a coach or mentor whose judgment may be affected by affection? As anyone who has fallen in love will attest, objectivity is not a lover's strongest suit. Favoritism may also occur in a backwards fashion, as one of the couple works too hard at denying advantages to the other. Such problems can jeopardize morale in the workplace and the morale of the enamored.

Another concern may be harder for a manager to perceive and address. It concerns the preoccupation of romance—even when attempting to work. The body language of the participants (whether games of "footsie" or obsessive eye contact) can prove distracting for everyone. Coworkers often come to resent the "cooing and fluttering" they experience around them.

Romances can also take time. Like other forms of addictive behavior, sweethearts require frequent fixes. Unnecessary visits, frequent intercom calls, lengthy E-mail missives, and other excuses for contact may abound. Real work may, at times, seem less important than the presence or attention of the other person. After all, it's hard enough to focus on work while being romantically involved with someone outside your work or office. When the object of affection is so close at hand, the temptation for distraction can prove overwhelming.

A romance occurring at work can bring out the best in some people and worst among others. For some, it's a healthy reminder. For others, it brings up resentments regarding their own work or personal life. What's really heightened interest within the couple may be perceived as greater distance or disinterest by others working with and around them. In work environments where close teamwork is stressed, a romance within or across team lines may prove disruptive. Employees may feel pushed or pulled as the romance advances.

In some cases, an office romance can raise moral or ethical concerns as well. One or both of the participants may be married—evoking discomfort and judgment all the way around. Similarly, same-sex relationships may evoke condemnation based on deeply held religious beliefs. These instances of discomfort often infect all kinds of operations. People may stop speaking to each other, avoid needed communication, or find other ways of acting out their displeasure.

Approach to Take:

1. The first and most difficult step for a manager when romance is detected is to verify its existence. We recommend the direct approach. Ask the couple if your hunch is correct. *Define the problem.* Before doing so, you may want to explain why you as a manager would need to know. Much of what's written above may help in justifying your curiosity.

2. Your concerns should be "on the table" so that the romantics understand their responsibilities to you, coworkers, and the organization as a whole. Be clear they are being asked for open and honest understandings with you—not restraint or the bridling of their feelings. Your role is not that of a liaison or confidante. In this case,

you're merely the boss—the central point of contact and the person who must be kept informed.

3. In larger organizations, you have more options for addressing this problem than you do in small organizations. You can move one of the pair to another department, thereby eliminating the temptation for them to waste time. One caution in considering a move—make sure you don't put one of them (traditionally this has been a female) at a career disadvantage. *Let the employees solve the problem.* Ask them to help you come up with a solution. If you have followed the first two steps successfully, they should be aware of the problems their romance is creating.

4. Another option, in both large and small organizations is to *get another opinion.* Ask colleagues and friends who may have encountered a similar situation what they did to resolve the problem.

5. In a small organization, you may be limited to having an open discussion with the employees. As the romance progresses, so may tensions both between the lovers and with coworkers. In many cases, the participants must be confronted and a decision made as to who stays or goes—for the overall health of the organization. As always, a history of honesty and open communication will make such an event less likely or more tolerable should it come to pass.

Preventive Measures:

Short of hormone therapy, we know of no measures that can prevent workplace flirtation and/or romance. Good clear training on sexual harassment may help clarify the difference between an office romance and an offensive work environment.

RUMORS

"Five employees approached me last week asking whether it's true we'll be laying off employees next month. It's not. I don't know where the rumor started, but my reassurances haven't really calmed the situation."

Most organizations have two main systems of communication—the official and the unofficial. The unofficial pipeline usually represents an effort to anticipate or better describe what's coming down management's line. It would be unusual for an organization not to have a grapevine or rumor mill. By the same token, the amount of time and communication devoted to this secondary source of information is usually reflective of management.

Where management is open, honest, and close to the employees who staff the organization, rumors tend to be less needed or credible. Employees who pick up on rumors will generally take them to management for validation. In less healthy workplaces, rumors are felt to be necessary. The grapevine carries information that management doesn't want to convey or prefers to sit on.

Unfortunately, the validity of rumors may be taken for granted—especially where information furnished by management is not always credible. For instance, where management may have received a safety inspection report indicating potential health hazards, individuals in management may prefer clarifying or rebutting the findings to disseminating them. Where this has happened, employees may come to view any and all rumors about safety hazards as believable.

Many managers react to rumors emotionally. Their immediate response is to find the individual(s) responsible. Such witch-hunts usually demoralize employees and are less preferable than letting them identify the gossips responsible and reassess the credibility of those individuals. It would be better for the manager to provide clear information that refutes the rumor and then begin to examine the reasons why false information may have been disseminated.

Although one possible source of false rumors is the gossip (see GOSSIP) who has simply run out of things to say or is looking to increase the interest of his audience, there are others as well. Quite often rumors are symptomatic of an anxious workforce. People whose health and security needs may seem threatened are likely to respond to scraps of information with reams of speculation.

Another cause may be an employee who cannot easily keep a secret. Some may just let information slip out, others find it impossible not to share, and in a few cases, a manager or employee may find it necessary in the interest of fairness to disseminate a rumor. In these cases, the rumor is not without substance. It only embarrasses management because the rumor arrived ahead of official management communication.

Approach to Take:

1. When you become aware of a rumor, three immediate options present themselves. The first would be to catch up with the grapevine by acknowledging the rumor, providing the official information, and explaining why such information lags behind. Another would be to deny the rumor, providing the employees with comprehensive and convincing information to the contrary. A third option is silence—leaving it to the employees to assess the validity of rumors without need for confirmation or rebuttal.
2. Beyond these immediate reactions, we suggest you interview or survey employees regarding the adequacy of communications in your organization. (See QUESTION-NAIRES AND SURVEYS.) You should acknowledge there is always the potential for a grapevine (carrying both reliable and unreliable information) whenever employees spend time with coworkers. If rumors have become persistent, or have an adverse effect on morale, it's time to find out why they're taking root. If asked honestly

and sincerely, employees may tell you what you need to know.

3. Where a rumor is particularly vicious or destructive, a manager may find it necessary to identify the source. If this is the case, we recommend you investigate openly. Let people know the nature of the information being passed, why you find it to be of particular concern, and why you feel it necessary to identify the perpetrator. You may also wish to ask the individual to identify him/herself in order to preclude the distress that an investigation would cause others.

Preventive Measures:

As the first three rules of the real-estate business are "location, location, location," so those in the business of management should remember communication, communication, communication. Where people have no cause to believe a rumor, they will also have no cause to initiate them.

SECOND JOB

"I have an employee who has called in sick on several Mondays. At first I suspected substance abuse, but recently learned she has a weekend job at a truck stop and may just be physically exhausted by Monday."

For any number of reasons, employees often find their earnings on the job you manage are insufficient. What's more, while you as a manager may consider any other employment to be secondary or moonlighting, the employee may not see it that way. While it's unreasonable to deny an employee the opportunity of additional earnings, it is acceptable to expect her to be ready, willing, and able to perform the job for which she's being paid.

Legitimate difficulties may arise if you require an employee to arrive early, stay late, or work on her day off or during her weekend. In some cases, despite efforts to find an agreeable arrangement, the employee's need for the second job and yours for the employee's services may stand in opposition.

Approach to Take:

1. *Define the problem.* Make sure you know what the problem really is. It's possible you're angry because you're afraid of losing the employee. At any rate, clarify the problem so you can discuss it calmly. Then meet with the employee and *say what you mean.*

2. As an alternative, *let the employee solve the problem.* Ask him what he would do if he were you. Enlisting his assistance can help you clarify the problem, and can enable him to be more empathetic with what you're facing. Remember, he's got decisions to make too. Yours may or may not be what he considers his primary employment.

3. Make a conscious decision regarding how much you can compromise in terms of attendance, distractions, and overall job performance. How much benefit of the doubt are you willing to give the employee? *Consider the costs vs. the benefits.* Consider the cost of losing the employee—including training a replacement—versus your concerns and frustrations with keeping him.

   When you've figured it out, we suggest you write it down, show it to the employee, and then stick to it.

4. If you've tried the first three approaches and are still really not satisfied that the problem is solved, AND you want to keep the employee and the employee wants to stay, consider mediation. Often hiring a professional mediator is cheaper than ongoing misunderstandings. One of the possible sources of mediators is your local affiliate of the American Bar Association. In addition, they're often listed in the phone directory under "Mediation Services." Always be sure to get—and check—references.

Preventive Measures:

It's perfectly reasonable to require employees to notify you of other jobs they're working. This is worth knowing not only for reasons of productivity, but also concerning issues such as health insurance, workers' compensation, unemployment, etc. If you have employees who are working additional jobs, you may wish to check with an attorney and/or various insurance carriers to be sure you understand the scope and limits of your liability for that employee.

Additionally, you may wish to advise employees concerning the need for their services outside required working hours (if any), and your expectations concerning their availability.

SECURITY

"This morning an employee told me that after working late he saw someone sitting in our parking lot drinking from a paper bag and making belligerent remarks. He alleges he wasn't scared; however, he worries about others, especially women, who might face the same problem in the future."

Security issues are important to employees. However, in the world of employment, most managers view security interests in terms of job security. The physical and emotional well-being of workers should be considered as well. Whether the issue is waiting for a bus during the dark hours of winter, receiving obscene phone calls, or fear of a break-in, employee concerns and misgivings should be taken seriously. These are issues where people would commonly prefer to leave an employer than to fight to be heard and understood.

Among the issues you as a manager may face are the following:

For those organizations that meet and deal with the public, access to your space may invite unwanted visitors. This can create a difficult balancing act. It's vital that customers be able to get to you, but it's also critical that employees not feel intimidated at the workplace.

When employees experience phone calls that are threatening, obscene, or downright belligerent, they may become scared to answer the phone. Again the goal is to find a solution that ensures employees don't feel harassed, and customers don't have to go to extraordinary means to make contact with your organization.

Some employees may worry about the security of getting to their car or public transportation. This is a particular problem in the winter months. (In the winter in Seattle it's dark by 4:30 in the afternoon!) You need to take these concerns seriously. It's a much happier situation to address these problems before serious incidents force you to confront them.

Banking is another area where security can be an issue. In every organization someone is responsible for carrying money to and from banking institutions. In most cases, this is done by an employee such as a bookkeeper, cashier, or accountant. There are many more alternatives than there used to be for banking. Electronic fund transfers and extended hours provide managers with options that weren't available a decade ago.

The final security worry is your computer system. Internally, there are ways to develop and use passwords to limit access to specific programs. For external concerns, there are programs and devices designed specifically to address this problem.

Approach to Take:

1. For those who are reading this entry while just casually perusing the book, you may wish to consider no news as good news. If you're not receiving evidence of employee concerns in this area, you may have no need to take precautions. You may, however, wish to mention to all employees that any security concerns can and should be brought to your attention. All of the following approaches assume there are professionals in various areas—police, the phone company, banks—who have thought about se-

curity issues and have recommendations for solving your problems.

2. If security concerns are raised, we urge you to consider using a combination of public and private resources depending on the nature of the problem. Where physical premises are your concern, we suggest contacting your local police precinct and scheduling an audit or walkthrough. Their suggestions are likely to be as well considered and explicit as any private contractor.

   Where employees are concerned as to who might be coming in and how they could ever get rid of them, you may wish to consider a buzzer system or a conspicuously placed video camera. If employees are concerned about break-ins, especially when working late, consider installing alarm devices or protective deterrents such as bars for windows, and deadbolts for doors. (See the section on KEYS TO THE OFFICE. You don't want to create new problems trying to solve old ones.)

3. Similarly, if problems center on your telephone system, you may wish to call the local phone company and ask for an expert in security matters. That individual should be able to answer all of your questions and address every concern. They may even provide employee training at little or no cost. In addition, they may be able to suggest devices that are centrally installed that would enable you to determine who's calling before you answer the phone. Such measures may include: caller ID, recording devices, or phone company taps.

4. To address employee concerns regarding walking to vehicles or public transportation, you may want to impose a rule that no employee work beyond certain hours without someone else present and able to leave at the same time (the buddy system). Perhaps it would be easier to call a local car or taxi service and investigate rates for taking employees to safe public transportation stops. You may also wish to consider security lighting in parking areas or on-call security escorts. If you want to consider a security escort, look in the Yellow Pages under security. As

with all contract services, be sure to ask for references before hiring a service.

5. Where the employee worries about being robbed or assaulted when doing the banking, you may wish to consider measures such as hiring a courier service, using specially marked deposit bags, making deposits at a different time each day, or driving to the bank rather than going on foot. In addition, contact your bank and discuss your concerns either with your personal banker or with the branch manager. They're interested in keeping your account, and may be able to help you address the problem.

6. With regard to the security of your computer system, look in the phone directory under computer system design and consulting. Always be sure to check references when hiring a consultant.

Preventive Measures:

In several issues raised here, the location of your organization may be the biggest problem of all. We suggest where this is the case, you do a serious analysis concerning costs and benefits of moving to a safer and more secure area.

SEVERANCE PAY

"I'm thinking about terminating one of my employees. He's a nice person; he just never really understood how to do his job. I'm ready to give him his notice, but I don't know whether or not to give him severance pay."

The issue of severance pay is one of policy and style. Except in the case of permanent workplace closings in a union environment, there are no laws governing the inclusion or exclusion of severance in terminations. Thus the decision is really more a matter of tradition, and possibly conscience, than it is conforming to a rigid standard.

There are several factors which contribute to the determination regarding severance pay. The most obvious is the circumstances under which the employee(s) is departing. If you have eliminated the job or the job classification (all senior engineers are being laid off), it's traditional but not required to make a final payment. This can be viewed as the satisfaction of a moral obligation, a contribution toward tiding the employee(s) over until new employment is found, or just good business with an eye toward future recruiting. Most large companies in the U.S. provide severance payments under these conditions.

The next situation where severance may be appropriate is where an employee will be terminated and you believe it would be harmful to morale to keep her around. Offering severance in lieu of notice is one effective way to get the offending (and usually, in this case, offensive) employee out of your organization, and still give adequate notice. In this case, the amount of pay is usually equal to the length of time the employer requires for termination notice. If the employee is required to give two weeks' notice, the severance payment will be equal to two weeks' pay.

The preceding example assumes an employee who has not committed any major infractions. It's generally reserved for employees who "just never quite got the hang of it." In cases where an employee has committed a serious infraction of rules, or has broken the law—cases where there is an incident which precipitates the termination—severance pay would not only be inappropriate, but is likely to harm morale and productivity for the remaining employees.

In addition to being tied to cause, the decision/amount of a severance payment generally reflects tenure on the job. Traditionally, especially in the first example above, the amount will be one week's pay for each year worked. An employee with ten years of service would receive ten weeks of pay.

Unless there are exceptional circumstances, we recommend against giving severance payments to temporary employees and those who are terminated while still in a probationary period. If you have permanent part-time employees—the bookkeeper who's worked fifteen hours a week for the last seven years—it may be appropriate to offer a severance payment. In this example, if you've decided to hire a full-time bookkeeper, and the incumbent is not interested in the job, we leave it to you whether you have an obligation to make a payment.

The final matter regarding severance pay is the possibility of such payments falling under the Employee Retirement Income Security Act of 1974 (ERISA). If you are making a one-time lump sum payment to one employee, ERISA will probably not apply. However, if you are offering a severance "package" and will provide the employee with the option of a lump sum payment or distributions over time, be sure to check with a tax accountant and a lawyer who is well versed in employment law before setting up such payments. The ERISA regulations are very complex, change annually, and have ponderous reporting and oversight procedures.

Approach to Take:

1. *Be consistent.* Whatever you decide for one employee, you must do for all employees in the same situation. If you decide that employees who are the focus of reductions-in-force (RIFs) will get one week's pay for each year of service, then give the same to all RIFed employees.
2. *Follow the Golden Rule.* If you must lay off employees, consider how you would feel if you were laid off with no severance pay. As we've said many times in this book, you don't want to bankrupt the organization trying to be fair. On the other hand, being without work and no severance pay can be a very tough place to be.
3. *Consider the cost vs. the benefits.* You must balance the cost of severance payments against the morale and productivity of the remaining workforce. In addition, consider the likelihood of needing to rehire existing employees or finding new employees in the future. The goodwill you create by making decent severance payments can make it much easier to find new workers down the line.

4. In the case of a termination for cause, again weigh the balance between giving notice and giving a payment in lieu of notice. If an employee has been disruptive, it may be worth it to you to get him out as soon as possible.

5. If you are thinking about making payments other than in one specific instance to one specific employee, check with an attorney who's versed in employment law and/or a tax accountant to make sure you're not running into ERISA regulations.

6. We recommend against trying to develop a rigid policy regarding severance payments. It's difficult to put together, and you'll always find exceptions. If you have a large organization, it may be a good idea, but in those instances you probably also have a human resource department that should be charged with this task.

SEXUAL HARASSMENT

"We recently received a videotape designed to train managers about sexual harassment. It's gotten me to the point where I'm not sure whether I can compliment an employee about a new dress or a piece of jewelry without getting into trouble."

By virtue of the Civil Rights Act of 1964, employment discrimination on the basis of sex or gender is illegal. While the Act itself focused on hiring, pay, promotion, and similar factors, it soon became apparent that women experience particular difficulties in the form of sexual advances and offensive work environments.

Legal requirements concerning sexual harassment have evolved through Equal Employment Opportunity Commission (EEOC) court decisions over several years. Based on cases brought by women, legal precedent has been set in three basic areas:

The first is the most obvious—that sexual favors or conduct of a sexual nature not be required as a "condition of employment." This means that no person (woman) should feel obliged to perform, witness, or be subjected to sexual acts and/or advances in order to keep her job.

The second should be just as evident: that submitting to or rejecting sexual advances may not be used in making any employment decision, such as performance ratings, promotions, freedom from discipline, etc.

It's the last form of sexual harassment, as determined by courts and the EEOC, that's most difficult to understand. It defines harassment as behavior that substantially interferes with the individual's ability to perform day-to-day work or which creates a hostile, offensive or intimidating work environment.

The first two forms of harassment should be obvious, and we believe anyone engaged in such practices does not deserve a job in your organization. The difficulty lies in the fact that most of these cases result in a credibility dilemma. Those accused of such offensive behavior don't admit it, even in the face of overwhelming evidence. The shame and embarrassment are simply too much. In making credibility assessments, managers often defer to the accused, partly because they're members of the same group (in most cases, both are male and managers) and partly because of a belief that no one should be disciplined—especially fired—without clear proof of guilt (something that's seldom available).

We know that harassment is real. We also know that the overwhelming experience is of women being disadvantaged by men. This has happened to so many working women that one is tempted, from an objective standpoint, to give the accuser the benefit of the doubt. Assuming every woman who alleges improper advances or working conditions is telling the truth would be almost as injudicious as accepting every boss's denial. Thus the dilemma.

When it comes to a hostile or offensive work environment, proof may be easier to come by. Such cases usually hinge on a pattern of behavior. Examples might be posting of explicit or clearly suggestive sexual material like *Playboy* magazine and suggestive posters, the telling of "dirty jokes" on a continuing basis, repeated physical acts such as fondling, brushing up against the other person, or slaps on the rear, as well as persistent remarks concerning the other person's body, sexual appetite, sexual habits, etc.

This area is obviously painted in shades of gray. It becomes easier to assess what's in or out of bounds by understanding women at the workplace and the indignities they've suffered for centuries. This is not easy for many men and may require the assistance of an outside expert . . . we recommend a woman.

One of the oddest provisions in sexual harassment case law is that a manager may be found guilty for having done nothing. Where you were or should have been aware of sexual harassment occurring within the workforce you manage, you can be found guilty of harassment yourself by allowing, condoning, or perpetuating such acts. In many cases, managers who didn't actively engage in any form of harassment still lost their job due to inattention or inaction. Beware!

We believe there's never an excuse for sexual harassment in the workplace. Like many other acts that are illegal—theft, exchanging trade secrets, and falsification of pay records—people get away with this behavior all the time. We think the only way to stop sexual harassment in the workplace is to quit tolerating it in any form at any time.

Approach to Take:

1. There may be no emotion known to man stronger than lust. Yet the law requires men and women to suppress their lust while on the job. It's the law. Those who cannot control their libido are simply not suitable for employment in the United States today. If you disagree with these conclusions, you need the best training available to guide you as a manager and/or employer. Spare no expense, as the cost of a lawsuit will likely dwarf any costs associated with training or expert consultants.

2. If you have any suspicion or are aware of sexual harassment occurring in your organization—either from comments made by employees or personal observation—

ACT. If you work in a large organization, seek guidance from your human resources office and document the conversation. If you have no such function in your organization, call your state or local human rights commission and an attorney who's versed in employment law.

Preventive Measures:

We think it's very important that all employees be made aware of sexual harassment laws and the differences between proper and improper conduct. We also think an organizational commitment from the top down is a prerequisite to any successful training effort. Therefore, shop around for good, effective sources of training. You can begin by contacting your state or local human rights commission, the National Organization for Women, or other similar sources for referrals.

Make sure you build into any training program the tone and specifics of your commitment. Work with the trainer to get her advice and assistance in coordinating this with the training itself.

Finally, practice what you preach!

References: *Personnel Journal,* "Answers to the Toughest Questions Being Asked about Sexual Harassment," February 1995, p. 36; "When Dealing with Sexual Harassment, Internal Issues Come First," p. 98; *Personnel Journal,* "Sexual Politics," May 1995, p. 50.

SHIFT WORK

"One of our swing-shift employees moved to another company for the promise of working days. There are no volunteers to replace him. Bringing a new employee onto the evening shift is always difficult. I fear I'll have to force someone to change shifts, and perhaps lose them down the line."

More and more operations are requiring two or three shifts in order to remain competitive and satisfy customers. With this change, come new challenges for management. Shift work is normally associated with blue- or pink-collar environments (grocery stores, twenty-four-hour restaurants, catalogue sales, manufacturing plants, etc.). Other round-the-clock employers include hospitals and police and fire departments. All such environments require special attention and experience special problems not associated with a daytime-only operation.

The first concern is what hours will comprise each shift. Usually there's a morning, afternoon or evening, and night-time or graveyard shift. In setting hours, many employers require an overlap or "turnover" to familiarize oncoming employees with the work of the outgoing. For instance, a nurse arriving at a hospital at 3:00 P.M. requires several minutes with the nurse from the previous shift in order to familiarize himself with the patient load and needs. Commonly employers will have shifts that run eight and a half hours with one half hour off for lunch and one half hour at the beginning and another at the end of the workday for turnovers.

The next concern is attracting people to evening and night shifts. Most people prefer working days. Evening is normally a time for family and/or entertainment, while late night and early morning hours are for sleep. Adjusting to an entirely different pattern looks quite unattractive to most of us. Many employers use pay differentials—some as high as 15 or 20%—in order to attract volunteers to the later shifts. While overtime rates are fixed by laws, shift differentials are not and, therefore, vary from one employer to the next. They may be negotiated where a union is present.

Where stable shifts (the same people work the same hours throughout the year) are not possible, either due to a lack of financial resources or logistical problems, rotating shifts may be the answer. In these situations, employees will work a number of weeks on one shift and then rotate forward or backward for a similar period of time. Obviously, rotating shifts can cause considerable stress as sleep schedules and home life must be continually adjusted to accommodate work needs.

Once staffed, night shifts may or may not require supervision and/or support staff. Back-shift employees require the same services and have the same needs as those working days. They may wish to talk to someone in personnel or payroll or ask a question of management, or may be injured on the job and require medical attention. This means staffing these shifts requires considerable attention to the needs and smooth functioning of around-the-clock operations. There's usually less organizational support available to back shifts, since most of the support workers and senior managers work days. Therefore, the need for competent, reliable, and respected management officials on evening and night shifts is very important—and no easy task.

One final issue regarding shift work is the morale of employees. Where an organization requires shifts, the sense of family or community within the workforce is often disrupted. In many organizations, blaming the workers on another shift is a common occurrence. Where stable shifts are used, you may have three distinct work groups having only a passing familiarity with one another. Moreover, issues of personal security, child care, sleep deprivation, and moonlighting are different for workers staffing the back shifts.

Approach to Take:

1. Most organizations that operate two or more shifts are unionized, with the exception of retail stores. This may be attributable to the stress associated with shift work. If you manage in an organization that's already unionized, you must assign, rotate, and compensate people based on the provisions in your negotiated agreement.

2. When shifts are required in an organization where there is no union, we suggest a labor-management advisory committee be established. This group would be chartered to ensure conditions are fair and reasonable, and productivity is maintained. Issues such as fixed or rotating shifts, method of assignment, and levels of supervision and support should be discussed and reviewed on an ongoing

basis. We suggest you defer assigning issues of compensation to the committee until they've had a chance to work cooperatively and understand differing points of view.

3. There have been many studies attempting to quantify the productivity difference between happy and unhappy employees. Nothing is conclusive. In the case of shift work, our belief is that attempts at improving morale will pay for themselves. Whether you use the committee recommended above, or simply increase levels of labor-management communication, employees, especially those working evenings and nights, should have a sense of belonging and caring about their work. If you have an internal newsletter or E-mail system, we recommend developing a "night news" or similar section devoted to those shifts.

4. Perhaps most important to the successful operation of shifts is the visibility of management officials. You must learn to adjust your own schedule so that frequent appearances on the evening and graveyard shifts are possible. Some managers stop by after supper or a movie; others may wake up with the chickens and arrive well before night-shift workers leave in the morning. The bottom line is that employees who can physically see and identify management officials are more likely to be responsive to organizational needs.

SHORT-TIMERS

"An employee who's worked here for thirty years plans to retire in two months. His energy and attitude have been flagging for some time, but since announcing his imminent retirement, he seems altogether indifferent."

When an employee's time with an organization grows short due to transfer, resignation, promotion, layoff, or retirement, it's often difficult for him to maintain a productive attitude toward his work.

Most individuals in this position are focused ahead and may find today's work or operations more of a distraction than an occupation. While a manager may sympathize, the difficulty in maintaining workplace efficiency comes first. The adverse effect short-timers have on coworkers and customers has often proven more than trivial.

One of the principal issues when managing these employees is their continued loyalty to the organization. Employees with short tenure and/or unpleasant experiences may carry some potential for theft, sabotage, etc. In work environments where employees are given days or weeks of notice prior to being fired, this potential is obviously much higher. Some employers may prefer paying an employee to remain at home during a "notice period" rather than risk the damage they could cause by coming to work.

Approach to Take:

1. Most of the problems associated with short-timers can be best solved by *saying what you mean.* You must define your expectations for their remaining time on the job. Basic organizational rules relating to calling in sick, use of equipment, personal phone calls, etc., must apply to these employees during their last days.
2. *Define the problem.* Be clear as to your fears, and look for agreement with the employee as to what each of you can expect during their final months, weeks, or days of employment. It's okay to say, "I'm still paying you. You can't spend all your time on the phone," or, "If you want to use my copy machine to make three hundred copies of your resume, ask me or buy your own paper."
3. In preparing for the employee's departure, you may wish to have her document various aspects of her job for use by her successor/replacement. This is especially true in small organizations or for employees in singular positions. Information relating to customer contacts, filing systems,

mechanical histories, etc., may be more useful than merely having the employee perform her routine job functions until the day she leaves.

If the employee has been terminated, or if resignation came just as you were considering firing, having the employee document her job may be a waste of time. In that case, try to think of tasks that will be helpful to you and keep the employee in question busy, and may be of some use after he's gone. This is a tall order and, as we said above, you may prefer paying him to stay home the last two weeks.

Many short-timers spend their last days scrambling to clear off their desk, vainly believing that their work will be current upon their departure (backlog will be eliminated). Again, a clear plan of action and realistic expectations are needed.

4. Where security is an issue, it's always preferable to pay severance pay and have the employee out of the office. In many large corporations, terminated employees are handed a check and escorted out of the office the same day. Although we find this to be an extreme measure, *consider the costs vs. the benefits* of how to address security.

Preventive Measures:

One of the hardest aspects of management is planning. Retirements, promotions, and resignations are much easier to manage when anticipated and openly discussed. Simply asking employees if they like their jobs, have plans for leaving, etc., on a periodic basis can provide a manager with invaluable information and an employee with less guilt, resentment, and/or confusion.

SICK DAYS

"I've run a business on my own for two years. Now I must hire an associate. One of the candidates for the job asked me about my policies concerning vacation and sick days. Regarding vacations I was pretty clear; however, I ended up confused as to how sick leave might work in a little office like this."

Most employers have policies concerning paid days off due to physical incapacitation. The task of writing such policies, however, can be much more difficult than you might imagine. Several issues present themselves, either immediately or over time. Among these are using sick days: for mental or emotional problems; for the illness of a family member; over long periods of time; and/or for a very short duration (one to two hours). Additionally, policies may need to address maximum accumulation of such leave, as employees with ten to twenty years' service may accumulate well in excess of 1000 hours.

Regarding the basis for using sick days (personal illness, family member, death in the family, etc.) a few external factors come into play. The Family Medical Leave Act of 1993 (FMLA) relates to serious illnesses in a worker's family, as well as maternity and paternity leave. While the guidelines speak only to unpaid time off in organizations over fifty employees, they should be considered when developing or reviewing your own sick leave policies.

Many firms and governments (including the federal government) have adopted guidelines relating to "family friendly" leave. Such policies allow workers to use sick time when caring for family members who are ill, rather than for their own medical needs only. Most employers have caps or limits on the number of such days that can be used. In some cases, these family-friendly days are dovetailed into provisions of the FMLA.

Even more fundamental economic issues arise when considering caps on sick leave vs. unlimited accumulations. Where an employer allows employees to earn one day of sick leave for every month of service, in nine years this would amount to over six months paid time off from work in the case of a lengthy or disabling illness. Many organizations lack the financial cushion to pay for such time, while also filling in behind the sick or injured worker.

The alternative is no prettier. Where employers have capped sick leave accumulations (at, let's say, thirty days or six weeks), employees become more likely to "get sick" as they see they must "use it or lose it." This creates a tension between management and labor—one party seeing sick days as a benefit while the other views it as an earned entitlement.

Efforts to compromise between unlimited sick leave and caps include awards for those who sacrifice excess days accumulated and diminished rates for earning sick leave after certain thresholds have been reached. Some employers are also using team-based theories and peer pressure in this area, by rewarding groups that demonstrate months of zero or low usage rates.

You may also wish to include a section in your policies concerning evidence of illness or injury. Some organizations require medical substantiation when absences exceed a certain period of time (say, three work days). In addition, your policy may require employees to provide medical certification for illness or injury of any duration, should suspicion of abuse be present. Such a requirement should be temporary in nature, so as to reflect a corrective rather than punitive outlook.

In our experience, employees who leave your organization with unused vacation days get compensated for those days, but they do not get compensated for unused sick leave.

Approach to Take:

1. Many human resource policy software programs have options for sick leave policies coded into them. While these may help, your specific situation may require broader input of ideas. *Let the employees solve the problem.* As always, we suggest you learn from your own workforce what policies would work best. While employees may imme-

diately think of policies that would suit their own interests, they will also balance these with concerns of
potential abuse and costs.
2. *Get another opinion.* Other organizations similar to yours
   may already have sick leave policies that are comprehensive. By requesting and comparing these, you and/or a
   group of employees may come to understand your needs
   and options better.
3. One other method for formulating sick leave policies is to
   informally ask family, friends, and even yourself where
   problems have occurred. The most successful policy will
   be the one that acknowledges the shortcomings of others.
   While there are no correct or perfect solutions, knowing
   how you and others have been dissatisfied with past
   guidelines should inject the broadest and best perspective
   into developing your own.

Preventive Measures:

People are bound to get sick and lose time from work. The
only way we know to minimize days lost to illness and injury
are effective safety and wellness programs that encourage good
health. See the section on PHYSICAL FITNESS.

References: *HR Magazine,* "Rx for an Ailing Sick Leave
Plan," March 1995, p. 67.

SLEEPING ON THE JOB

"Lately it hasn't been unusual to find one of my employees
dozing at his desk. I've been too embarrassed to wake him
and confront him on this issue, so I just make some noise
so he'll wake up and get back to work."

One of the basic tenets of the workplace has been "Eight hours
work for eight hours pay." Many jobs require an employee to
do nothing other than remain alert. This can become a prob-

lem; the more sedentary the job, the less likely most of us are to keep our eyes open and head up. Sleeping on the job is most common among guards, observers, and similar positions.

While many employers have moved away from the traditional five-day week and eight-hour day, there remains a presumption that employees will be awake, alert, and productively engaged during the time they're being paid. Most managers allow for short breaks or an occasional non-work conversation "on the clock." A catnap during lunch or break periods is accepted as being the employee's choice regarding how that time will be spent. Sleeping, however, crosses the line in every instance.

Approach to Take:

1. Before accusing an employee of sleeping, take a minute or two to observe him to assure you're not mistaken. Few of us can remain awake and alert during that time period without any discernible movements.

   If you're not positive, the employee still may be confronted concerning her lack of productivity during the time of your observation.

2. *Say what you mean.* Focus more on the need to accomplish work while being paid than on whether the person was sleeping or not. *Follow the Golden Rule.* Consider the possibility there may be mitigating circumstances.

3. Ask him to explain. *Let the employee solve the problem.* Suggest he come to you in a week with a solution. At that time, be prepared to listen to his suggestions.

4. Ask the employee to consider outside assistance (such as an employee assistance program—EAP) if concerns over income (two jobs), family (elder care), or health (excess medication) are at issue.

5. Where health, safety, or customer relations are compromised by the employee having napped, formal disciplinary measures are advised.

Preventive Measures:

Ensure that job duties are not so boring or repetitious as to make sleeping likely. Where this is the case, try adding variation to help employees remain alert. It's harder to fall asleep when work is fun and interesting.

Do not rule out personal problems. An EAP may be of greater long-term benefit than any policy, lecture, or enforcement mechanism that relates to sleeping on the job.

SMOKING

"I recently hired an excellent graphic designer. She is now complaining that a coworker's cigarette smoke is adversely affecting her health."

Issues concerning smoking at work and the effect of second-hand smoke on coworkers are among the thorniest a manager will encounter. They not only involve the issues of health, but also facilities (ventilation and outside facilities) and time away from the work site for those who smoke.

Smoke breaks can add up to an hour per day in some cases, while price tags associated with "adequate ventilation" may prove staggering. Many states have adopted laws relative to tobacco smoke in various settings—in public, offices, etc.

Approach to Take:

1. Call your state health department to determine what regulations apply to your site. This is particularly important if you are considering committing funds to alter your workplace.
2. *Define the problem.* Get clear about how smoking is affecting productivity. Confront the smoker concerning whatever job-related problems there are relative to her use of tobacco.

3. Explain policies, rules, regulations, or simply your own management needs. As an employer or manager, you have every right to expect your employees to work in exchange for a paycheck. When smoke breaks are out of control, they have an impact on efficiency and, therefore, on the organization.
4. *Allow the employee to propose a solution* that will, to whatever extent possible, maintain organizational effectiveness and productivity.
5. Ask the department of health what other organizations have done. *Get another opinion.* Find out what colleagues in other organizations have done to address the issue of smoking.

Preventive Measures:

One of the most effective measures you can take with regard to smoking is a smoking-cessation program. If your organization has a formal EAP, it is likely there will be a program already in effect.

If you don't have an EAP, call the local branch of the American Lung Association and ask them about smoking-cessation programs. Often they are free or low-cost. If you have enough people on the premises, you may be able to arrange a class in the workplace.

SUGGESTIONS

"We've always maintained a suggestion box outside my office. I hadn't checked it for a few weeks, and was surprised to find a lengthy contribution from one of our service representatives. It concerns new ways of conducting performance evaluations, determining bonuses, and gathering customer feedback. On the one hand, I want to commend her for the time and thought her suggestion represents. On the other, it could cost us hundreds of hours and thousands of dollars just to begin implementing these ideas."

Before Western management became interested in the Total Quality Management (TQM) theories of W. E. Deming and Joseph Juran, suggestion systems were more form than substance. Ideas were often rejected because they were premised on the inadequacy of current methods and/or management. Others were evaluated by individuals with little time or expertise. In all, creative employees often became turned off to the notion of improving work practices—either accepting the status quo or moving on to an organization where their insights might be more valued.

The most promising suggestions were ones that spoke to improved equipment or cheaper purchases. Tangible cost savings that did not reflect badly on other employees (especially managers) were the most likely suggestions to be adopted. Those that illustrated the inadequacy of practices or work methods were often evaluated by the very individuals who had designed the system under attack.

Many large organizations have changed their attitudes and practices 180 degrees regarding suggestions. With a new emphasis on employee empowerment and process ownership, managers are being trained to listen to employees as well as direct them. Current thinking emphasizes that without new ideas, organizations (even not-for-profits) lose competitive advantage and fall out of favor. While it was once believed that better mousetraps came from the top down, current wisdom points toward the employees for new ideas.

Making the conversion involves a profound change in managerial attitudes. Instead of saying, "It's always worked this way before," or, "This is the way we've always done it," a new mantra must be learned. "If we always do it the way we've always done it, we'll always get what we always got" implies fresh ideas are necessary and changes inevitable. This means managers must be flexible, open, and often self-effacing.

Any commitment to a suggestion system must be made real for employees. The first time someone waits for weeks without his suggestion being acknowledged, the erosion of credibility has begun. Simple ingredients are: timely acknowledgments, personal contact, open discussion, and a logical evaluation process.

Approach to Take:

1. If you want to make suggestions work to your organization's advantage, they'll have to be encouraged on several fronts. Through *regular staff meetings,* performance reviews, and informal encounters, let employees know you're looking for new ideas. If you believe work practices can always be improved, profess this openly—especially to yourself—and consider ideas for changing your own work habits.
2. Another way to draw attention to the need for fresh ideas and improvements is to announce the number and types of suggestions received on a weekly, biweekly, or monthly basis. The more you receive, the happier the report should appear to employees.
3. Develop a method to ensure you and other management officials are responsive to suggesters. Consider using suspense files or calendar entries to make rapid acknowledgments, frequent updates, and timely decisions. We suggest you also include face-to-face meetings between "process owners" such as you, procurement, marketing, etc., and the employee(s) suggesting improvements.
4. Most of us will profess our openness to and interest in new ideas, all the while resisting any form of change. In evaluating suggestions, you may wish to have both the suggester and evaluator try to acknowledge why even a good suggestion in the area being explored would be rejected. In other words, allow your organization to be up front about its own resistance to change. Make that part of the process.
5. Finally, consider how to reward those who are suggesting improvements. For those who find tangible savings that can be calculated, consider sharing the savings in some

meaningful way. Many suggestions focus on intangibles, such as management practices, employee morale, or improved time management. These suggestions warrant recognition as well. In some cases, the reward may equal or exceed those given in cases of clear dollar savings.

5. We recommend acknowledging and rewarding those whose suggestions are not adopted. After all, if the idea is to encourage employee involvement and to look for improvements, it may take a few misses before employees hit on the right ideas. You may want to put rejected suggestions into a quarterly lottery or have a committee nominate one or two particular ideas for a "close but not close enough" award. However you choose to do it, your efforts should be directed to your own and the organization's clear advantage.

TARDINESS

"Given the nature of our work, flexible hours are out of the question. I expect people to arrive on time just as I will pay them if they have to work late. That understanding isn't working with one of my employees who arrives late to work once or twice a week."

Hours of work is an area that's seen rapid and radical changes during the past several years. Not too long ago it was assumed that everyone showed up to work at a given hour, took lunch at approximately the same time, and left the office or plant as one. Now employees may be allowed flexible work hours, compressed work weeks, job sharing, work at home, and even telecommuting. Not every organization, however, can afford such benefits.

Fixed hours of work are still required of numerous organizations. Consider schools, hospitals, stores, banks, and airlines. All require employees to appear at work so that clients or customers will be served as expected. Arriving late can prove frustrating for both management and coworkers, as people wonder where the missing employee is, whether she will arrive, and if so, at what time.

At some point, everyone who works in such an organization will be tardy to work. Habitual or repeated lateness is the matter that proves most annoying and warrants management attention. In many cases, the reasons seem altogether legitimate—child or elder care, difficult commutes, etc. Over time, these reasons wear thin as the tardiness becomes a chronic condition.

Other cases anger a manager much more quickly. These employees seem to have a list of excuses next to the telephone, always offering the next reason why they couldn't arrive at work on time. It's almost comical to hear some of the stories they appear to invent—like a child alleging the dog ate his homework.

Approach to Take:

1. If you must deal with a tardiness problem, begin with your policy and a review of compliance. *Be consistent.* If others arrive late to work and are excused or overlooked, the rule has only limited value. Where this is the case, we suggest you inform *all* employees they are to be not only present, but ready to work, at the given start time.

2. If hours of work are being observed by others, put the employee on clear notice as to his responsibilities. *Define the problem.* If reasons/excuses are offered, counter with a referral to your EAP, as these are personal matters and your concern is timely arrival at work.

3. If the employee still isn't dependable after this initial confrontation, document each occasion you notice and write disciplinary letters advising that continued tardiness may eventually result in termination. The idea is to break a bad habit or allow the employee to find more flexible

hours elsewhere; therefore, your best bet is not to equiv-ocate.

Preventive Measures:

After some debate, we agreed that tardiness is a lifelong habit. If an employee is late for work, he's probably late picking up the kids, going out to dinner, and going to the dentist. There's not much likelihood that you will be able to convince him to change his habits.

> ### TEMPER TANTRUMS
>
> "When I told an employee her attire was inappropriate for our organization, she pitched a fit, telling me I was the last person to be commenting on issues of dress and style."

While many people whose upbringing did not allow them to vent anger and frustration might envy those who blow up on the job, temper tantrums at work present a major disruption and often appear to coworkers as a test or challenge to the ability of a manager to maintain control. In fact, whether it's a supervisor or subordinate who flies off the handle, the motivation may be fear. Certain people, when scared or embarrassed, become offensive or aggressive in an unconscious effort to throw the audience off balance.

Some organizations thrive on demonstrations of disagreement and frustration. Most prefer a "businesslike atmosphere" where temper tantrums have no place.

The most common model for tantrums is the explosive or fitful boss who feels entitled to berate or belittle errant employees. Certainly any organization that allows its managers, but not its employees, to vent spleen becomes less attractive and productive over time.

Approach to Take:

1. If it's you as a manager who has thrown a tantrum, the hardest part is to acknowledge rather than rationalize having done so. *Follow the Golden Rule.* Even if you don't mind similar behavior from others, you should acknowledge it can often have a chilling effect on those who work for you. Apologize. You stand to lose little and gain everything by doing so.

2. If an employee has flipped out, you need not request or demand an apology. When not volunteered, the words "I'm sorry" have little impact or meaning.

   Instead, an employee should be advised and be put on written notice that similar behavior may result in disciplinary action, or perhaps termination.

   We feel successive warnings and counseling sessions are usually futile. Once warned, an employee either can control his temper or he can't.

3. If you have an employee assistance program, use it. If not, consult a mental health professional and consider suggesting counseling for the offending employee. You are her supervisor, but you're not her mom. Temper tantrums are counter-productive and need to be dealt with assertively and decisively.

TEMPORARY EMPLOYEES

"Given our growth over the past two years, it's clear we need a full-time bookkeeper. A friend of mine insists it would be cheaper and smarter to hire someone from a temporary agency, even though the position will be permanent. She says hiring temps saves money in the long run."

The image of temps was once symbolized by the "Kelly Girl"— a clerical with enough experience to fill in for a month or two.

This is no longer the case. While many employers still rely on temps to fill more repetitive blue- and pink-collar jobs, temporary employment agencies commonly receive requests for doctors, engineers, and attorneys. In fact, it's estimated that over 25% of the U.S. workforce are contract employees.

As you might guess, the reason has to do more with money than management. Unlike the situation with permanent employees, many of the difficulties described in this book result in the immediate termination of a temporary. Beyond this simplicity, however, there may be fewer expenses associated with paying contract employees. Although agencies usually charge 25% to 50% above salary, they also provide services such as insurance, recruitment, payroll, etc. In addition, there's no expense for pensions, profit-sharing, or bonuses.

The ease of bringing on temporaries and letting them go is tempting. It means less time devoted to the ongoing needs of employees such as vacations, promotions, personal problems, and sick days. But the other side of the coin may appear more tarnished. Without long-term prospects, contract employees lack levels of commitment and loyalty common to career workers. They know they're here today and gone tomorrow and are unlikely to demonstrate loyalties which exceed your own.

Another issue temporaries raise is their integration with the permanent staff. Are they rewarded similarly to others? Are they invited to staff functions? Are they eligible to join the softball team? Some long-term employees will resent the answer to any of these questions, whether it's yes or no.

By the very nature of temporary employment, contract or leased employees may never really understand your needs as a manager nor your organization's culture. Where orientation of new workers is an important matter, temps may require more management time than you expected. They can't be expected to fully appreciate your way of doing things nor the requirements of your internal and external customers. Among all employees whose attitude is, "I show up, I get paid, I go home," contract workers top the list.

Where temporaries offer a distinct advantage is in the area of recruitment for permanent positions. While most temporary agencies charge stiff premiums to employers who hire away contract or leased labor, the price tag may be worth it. When converting a temp to full time, you've already assessed the person's character, work habits, job skills, and ability to fit into the organization.

Approach to Take:

1. *Consider the costs vs. the benefits.* Evaluate what kind of position you need to fill. Is it seasonal employment? Is it a specific project? Is it an ongoing position or maybe a new full-time job that's been done by an outside vendor in the past? Sit down and figure out exactly how much it would cost you to fill the job. Include all direct costs like unemployment insurance, Social Security, and health insurance or other benefits. (Remember that during an introductory probationary period you may not pay other benefits, but state and federal obligations begin at once.) Now you have a basis for comparison.

2. *Let the employees solve the problem.* Where you've been using a traditional, permanent workforce, consider bringing the issue of contract employees up at a *staff meeting*. Ask the employees to assess any effects your decision may have on them. Listen carefully. Adverse effects on the productivity or morale of your staff may cost you much more than a temporary employee could save.

3. Look in the telephone directory under Temporary Agencies. Pick three that are either in your neighborhood or specialize in your area of interest. *Get another opinion.* Check with colleagues in other organizations and get suggestions/references from them. Then interview three candidates. If you're going to get into the business of hiring temporary employees, you want to be able to have a long-term relationship with the agency. Ask them about their experience in your industry and how much they charge for what services, and get references. This is the time to make sure you're putting your trust in the right place.

4. If the job you're trying to fill is truly temporary, and the numbers look right to you, give it a whirl. There's little obligation and, at the worst, you may find it to be a "learning experience." If the job you're trying to fill looks permanent or ongoing, and the numbers are not unfavorable either way, go with your gut feeling and consider the feelings of your staff. By its very nature the decision to use temporary help is easily reversed.

TESTING, LIE DETECTOR AND HONESTY

"Someone broke into our office and stole several thousand dollars worth of equipment. The police have no suspects and are speculating that it was an 'inside job.' I want to have each employee submit to a lie-detector test."

Life would be a whole lot simpler for tens of thousands of managers if they could carry a truth meter with them at all times. They could hold it up to subordinates and superiors alike and find out what the real story is . . . on any subject. Lie detectors have always held this attraction. "Let's strap him in and find out if he's telling the truth" seems perfectly reasonable to those in charge.

For employees, the picture looks quite different. The ability of a machine to discern honesty from prevarication is doubtful. What's more, who knows what questions will be asked and what will be thought if they refuse to answer. Lastly, working in a place where one's integrity is officially questioned is a little like working for Big Brother.

In the end, the United States Congress agreed with the employee's perspective in almost all cases. The Employee Polygraph Protection Act of 1988 limits the use of lie detectors in almost all employment settings. Exceptions may exist for certain public employees, government contractors, security personnel, and drug company employees. Even in these categories, polygraph testing is limited.

The reason Congress acted as it did is based mostly on the

reliability of lie-detector testing. The style of interview may influence the results. What's more, the results themselves are subject to varied interpretations. Finally, not every liar shows up as such and, in many cases, honest individuals have been perceived as mendacious.

In the absence of lie detectors, a new industry has grown— honesty testing. Since the Employee Polygraph Protection Act only applies to electrical or mechanical devices, pencil and paper exams are allowable. Employers still looking for a predictor of honesty have turned to such tests. Unfortunately, there's considerable evidence indicating that honesty tests are no more reliable than lie detectors . . . just more legal.

Approach to Take:

1. We recommend against honesty testing, principally because studies show that a large population of truthful people score in with the dishonest. So these tests, while eliminating people whose integrity is in doubt, also works against large numbers of perfectly fine applicants. Our hope is good use of references, careful interviewing, and smart use of a probationary period will prove better predictors and safeguards than honesty tests.
2. As for lie detectors, they may be properly used when investigating documented instances of theft, embezzlement, etc. If this applies to you, we suggest you contact your human resource office or attorney concerning the propriety of using polygraphs. Then contact two or three security firms that provide this service and compare credentials.

Preventive Measures:

There are some people who will lie, cheat, and/or steal regardless of where they work, who works with them, or who manages them. Others may lean toward honesty or dishonesty depending on their feelings about work, and those for whom they work. Showing care and concern for your employees will lessen the chance the latter group would require the kind of testing described above.

TESTING, ALCOHOL AND DRUG

"My daughter recently applied for a job with a large defense contractor. They required a drug-screening urinalysis test before making a hiring decision. I'm wondering if we could do that here."

Recent surveys indicate that approximately half of the major employers in the United States are testing applicants for illegal drug use. Many are also randomly testing current employees. Of the companies that do not now test, most have plans to do so. These private firms believe that urinalysis screening is reliable, and that those who test positive are likely to be users, if not abusers, of the substance for which they're being tested.

Alcohol testing is far less prevalent. This is mainly due to the fact that alcohol is detectable for only a short time after consumption, whereas certain illegal drugs may remain in the body for a period of weeks after use. Alcohol tests (commonly referred to as breathalyzer tests) are most often performed shortly after an incident in which suspicion of intoxication is highest.

Alcohol tests, and especially drug screening, have been challenged in several cases raising employee rights of privacy. These Fourth Amendment challenges have, for the most part, been rejected by courts, as long as the testing procedure is unbiased, job-related, and technically reliable. The confidentiality of test results is a matter where the courts have found strong privacy interests. Employers must be careful that information regarding specific tests and personnel is released in accordance with law.

In certain industries, principally transportation and defense contracting, random urinalysis screening is required by statute of both employees and applicants. Under the Omnibus Transportation Employee Testing Act of 1991, certain transportation workers and officials must also submit to alcohol testing.

Under provisions contained in the Americans with Disabilities Act, alcoholism is considered a disability and, therefore, requires "reasonable accommodation" before action can be taken to terminate an affected employee. This is not the case with addiction to illegal drugs. Applicants or employees testing positive for drug use may be refused employment or terminated at the discretion of the employer. Those testing positive for alcohol must be offered treatment.

Although it's public policy to view alcohol separately from drugs such as marijuana, cocaine, heroin, etc., we see all of these as judgment-impairing (and in many cases addictive) drugs in the context of work and employment. Studies indicate that abuse of alcohol and licit (prescription and over-the-counter) drugs is far more prevalent than illegal drug use or abuse in the United States. In other words, the odds are much greater that you will hire or harbor an alcoholic than a crack- or pothead.

We feel preventing substance abusers from entering the workforce, or compromising safety or security once permanently on board, is an important matter. Substance abusers are less reliable, less safety-conscious, moodier, and costlier in terms of medical and other forms of insurance. While we don't advocate testing in most settings, we do believe that probationary periods should be used to your advantage, that being found "under the influence" (not necessarily legally "intoxicated") be a firing offense, and that managers should be actively encouraged to report suspected abusers to an employee assistance program.

Approach to Take:

1. If you're interested in establishing a drug or alcohol testing program, there are a few things you should consider at the outset.

   Who will you test? Will it be applicants only, or current employees as well? Will everyone in that group be subject to testing, or only those occupying or applying for certain positions? Will management officials be included? If you plan to screen employees, what percent of the workforce will be subjected to tests in a given year?

How will people be notified of a test? How much notice will they get? What happens if they refuse to be tested? Will they be advised that a subsequent test, at their own expense, may be considered favorably if their first test comes up positive? How will samples be taken, and who will handle them?

Who will write your policy? How will it be communicated to employees? How will equipment and/or laboratory services be selected and purchased? As laws and court decisions change, how will you be advised to modify your policy and program requirements?

2. *Consider the costs vs. the benefits* of the program you envision. Testing and screening can be an expensive deterrent. What's more, if no one tests positive, you'll never know whether the program itself deserves credit, or whether you're needlessly testing law-abiding and sober employees.

3. Obviously the services of an experienced attorney will be required. We suggest you interview other organizations that have worked with the attorneys you're considering before making a final selection.

4. Decide what you want to do if and when results come back positive. Will you offer employee assistance and/or rehabilitation services to those testing positive for illicit drugs? Will you give people a second chance or offer to retest? We believe a program which focuses on deterrence and rehabilitation is much more positively accepted than one focusing on detection and discipline.

5. Finally, make double sure testing and screening are performed with maximum attention given to employee confidentiality. Innocent employees, as well as substance abusers, need to feel confident about issues relating to their personal privacy.

TESTS, APTITUDE

"After years of hiring people only to find they must be terminated down the road, I'm now considering testing applicants every way I can before bringing them on board."

The business of testing both applicants and employees is booming. Standardized and validated tests cover such areas as intelligence, personality, honesty, and specific aptitudes. Along with this burgeoning industry, there is an increase in lawsuits concerning the use and misuse of these tests.

Aptitude testing is intended to measure or predict potential. In a blue-collar work environment, an employer may test for dexterity, as well as tool use and measuring skills. Tests that measure knowledge and skills are also referred to as aptitude tests, even though they're more properly referred to as achievement tests.

Finding and selecting appropriate instruments is a project in and of itself. Several reputable firms have developed any number of tests to measure any number of desired aptitudes. Specific companies can be recommended by a consultant or a human resource office in another firm. You may also scan copies of employee development/training publications, such as *Training* or *Training and Development*. Copies of these and similar periodicals are available in most public libraries.

The greatest jeopardy in testing applicants for knowledge, skills, or aptitudes is the potential for illegal discrimination. You have to be able to show a connection between what you're testing for and the skill(s) required to do the job. Since landmark court cases in the 1960s and 1970s, employers may not establish requirements that can be construed to be discriminatory. If you have any questions about whether or not your testing program meets the criteria, check with your human resource office or an attorney versed in labor and employment law.

Court decisions also require that the test(s) used be validated. Validation implies both that the test is related to an actual job-performance matter and that the test itself actually measures the appropriate skills or aptitudes. Most companies that sell aptitude tests have already performed validation studies. It's wise, however, to look through information they provide concerning validity before buying and using their product(s).

Approach to Take:

1. Many employers have learned of test instruments that are so cleverly devised and provide such interesting information they begin using them on applicants or employees before assessing the reasons why. We suggest you enter the world of aptitude testing with great care. Either hire or contract with a professional in the area of training, employee development, or organizational development. Ask your advisor what steps are required before a test can be procured and used. Get an estimate of the time and costs involved.

2. *Define the problem.* If you do decide on aptitude testing, you should also determine how you will use the test results. Will a certain score be grounds for rejecting an applicant or denying a promotion? Will test results be factored in with application or resume materials in some defined way? Will your method of using test results be employed consistently in each instance of hiring, promotion, retention, etc.?

3. In the process of validating the need for a test (not the instrument itself), you may wish to rely on employees. *Let the employees solve the problem.* Whether you say a particular skill or aptitude is important to success on the job may be less convincing than receiving the same information from employees who actually perform that work. Moreover, you may learn more about successful hiring from those you already value than you would from any expert or management official.

Preventive Measures:

While aptitude testing is itself a preventive measure, you may want to consider other ways of predicting success. In many cases, success is predicated more on work habits and work ethic than on talent or ability. If you believe this is true for jobs and people you manage, rethink the need and expense of testing.

THEFT

"After auditing our supply cabinet and making liberal estimates as to what we use, my hunch is that someone is stealing office supplies. I don't want to spy on people, nor do I want to mistrust them. By the same token, I don't want to harbor a thief among those whose salaries I pay."

By the time someone is old enough to reach the workforce, they should be aware of the Eighth Commandment: Thou shalt not steal. Yet some persist in old habits, unable to avoid temptation. Accordingly, correcting employees who steal is no simple matter.

Most legal interpretations of the term "theft" include the taking of someone else's property with the intent to convert it to personal use or gain. Legally this can be difficult to prove, as in any case where the employee's intent must be inferred. Therefore it would be wise to refer to such cases as "unauthorized possession" or "misappropriation." Should you find yourself in a position of needing to label the employee's misconduct, we suggest you consult your own attorney.

In many cases, it's hard to know when stealing is really stealing. When an employee takes home an office pen or pencil, wood scraps, employer-provided soft drinks, or other nominal items, do you, as a manager, consider it an act of theft? Different people have different thresholds in this regard. Many would say there is a normal or background level of pilferage in any organization. Others see misappropriation as the same act regardless of content or value. Some courts have found items valued under a certain level (say, $20 or $50) shouldn't cost an employee her job. Others have upheld firing actions when items were valued under $5.

Another area of confusion can be inconsistent enforcement. Where use of organizational supplies or equipment is tolerated within one group but not another, resentment is sure to follow. Employees who "steal" the organization's time or use equipment for personal matters may be as guilty as those who are outright supply thieves. In some such cases, the losses to the organization may be greater than those attributable to theft.

As discussed in entries concerning falsification and embezzlement, theft is an offense that attacks the trust upon which employment relationships are built. To tolerate stealing within the organization is tantamount to inviting a thief to live in your house. Where the bond of trust is broken, the damage is often beyond repair.

Approach to Take:

1. The idea here is not to catch anyone. Prevention or deterrence should be the manager's objective. If you suspect theft, then advertise the fact. Let employees know your tolerance for such activity is zero. Advise them that, if caught, they will likely lose their job. You may even encourage employees to report one another (anonymously, of course) in order to discourage anyone from stealing. While some of this may sound too heavy-handed for you, many battle-scarred managers would agree it's preferable to catching someone and having to deal with the fallout.

2. If you're fortunate or unfortunate enough to catch a thief, you may, depending on the circumstances and the value of the item(s) being pilfered, wish to contact law enforcement officials. If you fail to make this report, you cannot change your mind later. If you do contact the police, you may be able to drop any charges and deal with the matter administratively at a later date. Whether or not you

choose to contact law enforcement officials, we urge you to document the incident. Get factual information, including date, time, and items stolen—with values.

In either event, it should be the employee's job to save his job, assuming that's possible. You need not lecture him regarding the Eighth Commandment, nor the importance of trust, etc., etc. Let him know that it will take a lot of convincing to save his job, and let him try. Your job is to listen and perhaps take notes.

Preventive Measures:

If your organization is a tempting environment for someone with "sticky fingers," acknowledge your policies regarding theft loudly and often. Employees should be so convinced as to what they can expect that one who is caught would resign on the spot.

Where you use equipment that employees may want to borrow from time to time, develop a clear permission system that avoids the slightest appearance of stealing. Where employees can easily sign equipment in and out, they will be less likely to steal it.

A well-designed and maintained inventory system—both for equipment and products—can make it much more difficult for employees (or anyone else) to steal.

For more information, see January 1995, *HR Magazine*, "To Catch a Thief . . . and Other Workplace Investigations," p. 90.

THREATS

"Two employees got into a shouting match yesterday. During the most heated part of the conversation, one was advised she better back up everything she does on the computer because it could mysteriously disappear if she isn't careful."

Threatening remarks may be nothing more than jokes or the venting of anger. "I can't believe he took it seriously" is a common response from people accused of threatening others. In the end, whether a statement should be considered a threat depends on two factors. The first is the perception of the receiver. Did he honestly feel as if harm was on the way? Evidence of the receiver's concern for his welfare usually comes from the measures he takes after hearing such remarks. Did he report it to management or security authorities? Did he take measures aimed at protection?

The second factor involves the person making the threat. Is there any history that would lead a manager to conclude that violence or damage might result? Does the individual present indications of emotional instability, etc.?

In every case, if there's doubt as to whether a threat might be carried out, it should be taken seriously by the organization's management. While the world is not as violent as Hollywood may portray, instances of violence and vendettas in workplaces of all kinds keep increasing. It's a much better choice to over-react to a threat than to wish you had responded in time.

Approach to Take:

1. Err on the side of caution. If a threat that comes to your attention appears innocuous, approach the offending employee and check it out. *Say what you mean.* If it seems to reflect nothing more than a squabble, bring the employees together and develop a plan for resolving their differences. There needs to be management intervention.

   Where circumstances warrant, consider an agreement in writing to the effect that the threat will not be carried out, nor will similar instances occur in the future.

   In every such case, follow up with the receiver of the threat in a few days (Mark it on your calendar!) to see if peace of mind has been restored.

2. Where a threat appears to be serious and the offending employee not to be trusted in an informal manner, contact security or law enforcement officials as soon as pos-

sible. Also call an attorney who specializes in employment law. Not contacting such officials is often looked upon as evidence that you as a manager did not consider the threat a serious matter.

In all cases, document all conversations with employees.

3. If the situation is immediate and volatile, suggest the offending employee go home and cool off for the remainder of the day. Paying the individual for a few hours in such instances may prove to be a small price.

If and when employees threaten you or other managers, consider terminating their employment. *Think it over.* Do not haul off and fire a person who has threatened you without first contacting appropriate authorities.

Preventive Measures:

Where an employee appears to be overstressed, short-tempered, belligerent, etc., offer her employee assistance counseling early and often as a means of preventing future threats, violence, and similar disruptions.

TIME CLOCKS

"In the past year, the number of employees in our organization has doubled. Keeping track of hours and payroll seems more than twice as difficult. I'm thinking about installing a timekeeping system that will log employee comings and goings, making the payroll job easier and more accurate."

Punching in and punching out is an image that seems fixed in time. It reminds most people of factory scenes or of Charlie Chaplin's famous movie *Modern Times.* It also conjures up images of labor-management mistrust, as both sides rely on evidence so impartial only a machine could produce it. Yet many entrants into the modern workplace of flexible hours, compressed weeks, work at home, etc., suspect employees of shaving hours and misrepresenting their time and attendance. Bad habits don't necessarily die with the turning of calendars.

From a payroll standpoint alone, automated timekeeping procedures have some distinct advantages. The primary benefit, of course, is that you (or your bookkeeper) don't have to bug employees on a weekly or biweekly basis to turn in their time cards. If they are clocking in and out every day, you automatically have not only employee time reports, but also data you can readily use for statistical evaluations and comparisons year-to-year, month-to-month, etc.

The other obvious advantage associated with time clocks is their objectivity. Employees cannot clock in until they actually arrive at work. In cases of "non-exempt" employees under the Fair Labor Standards Act, clocking also provides reliable evidence of overtime. But mechanics are not foolproof. Since time-clocking began, employees have been "punching each other in" or otherwise trying to beat the system.

Knowing they must arrive at work on time, employees who play it straight will quickly learn to beat the clock. Thus time clocks mechanically enforce good attendance habits in many organizations. Machines, however, are never an adequate substitute for an employee who wants to come to work on time or even early.

Approach to Take:

1. *Define the problem.* If you're considering the use of time clocks, be clear as to why. Is this to facilitate payroll operations, demonstrate fairness to Department of Labor inspectors, or enforce proper attendance habits? Make your motives clear.
2. If employees dislike or resent automated timekeeping, find out why. *Let the employees help solve the problem.* List their concerns and have them list yours. See if a happier medium can be found. Time clocks are a negotiable item in many workplaces, so unions also raise the issue

where employees resent such a system. If the employees are convinced punching the clock is the best compromise, dissatisfaction will be harder to play on.

3. If you're still determined to implement an automated timekeeping system, you have a couple of options. One is to talk to your accountant about specific systems. She may be familiar with particular brands or vendors. Another is to check your telephone directory. There are several ads in the Yellow Pages for time clocks and payroll systems. Don't be afraid to shop around, and remember always to get references. You want to hear the good news and the bad news about new systems—before you install them.

   The object is to find a system that is the most compatible with your operation. If you're in a large organization with large numbers of employees arriving at the same time, you may want to consider multiple units. Contrary to the old stand-alone model, today's time clocks can be PC- or mainframe-driven. If your workplace has a computer network, you can use it to facilitate implementation of a new system.

4. Once you've clearly defined what's available in the market, *consider the costs vs. the benefits* of each option. Get a clear picture of what it costs to do your payroll now, and what it will cost when automated. In a small organization, there may be compelling reasons to purchase such a system (employees working at home or traveling, a bookkeeper who works outside the organization, etc.); in a large organization there may be reasons not to automate (although it's difficult to think what they could be). At any rate, make sure you're making a reasoned decision.

Preventive Measures:

As your organization grows, or as the character of your workforce changes, it's normal to feel that you need to make changes in your payroll system. There really aren't preventive measures, other than considering all your options for keeping track of employee hours.

TRADE SECRETS

"We've just instituted a new production process in our plant. It's a proprietary process that our competitors would love to get their hands on. Although we've applied for a patent, I'm concerned about my employees inadvertently leaking information."

A trade secret is information that allows you a competitive advantage in the market. In tough economic times, industrial espionage games intensify, often played for very high stakes. In order to retain legal protection for trade secrets, you must first determine whether or not you've got trade secrets. This determination is based on things like how far you'll go to protect the secrecy of information, the degree to which specific information is known to the public, the value of the information to you and to competitors, and the degree to which this information is known to employees.

Once you (and an intellectual property attorney) have determined you do, in fact, have trade secrets, you need to figure out what to do about/with the information. Although the laws protecting trade secrets may help to prevent theft of the information, patent, copyright, and trademark are also effective ways to retain control.

Trade secrets can only be protected legally if you take affirmative action to maintain secrecy, and if they are not divulged to the public. Once a trade secret becomes public knowledge, it's no longer a trade secret, and can no longer be protected. Although you can have employees sign trade-secret and noncompete agreements, it's still up to you to insure secrecy is maintained.

Although there are specific actions to take regarding trade secrets, this entry is particularly concerned with the employee's role in the process of maintaining/agreeing to maintain trade secrets. If you have specific questions about the law protecting trade secrets, contact an attorney versed in intellectual/industrial property law.

Approach to Take:

1. If you have just instituted a new procedure or acquired a new program that is proprietary, you may require employees to sign agreements regarding the trade secrets. Such agreements should include, but not be limited to, the fact that the employee will have access to the secrets, that she will not divulge the secrets to unauthorized employees or individuals outside the organization, and that she will notify authorities in the case of disclosure by others.

2. The fact of and procedures around trade secrets should be included in your personnel manual. This should be updated as needed on a regular basis, and should be reviewed with employees on an annual basis. Of course, all new employees should be apprised of the existence of trade secrets. Employees who will be working with the proprietary information should be asked to sign agreements; policies should be reviewed annually with employees who have signed agreements.

   Non-compete agreements should be signed by key personnel. To be enforceable, they should be as specific as possible regarding what narrowly described work may not be done, within what specific time period, and with what customers.

3. As obvious as this may be, don't forget about limiting access to trade secrets. In the fashion industry, this could mean a building with no windows and extra security on the cutting room door. In software design, it could mean a rigorous password/access system.

4. In the case of employees who have either quit or been terminated, you need to remind them of their obligations regarding trade secrets. In addition, make certain to retrieve any and all proprietary information, equipment, etc., that may have been in the employee's possession.

Preventive Measures:

Before taking any action regarding trade secrets, seek the counsel of an attorney. A well-written agreement, reviewed in advance by all affected parties, can go a long way toward alleviating problems later in the process. In addition, consider consulting an expert in security matters.

See also KEYS TO THE OFFICE.

TRAINING, REQUESTS FOR TUITION REIMBURSEMENT

"I have a request on my desk for tuition reimbursement from one of my employees. She plans to attend night school in accounting, and has requested I share the cost of tuition and expenses."

W. E. Deming, the late guru of Total Quality Management, felt the principle focus of employees should be improvement and "profound knowledge." In many instances, employees look to improve their knowledge, skills, and/or abilities by enrolling in seminars, workshops, and academic programs. Their hope is often that you, as their employer, will cover or help defray the costs associated with their self-improvement.

Training and education are essential components of many jobs. Employees and managers who keep abreast of changes in law, technology, and theory can be an asset to your organization. Similarly, those who improve reading, writing, and analytical skills are likely to be more productive.

Training and education fall into two categories: reimbursable course work after hours and paid time off to attend classes. An employee who wants to attend evening or weekend classes may be doing so for her own benefit, that of your organization, or both. What's clear is a sense of initiative or ambition and the fact that her time in class, studying, etc., will not be on your clock. If the course work is relevant to the job or her career, a manager's temptation should be to help out. Usually this help comes in the form of tuition and expense reimbursement.

Training conducted during working hours may include advertised classes at local facilities (hotels, community colleges, etc.), employer-sponsored seminars, interactive computer programs, or video training modules. In each of these cases, management is expected to bear both the costs associated with the training and the hours devoted to employee attendance. In some cases, employees may attend such course work with less enthusiasm or incentive to succeed. By the same token, if everyone needs to understand a policy or law (say, occupational safety and health requirements), employer-sponsored training is the only realistic answer.

In many organizations, requests for and costs of training and tuition can prove burdensome. The annual price tag often exceeds those of awards and bonuses combined. As costs become an issue (and they always do), it's often difficult to see a direct tie to productivity—especially when the class is Communications Skills or Stress Management.

When it comes to training and tuition, you must recognize and balance organizational costs and benefits along with employee motivation and morale. Saying "yes" to classes that are only marginally relevant may prove cheaper than explaining "no."

Approach to Take:

1. Accentuate the positive. Offer positive reinforcement to any employee who is motivated in the direction of education and improvement. Ask the employee what tangible benefit to the company will result from her attendance and participation.

2. *Be consistent.* Whatever you decide for one employee should, most likely, be the same for others.

3. *Think it over.* Determine whether the knowledge, skill, or ability that may be gained from the class or program is of real benefit to you and the organization. We rec-

ommend you ask the employee to do this. If his analysis of relevance seems sketchy or thin, persist until he appreciates the importance of this issue.

4. Do a *cost/benefit analysis.* Individuals in differing organizations may be treated differently. For instance, two cashiers want to earn four-year degrees in business administration. The one working in a large chain store may prove more useful to the employer than the other, who works in a neighborhood dry cleaner.

5. In some cases, requests for financial assistance relating to long-term (one or more years) educational programs may result in legal agreements that call for repayment in the form of continued service to the organization. If your tuition reimbursement program (and by the way, the employee must pass the class to get the tuition reimbursed!) calls for one year of employment for every year of tuition, the employee who leaves before that time will have to repay the extra years' tuition.

6. Some employers provide tuition reimbursement contingent upon a satisfactory grade in the course. If this idea appeals to you, find out the grading system at the institution providing the course and be specific as to what you mean by "passing" or "satisfactory." If the employee comes in below this level, the costs are hers.

7. If you're considering assisting employees in finishing high school or obtaining college or advanced degrees, things can become even more complicated. We suggest you contact the educational institution and have them refer you to other employers who have already instituted such programs. Learn all the good and bad news you can before making up your own mind.

Preventive Measures:

Training and development costs should be incorporated into your budget—along with salary, employment taxes, and benefits.

One effective way to project education expenses is to poll

employees at the beginning of the budget process to determine their best guess of their training/education wishes for the next budget year. (In organizations that have a human resource department, it may be helpful to have HR develop a list of potential classes that could be circulated to employees.) After you receive the requests, you can evaluate the extent to which you can honor requests. It is likely everyone will not get to attend all the requested training.

An alternative method is to apportion a certain amount to each employee for training. This is a benefit that can be earmarked specifically for this purpose—that is, if employees choose not to use it, they may not receive it in cash compensation. The challenge in setting it up this way is to assure each employee has the time available to attend classes.

TRAVEL EXPENSES

"An employee I supervise will be attending a conference out of town next month. She's asked to travel on Friday evening, visit with friends over the weekend, and then attend the conference Monday and Tuesday. She's explained her weekend expenses (hotel, meals, and rental car) will be offset by an excursion rated airfare. In the end, she says, the organization will save over $150."

Some employees look forward to travel assignments; others dread them. For many workers, travel is a way of life. Truck drivers, salespeople, consultants, and executives are expected to spend many days and nights away from home. While doing so, they're expected to live within an allowance or guidelines. Most would agree that reasonable or moderate expense reimbursement may be cheaper than staying at home, but others feel that reimbursement includes a certain margin or premium to compensate them for the inconvenience of being away.

Most organizations have a tough time establishing rules or

policies regarding travel expenses. Exceptions abound—many exceptions make common sense even as they seem to undermine organizational guidelines. There is one prevailing sentiment with which we agree—expenses should be recorded and never padded. As with other issues regarding falsification or stealing, an expense account is an act of faith. Once trust is violated, it's hard to repair.

There are nationally published guides that fix dollar values to each city in the country in terms of lodging and meal expenses. The federal government publishes similar statistics for civil servants' expenses. These guidelines, however, may prove too modest for a traveler who must spend the night in a downtown area, and too generous for someone who finds quarters outside of town along an interstate highway. Likewise, the traveler may have a ten-dollar hotel breakfast one morning, and the next morning be at McDonald's.

Some employers have dealt with the variation in daily expenses by paying each traveler a flat fee (called per diem)—especially for meals. The employee may live off fruit and yogurt from the grocery store and pocket the meal expense money, or dine at the best French restaurants and supplement the stipend. In either case, management need not worry over documentation of expenses or whether costs were reasonable. Few employers do the same for lodging. However, this process may prove more practical than payment based on receipts. The other benefit of a flat-rate expense policy is that fraud is no longer an issue. The money is the employees' to spend as they choose.

There are also travel issues regarding the need for the trip itself. Is the employee contriving a need in order to travel for personal reasons? Should the employee be allowed to stay the weekend out of town on your tab in order to save money on airfare? Eventually, exceptions outnumber rules and a subjective ("reasonable") standard must prevail.

Managers must balance the need to conserve organizational money against the comforts and hardships of travelers.

Approach to Take:

1. First off decide how you want to handle accounting for travel expenses. *Consider the costs vs. the benefits.* A flat-rate scheme (using some official reference as your guide) may save administrative costs and put extra dollars in the frugal traveler's pocket. If this idea appeals to you, consult the reference desk at your local public library concerning travel-expense indices, and your accountant regarding bookkeeping requirements.

   If you feel reimbursement based on actual expenses is more appropriate to your organization and employees, decide on documentation requirements. Will a cup of coffee require a receipt? You may also have to decide what is and is not reimbursable. Examples include tips for maids, hotel dry cleaning services, bar expenses on a meal ticket, and movies charged to the room. While we prefer the flat-rate method, principally for reasons of simplicity, we strongly urge you to work with your accountant in finding your own answer.

2. If you have a credit card in the name of the organization, and allow travelers to use it, decide who pays the bill. Will you remunerate travelers directly through the use of advances and reimbursements? If so, arrange with the card issuer to have employees receive the monthly statement. Make it clear that organizational credit cards are not to be used for personal expenses, except in cases of emergency, and that you expect payment to be prompt and in full. In addition, you need to do regular audits of those statements to make sure your guidelines are being followed.

   If you prefer having consolidated statements come to you, and paying the credit card issuer directly, there are a couple of extra considerations. You must decide how to deal with cash expenditures (no one charges at Burger King), and you must ensure that expenses unrelated to business travel not appear on that statement. If you choose this option, we recommend having the employee review bank card statements and initialing them before you send the check. This way you know she's reviewed the charges, and she knows you'll catch any non-company expenditures.

Consider the costs vs. the benefits of having credit cards that need to be paid in full at the end of each month. The advantage of using American Express or a similar card is that employees can't build up a big credit balance. The advantage of using Visa, MasterCard, or a similar issuer is that the organization may want to use the credit card for cash-flow crunches.

3. In the case where an employee is traveling by car—either her own or one of yours—we strongly recommend a log that can be left in the car. (This is also the case when you're reimbursing employees for mileage around town.) If you are going to represent this on your taxes as a business expense, you need to be able to justify it. Include date, beginning and ending mileage, and a brief statement of destination.

4. Most travelers are allowed at least one personal call per day at the organization's expense. While we advise against concerning yourself too much with the details, you may want to advise employees you expect the calls to be of moderate duration. There may be times when that means five minutes, and there may be times—if an employee is having family problems—when that means sixty minutes, but at least you've mentioned it.

5. Laws concerning compensation for time in a travel status are complicated, to say the least. According to the Fair Labor Standards Act, you must first determine whether the employee is "exempt" or "non-exempt." Beyond this, there's another law entitled the Portal-to-Portal Act which speaks to compensation for time spent traveling. In most cases regarding travel away from home and overnight, compensation begins and ends during the employee's regular hours of work—say, 9:00 A.M. to 5:00 P.M.

But time spent beyond these hours on weekdays and

weekends may differ and it should be your accountant who makes the call. Employees obviously want to be compensated for time spent traveling. We urge you to consider this when looking at whether to pay straight or overtime pay for time in the air, on rail, or in the company car. Money you save in direct compensation you may end up spending elsewhere in terms of morale and productivity.

6. Travel expenses are one of the most common areas of employee falsification/theft. The temptation to pick up a few extra bucks on a supper, or even to doctor a hotel receipt, may be too much for some travelers. If your organization has many people traveling out of town, we suggest you consult with a security specialist who has experience in travel fraud. Upon reviewing receipts and records, he can show you areas and items to look out for.

Where outright fraud is clear, we suggest confronting the individual and giving her a chance to save her job. *Say what you mean.* Where a review of records casts doubt on the veracity of an employee, let him know what you found and what you're thinking. The odds are excellent you'll change his behavior and solve the problem right then and there. Another option is to have his travel claims investigated over time to either confirm or refute any suspicion. If you choose this option, do not confront the employee or otherwise "tip your hand." Just wait and see.

Preventive Measures:

The best way to minimize travel expenses and prevent suspicious claims is by setting a good example. Employees generally follow the lead of management in matters such as these. If you stay at the Ritz, so will they, unless they know on the next trip you slept in a Motel 6 . . . and why. As you relate your travel habits and justifications, they will usually adopt similar behavior.

If you have frequent travelers, don't pretend the temptation or likelihood of padding expenses isn't there. Discuss what is and isn't reasonable, communicate guidelines, and remind employees of questionable items.

Before leaving the subject of travel expenses, consider whether out-of-town or overnight travel is required at all. Computers and telecommunications equipment have become so sophisticated that face-to-face attendance may no longer be required or may be accomplished through the use of video cameras and fiber optics. While the cost of a video conference studio may seem prohibitive at first blush, the equipment, personnel, and space—or the rental time for a contracted service—may look small on an annual basis when compared to travel costs.

TURNOVER

"Our receptionist has just given two weeks notice. I'll have to hire someone to fill that job for the third time this year. This rate of turnover is costing me too much, mostly in terms of my own time."

Lifetime employment in a single organization was once the norm. Now it's the exception. It's not uncommon for resumes to show ten or more previous employers. As people look for employment under a variety of circumstances, so they leave for many differing reasons. Some organizations consider high rates of turnover normal and expected in their industry. Others can suffer serious disadvantage when even a single employee pulls up stakes.

Generally speaking, people leave a job before retirement under one of two circumstances—they either have something different or better toward which they are looking, or they find their current conditions too distasteful to continue. When a spouse is transferred out of town, a parent becomes disabled, an opportunity to finish school presents itself, or the employee wins the lottery, you need not take it personally. In other cases, employees simply don't know what they want, and move aimlessly from one job to the next. You just happened to be a marker on the trail.

Despite all these normal instances of turnover, we all know many people leave work because it's just not worth staying. The job isn't fun, the pay doesn't increase fast enough, the benefits are lousy, or the boss stinks. High rates of turnover are often a reflection of an unhealthy workplace.

High turnover is also an area where costs may not be readily apparent. The cost of turnover can be found in recruiting, orientation, training, and customer service. In an organization where workers depend on one another, a new employee can disrupt the flow, require communication adjustments, and present new issues relating to teamwork. Unlike salary or utility expenses, costs like these can get lost and not be considered when analyzing operations.

The impact that may be least understood is the effect on customers, who develop a relationship with an employee and find it difficult to adjust to her replacement, then his replacement, and so on. Any beautician, theater manager, realtor, or auto mechanic can tell you that a personal relationship with customers is the key to continued success. Turnover hurts.

If people are leaving your organization for reasons more of your making than theirs, consider the following: Are you paying a competitive wage or salary designed to retain good employees? Are employees' skills and talents being used to the extent that they're not bored on a daily basis? Do people get along with each other at work, or are they impersonal and occasionally petty with one another? Do benefits and/or retirement plans add to an employee's sense of personal security or lead them to look elsewhere? Any or all of these may contribute to problems with tenure.

Approach to Take:

1. *Define the problem.* Consider the true costs of turnover in your own organization. Ask employees to identify how people leaving and replacements coming on board affect

productivity and customer service. Take a few hours and attempt to quantify these costs—first in terms of hours, then dollars. Before you can decide what, if anything, to do, you need to understand the actual extent of the problem.

2. Assessing turnover is a project for which most managers are ill-suited. Happily, it's almost the perfect project for a business or organizational development consultant. We recommend an outsider interview current and former employees to assess the reasons for high turnover and report findings and recommendations back to you. This is a clear and defined package of work that should not run into excessive time or costs.

3. If you follow the previous recommendation, be prepared for the worst. The problem may be you. Endless studies have shown that managers perceive themselves to be more sympathetic and better communicators than employees perceive them to be. The disparities are often enormous. Your own management skills and abilities may turn out to be the principal reason for high employee turnover. Brace yourself.

4. Consider low-cost ways of making yours a more fun and enjoyable place to work. One to five thousand dollars a year spent on recognition and frivolity may prove a small price when compared to the costs of turnover. A fun place to work is a hard place to leave. (See the section on AWARDS AND BONUSES.)

Preventive Measures:

Two ongoing practices you may wish to employ are:

Exit interviews. Make a habit of getting information from employees on their way out about their reasons for leaving. If they're not comfortable talking to you, and you don't have a human resource office, choose a member of your staff to conduct the interviews. Develop a standard set of questions to ask each employee who leaves.

Industry salary and benefit surveys. You need to understand

whether you're offering competitive salaries and benefits. The best way to do this is to find out what the industry averages are. If you have a trade association, they should be able to help you. If not, try a trip to the business desk at your local public library, or call your local SBA office to see if they have salary surveys available. Part of your problem may be nothing more than salaries or benefits that have fallen behind the times. Although this is unlikely to be the underlying cause of high turnover, it may be a contributing factor.

UNEMPLOYMENT COMPENSATION

"I have an employee who's really not doing her job. I've counseled her and told her she really needs to start doing better or I'll have to fire her. The last time we talked, she said if I fired her she'd pay me back by collecting unemployment."

Employers have been confused about unemployment compensation since the program was established by the Social Security Act of 1935. Originally, the primary objectives of unemployment compensation were to provide a weekly cash benefit for workers involuntarily unemployed, provide job training/assistance in job-hunting, and induce employers to maintain a stable workforce. Although we've gotten further and further away from these original objectives, the spirit of the program lives on.

Although unemployment insurance (UI) programs are administered by the individual states, the federal government has established basic minimum standards for eligibility, length of benefits, and benefit amount. These standards have changed over the years, with administrations and economic conditions. Currently there is a minimum benefit period of twenty-six weeks. In some areas of high unemployment, a thirteen-week extension may be granted. In most areas, there is a one-week waiting period before UI starts paying benefits.

In all but five states (Alabama, Alaska, New Jersey, Pennsylvania, and West Virginia), the UI premium is paid by employers. The amount of the premium is based on "experience rating." The amount paid is a function of the organization's claims experience. The more successful unemployment claims a firm has had filed against it, the higher the rate paid.

To be eligible for unemployment, a worker must; be ready, willing, and able to work; actively seek work; and have earned a certain minimum amount and worked a certain number of quarters before becoming unemployed. The number of quarters is generally two of the last five quarters. The amount earned varies widely among the states, from a low for the base period (four of the last five quarters) of about $200 to a high of almost $4,000. Employees who earned less than the minimum for the base period will be disqualified from receiving unemployment.

The most important thing for the employer to remember is unemployment must be *involuntary* for the employee to qualify. If an employee is fired for misconduct, or quits because she doesn't like her job, the claim will likely be denied. The exceptions to this are compelling reasons for quitting, such as sexual and other forms of harassment. In most jurisdictions, workers are entitled to two appeals on a denied claim.

Approach to Take:

1. If you have employees, and you're not currently making payments for UI, you need to start. Look in the State Government section of your telephone directory under either Employment Security or Department of Labor to get the number for your state office. Call and find out what's required to register with your state. They can also give you information about what to expect in the way of premiums. In addition, they can give you information about the federal UI requirements.
2. If you have a former employee who's filed for unemployment, you'll generally get the paperwork on the claim within a week of filing. You then have a certain number

of days to approve or deny the claim. In most cases, this is a fairly straightforward decision. Keep in mind if you deny a claim, the employee still has the right to appeal. As mentioned above, there may be cases where an employee has quit under duress and may win an appeal for unemployment benefits.

3. If you have a serious question about whether or not to deny a claim, call either your human resource office, the state employment security office, or your attorney to determine what latitude you have.

Preventive Measures:

The best preventive measure is to be fully aware of your rights and the rights of employees before you have the need to terminate. If you follow the suggestions made in item 3 above as soon as you finish reading this entry, it may save you problems later.

UNION ORGANIZING

"I was advised today of a rumor spreading among employees. The word is that a union is coming, and there will be an election soon to see if they will represent workers and bargain a contract with us."

There are two old sayings about unions that hold true in most cases. The first is, "Any management that gets a union deserves one." The implication being a union is bad news and a response to bad management. The other saying is, "When a union arrives in an organization, something special leaves." Where you once thought of the workplace in terms of family or community, a union is a reminder that managers and workers are more separate than you thought.

Unions usually arrive on the scene at the invitation of one or more employees. While there are cases where unions independently target certain employers, more often than not they're invited. If they arrive to discuss organizing with your employees, their first job is to determine what level of interest or support they might find. Professional organizers are being paid from union members' dues and are loath to invest time in organizing where success seems unlikely.

Guided by the National Labor Relations Act of 1935 (NLRA), a federal agency known as the National Labor Relations Board (NLRB) oversees union organizing and disputes throughout the country. Most of the NLRB's staff are attorneys—familiar with both the law and sixty years of court decisions relating to it. Hence many organizations rely on professional consultants familiar with the legal ins and outs of union organizing.

The union's usual technique is to contact workers who are likely to support union organizing and eventual representation. These individuals are asked to sign cards or a petition indicating their desire to have a union. While thirty percent of the workforce is enough to justify an election, most union organizers aim for a majority of employees signing cards.

These are then presented to the employer. If they are examined and/or accepted as authentic, they may result in what is known as a "consent agreement" to have union representation and commence bargaining a collective agreement. Most labor-relations consultants urge you, as an employer, not to take the cards, acknowledge their authenticity, or otherwise indicate that employees favor union representation. While this is an odd posture, it would be stranger still to have arrived at a consent agreement without realizing it.

Where an employer does not acknowledge that the staff desires union representation, a hearing and eventual election are conducted by the NLRB. During the hearing, employees eligible to be represented (and, therefore, to vote) will be defined. Likewise, the date of an election will be set. During the ensuing campaign, management may legally express its opinion concerning why employees might wish to vote against the union. In this regard, you must be very careful as to what rhetoric is in or out of bounds. In the end, if a majority of those voting does not vote for the union, your efforts aimed at preventing exclusive representation have succeeded.

If you find yourself shopping for a consultant, you shouldn't have a problem finding one. This is an industry approaching $1 billion a year, due primarily to management's fear of or antipathy toward organized labor. Many organizations feel that keeping unions out is worth any price . . . and that's what they usually pay. Some estimates of consultant costs are $700 per employee and up. In many cases, it would have been cheaper to bargain a collective agreement. Where consultants succeed, the union may reappear after a year's time and start the entire process again.

Consultants build their reputation on previous successes. Being able to say they prevented union victory eighty, ninety, or even ninety-five percent of the time seems impressive. Our concern is what they might have done to achieve this record. Many consultants have a record for committing questionable and even illegal acts in an effort to frustrate and ultimately defeat organized labor. After they have left, management and employees must pick up the pieces and try to reestablish their relationships.

Approach to Take:

1. If you receive any news or rumor to the effect that union organizing has begun, take it seriously. More than one organization has been surprised to learn that sufficient signatures had been gathered without them knowing it. We suggest you speak to your attorney about finding an advisor with a background in labor law. Discuss with your attorney what attitudes or qualifications you feel are most appropriate, then let her make recommendations and define options.

2. If you're approached by a union organizer, do not discuss matters unrehearsed or off the cuff. Make an appointment with him, and then call your attorney for advice as to how you should conduct yourself. In many cases, she

will want to sit in on the meeting with you or have a labor-relations expert do so.

In many organizations, a human resource manager (HRM) or specialist is on staff to handle personnel matters. Unless that individual has a depth of experience with labor-relations matters, and especially union-organizing drives, we suggest you not hand responsibility off in that direction. You may want the HRM to find the expertise required in lieu of the attorney doing so. That, however, should be the extent of his involvement.

Preventive Measures:

The best strategy for keeping a union out is not to commit the errors and practices that invite them in. Generally speaking, where management wants the best for employees and is willing to share in the success of an organization, unions are not needed. It's where employees feel underpaid, insecure, unjustly treated, or disempowered that unions are seen as a welcome option.

VACATION AND PERSONAL DAYS

"One of my employees is forgoing a vacation this year. He tells me he's saving his vacation time so next summer he can spend five weeks driving across the country and back with his family. I don't know what would happen if he were gone for five consecutive weeks. My gut reaction is that his plans for a marathon vacation would put the organization at a serious disadvantage."

Virtually all employers in the United States provide paid vacation to their staffs. Some employers refer to this time off as vacation time, while others call it annual leave. Most pay for greater amounts of time off as employees gain tenure. Most also require an employee to have worked beyond a probationary period, or some other interval of time (usually six months to a year), before she's eligible to use vacation days.

Some employees use annual leave as quickly as they earn it. Others accumulate as many hours as they possibly can. Those who use up their vacation days often find themselves in a bind. An emergency comes up, they need a day or two off work, and there are no paid days "in the bank" for them.

Leave-savers present a different problem. Unless they use some of their accumulation, it becomes a liability on the books of the organization. If they were to leave before retirement, a hefty payout would be required. If they continue working an entire career, one or more years of vacation time could accrue. Most employers, therefore, put caps or maximum accumulation levels on vacation time.

For most employers, annual leave falls into two basic categories: scheduled and unscheduled. Scheduled leave would include a fishing trip, a week at the beach, or a day of home repair. The further in advance vacation time is scheduled, the easier it is for you as a manager and for coworkers to adjust and compensate for the employee's absence. Scheduled leave often creates conflicts—especially around holidays. Where two or more employees in a small work area each want the week between Christmas and New Year's Day off, someone may be denied his request. Managers should anticipate this and have a policy (for instance first come, first served) for resolving conflicts.

Unscheduled annual leave, like sick days, presents a greater inconvenience to management. Receiving a call at the beginning of the day advising of the employee's absence makes workload adjustments much more difficult. Moreover, a few employees may come to abuse vacation privileges by never scheduling annual leave. A manager could swear the employee has a list of emergencies by the telephone, describing a different one with each day off.

Another managerial headache may come with requests of advance vacation time to an employee who needs it but does not have it. In most cases, this is because the employee either has not maintained a sufficient accrual or balance to cover unplanned absences, or because the employee hasn't worked for your organization long enough to save up sufficient days. It's unusual for an employee who uses vacation time responsibly to request an advance. But it's these cases that prove the most compelling.

Tenured employees who must tend to personal matters over weeks or longer may find themselves out of leave yet not out of the woods. Most employers have a firm policy in all cases that leave is earned in increments (say, one day at the end of each month) and will not be advanced. Some prefer allowing employees to use any and all vacation time they will have earned by year's end whenever they choose. In such cases, if the employee resigns or retires with a vacation debt, repayment for those days is deducted from her final paycheck.

Leave habits of employees add to the seemingly endless complications surrounding vacation time. Some prefer a three-day weekend as often as possible. Others want a long vacation out of town. And, of course, there are those who prefer taking vacation time in intervals of a day or less, and invariably, at the last minute. In response, many employers require vacation days to be used a day at a time. Others allow it to be broken down in terms of hours and maintain leave records in those terms. While the latter policy may seem much more complicated, employees generally prefer it.

As a manager you should be warned that granting leave on an hourly basis to "exempt" employees (see OVERTIME, FAIR LABOR STANDARDS ACT) may create an unintended liability. Past court decisions have determined that such policies, especially if they lead to unpaid hours off work, often put a salaried employee into an hourly status, making him eligible for overtime compensation. Some employers have been found to owe hundreds of thousands of dollars due to an hourly leave policy for such personnel. We advise you to consult an attorney when formulating or reviewing your policy.

Quite often employers will require use of annual leave where sickness or death in the family requires the employee to be off work. For them, there is no special category of bereavement leave, nor are sick days to be used for anything other than the employee's own medical needs. As in all of the cases above, employees may still, with your permission, take days off work without pay.

Approach to Take:

1. Annual leave policies are difficult to write. We recommend examining examples from firms that sell generic personnel policies, either as software or in writing. *Get another opinion.* It would also be a good idea to ask other employers in organizations similar to your own for a copy of their policy. While it would be nice to have guidelines regarding vacations that are short and to the point, we suggest one that is comprehensive enough to address the kinds of issues discussed above.

2. Each organization must develop vacation policies that suit management, employees, and customers best. No one philosophy can be recommended. *Be consistent.* Whatever your policies, the temptation over time to make exceptions will feel compelling. We urge you to be consistent—to the extent you possibly can. Disparate treatment is usually noticed and resented.

3. Whatever policy you decide on, be sure to develop a complementary process for documenting vacation time. Most automated payroll systems provide for a way to keep track of vacation leave accrued and used. If you're doing the payroll manually, be sure to keep clear, updated notes on vacation time.

4. If you're unlucky enough to have an employee who uses vacation time on an unscheduled or emergency basis, our condolences. We think it's time to let the individual know that in the future such absences may not be credited as annual leave but rather unpaid days off. *Say what you mean.* Let him know the inconvenience you and others experience around unplanned absences. Be clear that he's responsible for his regular attendance at work, and offer a referral to the EAP if you have one.

   You may also want to discuss the employee's chronic

excuses. Explain to him others are able to manage their personal lives at a completely different level. You may also want to advise him that future emergencies preventing on-time arrival or attendance at work may require some form of confirmation or substantiation. For example, if he alleges the power went out in the middle of the night affecting his alarm clock, you would request confirmation from the power company as to an outage in his neighborhood. If the habit persists and/or documentation is absent/unconvincing, take progressive disciplinary action.

5. If and when the question of advancing vacation time arises, we recommend against it—not because we advocate heartless, rule-bound management, but because any other policy will lead to inconsistencies over time. Those inconsistencies are likely to provoke discontent among affected employees. In a more litigious setting, they may also precipitate grievances and/or formal complaints. Such a firm policy does not preclude you from allowing employees additional time off work. It only means if no leave is accumulated to cover that time, it will go unpaid.

VEHICLES, COMPANY

"I just received an anonymous call alleging that one of our cars had been parked in a residential driveway for an hour. The caller alleges one of my employees is using the car to visit a 'lady friend' during the day."

Buying and maintaining vehicles for organizational use represents a serious financial investment. The costs of the vehicle, upkeep, and insurance should be outweighed by advantages in productivity, efficiency, and customer service.

Employees assigned to operate these vehicles should, in all cases, be advised as to the limitations on their use. Issues such as personal use, additional riders, smoking, scheduled maintenance, and reporting accidents should be clear, written, and periodically reviewed.

In some large organizations, special licensing procedures are developed and implemented. Driver reports and fleet maintenance are likely to be handled by a separate arm of the organization. In smaller businesses, however, written agreements may be developed and maintained by line managers/owners.

Approach to Take:

1. *Be consistent.* In most cases, misuse of an organization's vehicle should result in confrontation, counseling, and agreement on a long-term solution. Some offenses, if they had occurred at the workplace, would require discipline (i.e., using foul language in public, conducting an affair on company time, etc.). Violations that would result in discipline at work should pertain to operation of a vehicle.
2. In cases where the vehicle sports the company logo or name, employees should be advised that their operational habits are a reflection of the organization's public image.
3. *Consider the costs vs. the benefits* of revoking driving privileges where employees violate laws. In some cases, "clean" driving records should be made a "condition of continued employment" to ensure the least possible liability.
4. Personal use of the vehicle should fall within explicit guidelines, including logged mileage. Even with employees whose jobs require them to spend a lot of time in the car, make it clear the vehicle was purchased by and for company purposes. Rules for personal use should be clearly developed, including input from the employee.
5. Failure to maintain or clean the vehicle as prescribed should be considered as would similar failings in an office or plant setting.
6. Any problems related to the safe operation of the vehicle should be dealt with seriously. There may be times when firing the employee may be appropriate. When making

such decisions, a manager should consider the potential costs associated with recurrent failures.

Preventive Measures:

Maintain copies of written operational and maintenance procedures in the vehicle.

Keep logs relative to vehicular use and maintenance.

Provide refresher training and/or procedural reviews with vehicle operators on a scheduled basis.

WHINERS

"One of my employees is a chronic complainer. Yesterday she stopped by my office to tell me that after three tries she still couldn't get an answer from one of our suppliers. Today she pointed out the office carpeting is not being properly vacuumed by the janitorial service."

On the one hand, when things go wrong and no one points it out, a manager can be left holding the bag. On the other, an employee can point out so many problems, shortcomings, dilemmas, and deficiencies that a strip of duct tape across the oral cavity seems like a modest response.

Whiners and complainers often conceal their behavior from the boss, choosing to inflict it on coworkers. They stifle cooperation and teamwork, as few will ask them for help and fewer still would offer it to them. In essence, the whiner exacts a psychological fee for many, if not all, services rendered. The prevailing sentiment in the organization becomes one of "I'd rather do it myself than ask him." Lest we complain too much about the whiners, perhaps we should give thanks not to know their parents.

Approach to Take:

1. *Say what you mean.* Tell the whiny employee that the complaining has to stop. This weakness on the part of the employee tends to obscure whatever strengths might otherwise be apparent.
2. *Let the employee solve the problem.* Ask him how you can count on him to propose more solutions and fewer problems as long as he's employed by you. If he needs something from you, be prepared to give it to him—but don't let him derail your intent.

Preventive Measures:

This is a case where you need to be clear and assertive. Some managers are intimidated by whiners, preferring to put up with them rather than confront them. This is one management problem where decisive action is the most effective solution. If you have problems dealing with whiners (or with other problem employees), consider skills training for dealing with difficult employees.

WORKING LATE AND WEEKENDS

"When I arrive at work, one of my employees is already hard at it. She's often still working when I leave in the evening. Other employees have begun complaining that she is 'a brown noser' and 'has no life away from work.'"

It's hard to complain when an employee's efforts exceed 100%. By the same token, it can breed dissension among others where they perceive the motive is a need for greater recognition from you. Extended work hours/weeks may also indicate an employee's inability to perform the job within reasonable time limits.

They may be less competent than their peers, or the job may have grown beyond anyone's ability to manage.

In accordance with the Fair Labor Standards Act (FLSA), work beyond eight hours in a day or forty hours in a week may require compensation at one and a half times the basic rate of pay. Certain types of jobs may not elect to "volunteer" extra hours at work.

For those employees "exempt" from the provisions of FLSA, extra hours are often necessary due to fluctuations in the work-load. Ongoing work weeks in excess of fifty hours may prove more detrimental than beneficial—some people burn out when they lose track of the balance between work and their personal lives. Similarly, workers often perceive the additional hours as an expectation rather than their choice.

Approach to Take:

1. Your expectations regarding work hours should be clear to each employee on your staff. Whether they are hourly, salaried, or supervisory, the employees should understand your position as it relates to extra work hours.
2. *Define the problem.* Do you personally have a problem with the employee putting in long hours? Do coworkers? Are you concerned about the employee's personal health and well-being? Before speaking to an employee, you need to be clear about the problem.
3. Where an employee's hours/days of work are becoming excessive, meet with that individual and discuss the matter. What you want is his perception about why he's working so many hours.
4. *Let the employee solve the problem.* Be sure to show your gratitude for the employee's extra efforts, as well as your concern regarding the longer-term implications. Ask the employee what she thinks would fix the problem. Be available to reply to suggestions, and be open to a flexible response.

Preventive Measures:

Develop a policy regarding overtime, and communicate it to all your employees. Make it clear you expect exceptions to be discussed, as much as possible, in advance. Many organizations require written approval for overtime. This depends entirely on your situation and your feelings about this issue.

If you don't already have a policy regarding working late/weekends, consider soliciting opinions from the staff before you create one.

ZEROS

"I was transferred to supervise another section last month. One of the guys who works here seems to be without a clue as to what he's doing, why he's doing it, or how it will affect others. He's been here two years, yet as far as I can tell he's utterly worthless."

Every A-to-Z book requires a final entry representing the twenty-sixth letter of the alphabet. Here's ours. If the example looks far-fetched to you, congratulations.

There are other readers, however, to whom we extend condolences. Like many zeros in arithmetic, the person described above serves no purpose other than to occupy space.

For those readers who remain incredulous, you should know that zeros are a by-product of managers who are afraid to act. Perhaps the employee threatened or actually filed a complaint of discrimination or sexual harassment. Perhaps he's someone's nephew or a member of the right fraternal order. What's certain is anyone who works, grows to resent him.

Approach to Take:

1. It's time to confront reality. If managers above you refuse to act or support you, try documenting the annual dollar cost of a zero. Include the costs of salary, benefits, and other extras (even the square footage allotted to her) that's being lost. Do your best at estimating these costs in dollar terms. Don't forget the time others spend working behind her and your time spent compensating for her lack of productivity. Submit the grand total, with itemization, to senior management, merely asking for acknowledgment.

2. *Consider the costs vs. the benefits.* Dealing with a zero may be arduous and expensive. It is, nevertheless, a one-time cost. Once the dust settles, it's over. There may be a risk of having to reinstate the employee if and when she's fired. The costs computed above, however, are annual. If the employee were to continue another five years in the comfortable position she now occupies, the cost/benefit ratio may favor action.

3. If it's clear you will be unable to deal with the zero, we suggest you seek permission to tell him so—laying your cards on the table face up. There should be no pretending that he's a valued or productive member of the team, nor that you're accepting of his performance or behavior.

AFTERWORD

In many areas of this book, we recommend you turn to employees for ideas, plans, strategies, and so on. Like many current management thinkers, we ascribe wisdom and leadership ability to those who traditionally have been told what to do and how to do it.

Many employers are subscribing to the use of "process action teams," "quality circles," and "quality improvement teams." Recent rulings from the National Labor Relations Board (NLRB) indicate that, in some cases, these are the equivalent of employer-dominated unions and are, therefore, illegal.

The National Labor Relations Act (NLRA) prohibits employers from creating or dominating a union. In a recent decision, known to most as *Electromation,* the NLRB determined that where an employer assigns or empowers employees as representatives in determining personnel policies and practices or working conditions, an employer-dominated union may have been constituted. In other words, particular employees have been selected by management to represent themselves and others in the workforce, without the elected or democratic structure of a labor union. In a legal sense, these employees may have taken on the mantle of labor representatives at your designation rather than having been elected/chosen by their coworkers.

A tremendous alarm has been sounded within business groups and associations concerning this situation. Some of it is well-founded and much of it is irrational. If used to provide input and *not* decisions, employee teams and/or employee-management teams are usually legal and very useful. It's only when employers assign members to the group and then empower that group as a decision-making body that the NLRA would even apply. Even in those cases that are currently considered illegal, who will report or catch you—especially if the outcome is improving both morale and organizational performance.

At this writing, there's talk within the Congress of revising the NLRA to accommodate such practices. Regardless of the outcome, we think employee ideas and input are important ingredients to success. Consult with an attorney if you have concerns in this area, and follow the guidance provided. You may be advised to work with volunteers only, format feedback in terms of options rather than recommendations or decisions, etc. Such advice should not, however, preclude you from obtaining advice and assistance from within the workforce.

BIBLIOGRAPHY

If you're interested in doing more reading on the subject of human resource management, here are some suggestions.

Batten, Joe D., *Tough-Minded Management*. American Management Association, 1978.

Brounstein, Marty, *Handling the Difficult Employee*. Crisp Publications, 1993.

Coleman, Ron, and Giles, Barrie, *525 Ways to Be a Better Manager*. Gower, 1990.

Cox, John, *Straight Talk for Monday Morning*. John Wiley & Sons, 1990.

Drucker, Peter, *People and Performance*. Harper & Row, 1977.

Fournier, Ferdinand F., *Why Employees Don't Do What They're Supposed to Do—and What to Do about It*. Liberty Hall Press, 1988.

Fried, N. Elizabeth, Ph.D., *Sex, Laws and Stereotypes*. Intermediaries Press, 1994.

Gardiner, Gareth, *Tough-Minded Management of Problem Employees*. Smith Collins, 1990.

Kindler, Herbert S., Ph.D., *Managing Disagreement Constructively*. Crisp Publications, 1988.

Mansfield, Clay B., and Cunningham, Timothy W., *Pension Funds: A Commonsense Guide to a Common Goal*. Business One Irwin, 1993.

Miner, John B., *People Problems—The Executive Answer Book*. Random House Business Division, 1985.

Rosenbloom, Jerry S., editor, *The Handbook of Employee Benefits—Design, Funding, and Administration*. Business One Irwin, 1992.

Solomon, Muriel, *What Do I Say When . . . A Guidebook for Getting Your Way with People on the Job*. Prentice Hall, 1988.

Werther, Dr. William B., Jr., *Dear Boss—Things You Always Wanted to Say to Your Boss*. Meadowbrook Press, 1989.

Robert Kunreuther is Director of Government Personnel Services, a firm that provides human resource training and consulting to government agencies. He conducts seminars throughout the country concerning performance appraisal, managing difficult employees, and cooperative labor and management relations. He's been in the field of employee relations for fifteen years.

Victoria Kaplan is Fund Manager of The Millennium Fund, L.L.C., a privately capitalized equity fund investing in minority- and women-owned businesses in Seattle. She has a master's degree in Business Administration, with an emphasis on finance and organizational behavior. Kaplan has been an enthusiastic observer of people in organizations for over twenty years. She has a wide variety of management experience from managing a chamber orchestra to working as a corporate financial analyst.

Both authors live in Seattle, Washington.